Dog Tails
Fish Tales

DOG TAILS
FISH TALES

AND

OTHER MISADVENTURES

Short Stories about
Dogs, Guns, Hunting, and Fishing Experiences

BY ASH CUTCHIN

Illustrated by
Ginna Cutchin, Cathy Gornto,
Caroline Gornto, and Courtney L. Weaver

First Edition.

ISBN 978-1-62806-115-4 (print | paperback)

Library of Congress Control Number 2016956294

Published by Salt Water Media
29 Broad Street, Suite 104
Berlin, Maryland 21811
www.saltwatermedia.com

Cover design by Stephanie Fowler of Salt Water Media

Photographs by and/or used with permission by Ginna and Ash Cutchin

Interior illustrations by Ginna Cutchin, Cathy Gornto, Caroline Gornto, and Courtney L. Weaver

DEDICATION

In memory of the following:

First: My parents, LaRue and Adolph Cutchin, who sacrificed so much that I might have so many opportunities; next my aunt Lizzie Mae Cutchin who taught me to love books; also Ethel Raveling, my high school English teacher ("Remember, whether means whether or not") and Professor Dr. Markham H. Peacock, who encouraged me to "do what you do best."

Next: My good friends, fishing buddies, and fellow Pan Am pilots, Jack Meyers and Erroll Johnstaad, and my very good friends and bird hunting partners Frank Holladay and Chet deGavre. Rest in peace, gentlemen.

Finally: The crew and passengers of Pan Am 103, December 21, 1988.

CONTENTS

PREFACE

I come from humble beginnings, a descendant of farmers and blue collar workers, themselves the offspring of Scottish and English immigrants. Both my parents' generation and my grandparents' generation lived through the Great Depression, and I frequently heard stories about how hard they had to struggle merely to survive during the nineteen twenties and thirties.

Born in Southeastern Virginia (aka Tidewater) six weeks before the attack on Pearl Harbor, I grew up during WW II and the post-war, cold-war era. We were not poor or if we were, I was not aware of it, but neither were we members of the country club. We never had a new car. Our one great material asset was the family farm and farm house passed down from my paternal grandmother, mortgage free. My father was too old to serve in the military in WWII. Instead of farming, he worked as a refrigeration and air conditioning technician in the Public Works Department at the US Navy Yard in Portsmouth, Virginia and he rented our crop land to his cousin. I remember his saying that the farm rent paid the real estate taxes. Twice during my childhood he sold a few acres of the timber.

In the days before chemicals were the herbicide of choice, I remember waking many summer mornings to the sounds of African-American field hands singing as they hoed and chopped the weeds in the peanut, cotton, and corn fields. I had one cousin who lived nearby—he was older and I wore his hand-me-down clothes and he often bullied me—but my main playmates were my younger sister and the children of the farm workers. I picked cotton by hand at age nine.

My aunt Lizzie Mae had been a school teacher, but by the time I was born she was the town librarian, and that is where I spent most of my Saturday mornings, reading whatever she thought was appropriate for me. I learned to love books. Mark Twain, Robert Louis Stevenson, Jonathan Swift, and other writers could whisk me away from the family farm to exotic places where there were exciting things to see and do. Of course, I also had to read about Joseph and his colorful coat and how his brothers sold him into slavery in Egypt, and about Daniel in the lions' den, and about Nebuchadnezzar and David and King Solomon. We were Southern Baptists before I became an Episcopalian. Thanks to my Auntie Mae and my mother, by the time I entered first grade I was reading at third grade level, and my love of books has never waned.

I hated shoes! Almost all my summer time was spent going barefoot. It was fun and not so bad except when my dad would let our chickens roam free in the yard each afternoon. I had trouble avoiding their droppings. One time I stepped on a piece of broken Coca Cola bottle and cut my right instep rather severely, but I still had a dislike for shoes. My mother made me wear them to school. In the first grade I would walk to the school bus, wave goodbye to my mom, immediately remove my shoes and socks, and hang them over the steel bar on the seat backrest where they remained throughout the school day. I put them back on during the bus trip home. As the weather began to get colder in October, my teacher and the school principal visited our house one day after school and told my mom that financial assistance could be made available if needed to help buy me some shoes. My mother was not only embarrassed, but she was furious with me. She thanked them very much, showed them my Buster Brown shoes, and she assured the ladies I would wear them during the school day. I did.

The farm was within a half mile of the local airport which was a Naval Auxiliary Field, and at night it was frequented by Navy planes from nearby Norfolk. The carrier-based pilots practiced night touch-and-go landings hour after hour after hour. I am sure many of those men went away either to WWII or Korea and fought the Nazis, the Japanese, and the Communists, some becoming national heroes. Those pilots were also my personal heroes. I knelt at my bedroom window watching them fly over my house, utterly amazed at the huge flames streaking from the exhaust pipes as they revved their engines on final approach, thereby clearing any carbon buildup and ensuring that power would be available when they needed it for the 'go' portion after touchdown. Because of the trees and some hangars and apartment buildings, I could not actually see them touch down, but I could hear the roar of those powerful piston engines as they made their take-off rolls after touching down briefly on the pavement. It was exhilarating. It was wonderful. It made a powerful and lasting impression on me. I decided that I could be a pilot and travel to far-off places, places I had read about such as: the Mississippi River, the Oregon Trail, Treasure Island, Pitcairn Island, and Tahiti, maybe even Africa or India. First I had to get an education.

I was never really a teacher's pet, but I can truthfully say that I did not have to struggle through public school. As I grew older, I became more and more aware of my father's limited knowledge of correct English grammar; he had quit school in the tenth grade following his father's death. After we got a television set and I joined him watching baseball games, I realized that he talked exactly like sportscaster Dizzy Dean; "I seen him when he come around second base and slood into third." I would strive to do better. I loved my father dearly for all the affection he showered upon me, all the sacrifices I could see that he made for my sister and me, and for teaching me how to get along in the woods and how to shoot and hunt and fish safely and ethically. I imagined that I could survive if ever my plane crashed in a jungle. But I listened to my school teachers and did my homework and continued to read.

I struggled with many subjects in college, especially chemistry, physics, and most math courses, but thanks to a very kind and caring professor, Dr. Markham H. Peacock, head of the English Department at Virginia Tech, I was steered toward a major in English. I finished my studies at William and Mary in 1963 and entered the US Army. I remember calling home from Ft. Sill, Oklahoma, after I received my first paycheck as a Second Lieutenant. My father was excited and pleased—it was larger than his paycheck after working at the Navy Yard for twenty-two years. He was proud of me and he told me so.

In 1975 after we bought a second-hand 1971 Mako 22-foot center-console fishing boat (Hull No. 371) with a 125 HP Evinrude on the transom, my father-in-law gave me a little plaque which I glued in place beside the ignition switch. It reads: "A boat is a hole in the water into which one pours money." Truer words were never written or spoken. That boat provided my girls and me with many, many fun-filled adventures most of which were routine and unspectacular. Some were not. I write about the most interesting and unusual...and sometimes the most surprising.

My military and airline careers provided me with many opportunities to see some things that many people see only on the Discovery Channel. I have travelled to seventy-eight countries. I have been blessed. My wonderful and lovely wife Ginna and I have tried to remain thrifty and to teach our children and grandchildren to do the same. Several second-hand pickup trucks, two second-hand boats, four used tractors, hand-me-down fishing rods, and a couple of guns bought at pawn shops have been some of my possessions. Through it all, I have continued to read as many as three or four books a month. In the late nineteen eighties I decided to share some of my experiences with others by writing short stories, some of which were published in magazines such as *North Dakota Outdoors*, *Shooting Sportsman*, and *Gray's Sporting Journal*. Seven of them are reproduced here. Many were rejected, but that did not discourage me; I continued to write. Sometimes on an airline layover I would wake up in the middle of the night in Madrid or Rome or Paris or London with a story aching to be put on paper so I wrote it, sometimes on hotel stationery.

The explosion and destruction of Pan Am 103 over Lockerbie, Scotland, on December 21, 1988, Pan Am's ultimate downfall, and other events in the early nineteen nineties precipitated a career change and a temporary halt to most of my story writing. However, the events about which I write are etched so vividly in my mind that, now that I have officially retired from my second career, I have returned to the keyboard using only my two index fingers and occasionally a thumb.

I made it to many of the places I read about as a child including Tahiti and India. I have been many times to Africa but not on a safari, and I have never shot an elephant. I write about things that have happened to me or to my close friends, things that could have happened to you—some good, some bad—things which I think are interesting to others. I try to put you, the reader, right beside me in the field or out on the marsh, at the vet's with the dog, or in the boat reeling in a fish. I have had many hunting and fishing trips during which nothing especially interesting or exciting happened. They were boring and I do not write about them. I write about the unusual, the out-of-the-ordinary events, some of which I call misadventures. I hope and pray that you find them worth reading and that you enjoy my efforts. Please note that almost all the names of my friends and companions are real, however, in one or two instances the names have been changed to protect the innocent or guilty.

Unfortunately, in my way of thinking, television videos on several channels have become the twenty-first century way of sharing the adventures of other sportsmen and women. They are all right, I suppose—even though the dubbed-in music is annoying and most of the hosts and many of the guests murder our language, sounding like Dizzy Dean…"Me and Bubba, we both seen them two coyotes when they come up outta that draw. They shoulda went the other way"—but I still think Zane Grey, Ernest Hemingway, and Robert Ruark, Gene Hill, Jack Samson, and George Reiger, none of whom ever made a hunting or fishing video, captured the essence of their exciting adventures, using words from our beautiful language. I have tried to do the same.

Ash Cutchin,
Courtland, VA
July 1, 2016

ACKNOWLEDGEMENTS

I have always felt empathy for authors who have had to write an acknowledgement page, because I figured that if I ever had to I would surely—albeit inadvertently—omit someone important. If that is the case here, and you are the one omitted, please accept my sincerest apologies. You may rest assured your assistance has been vital.

First I must thank my lovely and patient and understanding wife, Ginna Cutchin for putting up with me for 53 years, for tolerating me while I composed these stories, and for illustrating many of them so skillfully. Next I thank my daughters, Cathy and Betsy, for accepting all my idiosyncrasies during their youth, and for their encouragement while an old man tried to recall events that happened so long ago. I must also mention my granddaughters, Courtney L. Weaver and Caroline Gornto as well as my daughter, Cathy Gornto for their contributions to the illustrations. I know you worked hard on them.

I cannot forget to thank my very good friend Jerry Saunders, his son Deacon, and his sister Nancy Koehler. They accompanied me on many of the misadventures contained in this book, and their encouragement to put it all on paper has helped see me through the process. Thanks for being my friends. You, too, Roger Anderson and Lee Johnson and Jim Weldon and Carey Roberts. Thanks to dear friends Dolores and Dave Tyler. Thanks also to my special friends Bette and Daryl Belik of Ross, North Dakota, on whose ranch many of my adventures took place and who are the very best of hosts.

I must also acknowledge writer Gene Hill (1928-1997) whom I never met but whose wonderful stories have been an inspiration to me ever since I read the first one. Rest in peace, Gene. Rest in peace.

Thanks also to Harold Umber, Tony Clark, Elliott Cobb, Rex Alphin, and Phyllis Speidel. Thanks also to my friend George Reiger, author of *The Wildfowler's Quest* and other books. Many thanks go to Curtis Badger, well-renowned author of more than thirty books, for his support and advice. My friend and W&M classmate, Marshall Williams, attorney, author, and gun expert extraordinaire, gave me lots of sound advice and much encouragement. Thanks Marshall. Thanks to Willie Crocket, famous wildlife artist, for his support, assistance, and kind words. Thanks also to Stu Apte for his encouragement and his generous review. May you continue to break fishing records and live to be a thousand, Stu. Thanks also to author Bob Gandt for his encouragement and his flattering remarks. You are too kind, Bob.

I must also thank my good friends Lew Carr and Toni Phillips, for their faithful and enduring job of proofreading my text, ensuring that my spelling and grammar are reasonably acceptable (even the odd-appearing dialogue in many instances). Thanks guys, for your hard work and your enthusiasm.

Without you, the readers, this project would go nowhere. Many heartfelt thanks to all of you.

I must also acknowledge and thank my departed, devoted, and faithful four-legged companions who accompanied me on many of my adventures while we made memories together. Thank you Rusty, Freckles, Sammy, Lee, Daisy, Bogey, Christie, Casey, Emmy, Sonny, Tasha, and Dot. You are sorely missed.

And a special thanks goes to Stephanie Fowler for her unwavering encouragement and assistance, including the final editing and of course, the printing.

A Certain Place

Author's Note: Except for a couple of very short stories in news-papers (for no pay) this is one of my early stories published in a magazine (also for no pay). Thanks to my good friend, and former editor, Harold Umber, this one appeared in the September-October, 1992 issue of North Dakota Outdoors *magazine. Harold and I have walked many a mile together on the prairies of North Dakota.*

All my life I've heard it said that if you don't like the weather in a certain place, stick around a few minutes and it will change. Well, friends, I think I've finally found that certain place—Mountrail County, North Dakota.

We first began hunting prairie grouse back in the early eighties, and a September trip to the Dakotas has become somewhat of a tradition. In 1990 we arrived late, only to find that the birds had been hunted hard, and were very spooky. Many sharp-tails, in fact most of them, flushed wild—as much as 300 yards ahead of us. Those birds are survivors, I know, but only if they are in very thin cover, or have been shot at a few times do they spook so easily. Same for Huns. The cover was fine. I decided not to replay 1990.

For 1991 we were determined to go someplace where nobody had a two-week head start on us.

A few phone calls and a letter or two put us in touch with some of the friendliest people I've ever met in nearly fifty years of hunting on three continents—the folks who live in and around Stanley, North Dakota. Except for three days of really weird weather, weather which almost defies description I might add, I had a wonderful experience on the prairies and wheat fields of Mountrail County, truly a certain place, a special place.

Because of prior commitments we had to travel on opening day, therefore missing what was described as a perfect day for hunting. "A little warm," said the man from Minnesota. "Seventy-five degrees. But your little pointer there wouldn't have had any trouble being as how you're from the South. A couple of our Brittanies had trouble with the heat."

"No problem at all with seventy-five," I said. "We've been putting in two or three hours a day of exercise and training in the low nineties. See many birds?"

"Well, in the best section we hunted, over by White Earth, the dogs pointed eight separate coveys of Huns. We saw a few sharp-tails but we didn't shoot them. We don't shoot birds unless the dogs point them. Besides, we don't like to eat sharp-tails anyway."

"I love 'em," I said. "Bone the breast and leg meat, dust it with flour, and cook it with sautéed onions and mushrooms, and a little wine. Ummm-ummmh. Hard to beat."

He smiled.

My wife and I went to bed that night dreaming of fantastic shooting the next day. At midnight it began to rain. Hard. At 6 a.m. it was raining even harder. An inch-and-a-half had already fallen earlier in the week, and now it was coming down like there was no end to it. Discouraged, we ate a leisurely breakfast, watched a movie on TV, and lounged around the hotel room until the roof started leaking. We changed rooms.

"Let's do a little recon," I suggested. "We can check out some of those places on the map, and then we'll be familiar with the area when the rain stops." It stopped at two o'clock. We hunted, succeeding only in getting soaked from the waist down because of the wet grass. Some of the roads we wanted to take were too muddy for our rent-a-car, but all in all it was a beautiful sunny afternoon. For two hours. At four the skies opened up again, sending another deluge. We met some friends and visited with them at their hideaway on the shores of Lake Sakakawea, where we dried ourselves and our clothes beside the wood stove. It was a relaxing afternoon, but so far we had only four birds.

"Tomorrow will be better," said my friend. To a certain degree he was right because it did not rain. But we slogged around his ranch in the mud and across section after section of wet Conservation Reserve Program (CRP) cover, and by noon we felt like we had been dragging a fifty-pound weight tied to each leg. The dog had fun and the birds cooperated with the dog, and we had a few more birds to show for our efforts. We took only three or four Huns from a covey before moving on. Most coveys typically contained ten to twenty birds. We called it a good day and went to bed Monday night tired but comfortable with the thought that Tuesday would be an even better day. Having traveled two thousand miles to reach this certain place, we thought we certainly deserved a better day.

During the night a cold front dropped down from Alberta and Saskatchewan bringing strong winds and freezing temperatures. Another leisurely breakfast for sure because there was no need to be in a rush. The guys from Minnesota with the eight-dog trailer went home. So did two other groups of hunters. I decided to give my little warm-weather pointer a break, and my wife decided it was too cold for her to shoot, with a gun or a camera, even on a sunny day. She chauffeured me around to some likely-looking cover and I hunted alone, discouraged that the week was not turning out as I had expected. With the wind at my back part of the time and a sharp-tail or two occasionally flushing from the wheat stubble, I was having a modicum of fun. At least it was clear and sunny—

for about an hour. Then the sleet came. It came in flurries, blown across the prairie on a thirty-knot wind. I shot two sharp-tails, but I had to shield my face from the stinging sleet which hit me like tiny bird shot as I returned to the car with my birds.

"About six landed over there in those weeds beside that grain bin," said my wife as we sat in the car watching the sleet flurries come and go. In a few minutes the ground was covered white. Just as quickly as they came, they left, moving south on the wind. They were followed by patches of warm sunshine. Soon the ground was visible again, the white sleet having melted away. She convinced me to try for the sharp-tails she had seen less than two hundred yards from the car.

I moved quickly toward the spot. They flushed just as quickly beating a hasty retreat with the wind on their tails. Two of them didn't make it, but as I searched the heavy waist-high CRP cover looking for them, I felt that now-all-too-familiar sting on my face. Another flurry hit me, reducing the visibility to a few feet. I retrieved the birds, and as we sat in the car lamenting our situation, being in this certain place during this ungodly weather, I commented that I had never before gotten a limit of sharp-tails in less than thirty minutes. I never expected to do it in goose weather either. It sure was goose weather. But stick around awhile, etc. etc.

As we arrived back at the hotel it began to snow. The men from Texas in the big four-wheel-drive Suburban checked out. We decided to stay because most of the expense of the trip is in the coming and going, and once you've already reached that certain place why not persevere—surely the weather will get better. But secretly I felt like Noah must have felt during those famous forty days.

Wednesday was still cold but the wind died down to about ten knots and the sun occasionally peeked out from behind the clouds. It was twenty-five degrees. On TV Willard was in Washington where it was ninety-five. In Mountrail County some snow lingered, clinging tenaciously to the north faces of the trees and fence posts, and hiding from the sun in the shadows, but the air was crisp and clean and invigorating and the birds were there. Little Dot, the pointer, did her job. We had some good shooting with both the Huns as well as with the sharp-tails and with the camera as well as the guns. It was a nice day, cold but nice. If you don't like the weather stick around awhile, it will change. Thursday it was sixty and Friday it was eighty, and I stripped down from my wool-lined Barbour raincoat to a short sleeve shirt. The shoulder-high weeds were a bit scratchy on the arms but bearable nonetheless. We felt like we could endure almost anything because it was good to be warm again, but because of the heat, the dogs needed water frequently. There was very little water left standing, considering all the rain that had fallen.

One fact impressed me about the CRP—we found very few birds in it. I commented on the lack of birds in the CRP acreage to my friend, Daryl, and he replied that the secret of the CRP is nesting cover. "That's where all these grouse and partridges you've been shooting were hatched," He said. "Without the CRP and, of course, the rain this year has helped too, but without the CRP you wouldn't have seen nearly as many birds."

Thanks to the CRP and some moisture relief from a few dry years we saw lots of birds. The sharp-tails were lounging in the shade of the tree rows eating choke cherries, and a few of them flushed within range. The Huns were mostly near the stubble and they held well for the dog's points, but damn, they're fast! But exciting! Very exciting! A miss here and there but most of our shots were successful and before we knew it, our vacation was over.

We were sad to have to leave, but I'll be honest with you, my wife had not been extremely enthusiastic about going in the first place, what with everyone being strangers. She's always reluctant to blaze a new trail. But let me tell you, we did not meet a stranger—everyone treated us like we were prodigals returning home after having been lost. Kill the fatted calf. Bring out the best wine.

Now my wife is planning this year's trip to that certain place. I can hardly wait.

OUTSMARTED AGAIN

Author's Note: This story appeared in the February/March 1990 issue of Shooting Sportsman *magazine, accompanied by a beautiful photograph of five swimming geese by photographer Garry Walter. It is the very first of my stories to be published in a magazine (for $1,350).*

Get down! Be still! Here they come! Who am I talking to? I ask myself when all of a sudden I realize I am alone. My hunting partner decided to sleep in this morning and here I am wet, cold, and alone in 200 acres of wheat field. Alone, that is, except for the sixty shell decoys surrounding me, looking for all the world like sixty contented geese munching away on the tender, young shoots of wheat. At least they look that way to me, as I scrunch down even lower, trying to blend in with the wheat and the mud.

"H'ronk! H'ronk! Thirty eyes look down on me from a hundred yards above as fifteen wary geese perform a perfect low-level recon pass, safely out of range, but close enough to check me out. Now I know what it is like to have the shoe on the other foot. I have performed many low-level recon passes myself, hopefully also safely out of the range of fifty caliber and thirty caliber anti-aircraft guns and other such menacing weapons hiding in the jungle. Strange, after all these years (how many, now, twenty-four? Yes.)... strange that I never made the comparison before today. Perhaps it is because I am all alone out here in this field, looking up at the squadron of Canadas slanting by on a downwind leg, looking down at me. The game's the same, but somehow different. The recon pilot has become the target, and the thirty eyes win. *Damn!* I think to myself as they turn east and continue flying. *What have I done wrong? What is it they see that makes them stay out of range and then fly away?* Of course I secretly admire their caution and their survival techniques, as I hate them for being so smart. *All the dumb geese are dead*, I think, *and that leaves the smart ones to become the breeding stock.* But I would like at least one goose dinner before the season ends. I hear there were lots of geese around while I was away.

"Man! You shoulda been here last week...geese was thicker'n mosquitoes. Ol' Sam (you know Sam don'tcha?) Hell, Ol' Sam he got twenty with one shot! You shoulda went with him." Not me. Not my kinda sport. Did I say sport? Not my kind of slaughter, I mean. I've seen the results of that kind of shooting...twenty dead, perhaps, but another dozen or so crippled, a wing broken or gut shot, struggling off to the marsh to die at night or a few days later, alone on the marsh—food for the foxes or the raccoons or the buzzards. No sir, not my kinda sport. A goose deserves a kinder adversary than a cowardly flock shooter or an outlaw gunner. Perhaps it is because I myself have been there, "slipped the surly bonds of earth and danced the skies on laughter-silvered wings; Sunward I've climbed...and done a hundred things you have not dreamed of..." as pilot/poet John Magee wrote, that I feel a certain kinship with the goose. Perhaps it is because I also wander the skies like a homesick angel, searching for who knows what. But whatever the reasons, I do, indeed, have a love/hate relationship with the venerable Canada goose.

I love to see them flying overhead as the first cold snap of late autumn sends a few winging their way southward to spend a few months along the shores of the Chesapeake. I treasure the sound of their haunting cry which has excited me for years, as I'm sure it has excited others for generations. It gives me great pleasure to see them swimming on the creek in the late spring, as two or three pairs from my neighbor's captive flock raise their young near civilization, far from their native homeland. I really enjoy watching them twist and turn, pitch and roll, killing lift and losing altitude rapidly, as they first cup their wings then spread them, just before lowering their landing gear and touching down. From a pilot's viewpoint I truly admire such maneuverability. I also fancy them roasted to perfection, tender and juicy, and served with wild rice and homemade biscuits the way my wife does it. Yes, I love Canada geese in many ways.

Right now I'm hating them as the first fifteen to come my way fly across the ditch and pitch into the next field about five hundred yards away. Knowing that my decoy rig cannot compete with 'live' decoys, I scramble out from under my weeds and such and begin the long trek to chase them away. I take my gun, on the slim chance that I might get a pass shot if some others fly by. You never can tell about geese.

"H'ronk! H'ronk! H'ronk!" Oops, now I've done it. Here I am halfway between my plastic geese and the real McCoys, and suddenly the sky is full of geese. Three, no four flocks! Twenty there. A dozen over there. Another forty over by the trees. And look, that small flock of nine right there where I was just hiding, pitching right into my sixty plastics. Not my lucky day. If only I'd stayed. What do I do now? I mean, here I stand, helpless, only partially hidden in some skinny weeds along this ditch bank, easily visible, and yet, there they go landing almost on top of my decoys. Why couldn't they come just a little closer? Why couldn't they cruise by on over here where I am, and go check out the live decoys over there in the other field? I mean, what am I doing standing here, standing in the rain, betwixt and between, with nothing to shoot at but my foot? I feel like the cartoon villain who used to say, when I was a kid, "Curses, foiled again." Do cartoon characters still say that? Probably not, but that's the way I feel, foiled again...outsmarted again. But while I regret the sad comedy I find myself in, I delight at being outsmarted by such a noble creature. I admit defeat and decide to make the best of the situation. I try to get a little more comfortable (if, indeed, onc can in forty degree rain—it's like being in your refrigerator with the ice trays leaking on your head) and tell myself I'm having fun. Here come some more geese. I sit and watch, as first one small flock and then another fly in to join the party. Soon there are about two hundred in the field; some feeding, some standing sentry duty, some merely hanging out. But there is always motion. One chases another a few yards away. "Get away from my wheat (or mate or youngster)" or whatever it is that the chaser says to the other one. A few spread their wings now and then as if preparing to launch. Or are they simply stretching? Some one or two of them look like giant dragonflies, newly hatched, drying their wings. But one truth is evident—there is constant motion. I don't suppose I ever watched them before for so long or so intently. But now I become suddenly aware of one thing lacking in my decoy spread...movement. Not movement by the goose hunter, there's probably enough of that, but movement by the geese. Five dozen lifeless plastic decoys, no matter how realistic they might look, simply do not look like sixty real geese, hustling and bustling about. I've heard about 'flagging' by professional guides. Now I can understand why it works. It's easy to see why live decoys were so effective. What I really need are two or three battery-powered, motorized decoys, strutting around in the spread. But would that add to the fun, or simply add to the frustration?

Geese don't always offer me the consistent sport that upland birds have offered me over the years. Sometimes in the past I can remember few, if any, geese around until after the season was over. Too much good corn up in Maryland or grass on Connecticut golf courses. Weather didn't cooperate. Poor breeding conditions on the tundra. But I also remember a few good years here in Virginia when conditions were right and my schedule allowed it. A couple of good days before Christmas, maybe a day or two in January, and Bingo! six or eight geese. Why I guess I've had goose for Christmas Eve dinner five or six times during the past ten years. But not this year. Maybe I try too hard. One thing I know. A pit works. I don't have a pit. I have to try and hide my big ol' ugly self on top of the ground, and that's not easy. Someday maybe. Maybe I can convince my farmer friend that with reasonable caution his hired hands won't drive his tractors or his combine into the pit. That seems to be his biggest fear. Maybe, however, he secretly admires and respects the geese as much as I do, or more, and he doesn't want me to become too successful. Maybe, just maybe, he gets a thrill knowing his geese have outsmarted me once again.

"Heh, heh! Boy that ol' Ash is something, ain't he? Laying out there flat on his back in the mud tryin' to fool them geese. Thinks he's smarter than they are, he does. Them geese is a whole lot smarter'n he is, and prob'ly better flyers too. Look at 'em. Jes look at 'em...flyin' around all over th' sky out there and waitin' until he's outta position before they land. When is he ever goin' to learn?"

But that's all right. I don't mind. I'll keep trying as long as he lets me. Sometimes I'll win, but most times I'll lose. No, that's not right—lose is not the right word for it. I win every time. Sometimes I don't have any geese to clean, but that's not a loss. Just seeing them and hearing their beautiful voices calling to each other, and to me—knowing they'll be around for my grandchildren to see and to hear into the next century—that's a win no matter who keeps score.

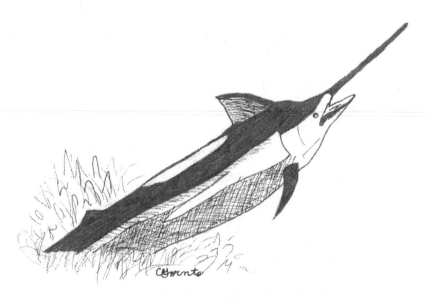

A GREAT FISH

Author's Note: This is one of those very short stories in newspa-pers (for no pay) I mentioned earlier. It first appeared in the Eastern Shore News, *a local paper on Virginia's Eastern Shore.*

A few years ago one of my best friends handed me a book, saying "I know you enjoy good books. Read this one and let me know what you think." My friend knows I'm a frustrated writer, always on the lookout for some inspiration to bring out of me that Great American Novel hiding inside.

The book he loaned me was *The Great Fish*, by Jack Samson. I had already read Mr. Samson's book *Line Down* and numerous stories in *Field and Stream Magazine*, so I knew I was in for a real treat. I expected some novel about a fish or a man, or both, similar to *Moby Dick* or *The Old Man and the Sea*. What I found, instead, is a perfectly delightful book of short stories Mr. Samson has com-posed about some of the great experiences he has had both catch-ing (and losing) various game fish around the world.

Yesterday I met one of those Great Fish! It was an experience I will never forget even though I was merely a bystander, and observer—a witness to the battle. This little tale is a tribute to that Great Fish and to the young man who so nobly did battle with him for nearly eight hours.

I was a guest aboard the boat *BOZO II*, sailing out of Wachapreague, captained by Carey Roberts. The other anglers were Rob Bloxom and Stewart Keating. We plunged through a rough inlet at 6:15. headed for Norfolk Canyon and blue water. We were slightly concerned about the weather and the sea since the entire east coast was being bombarded with gigantic eight-to-ten-foot swells, courtesy of Hurricane Gabrielle, one thousand miles east and north of us. She had graciously passed us at that distance, but was, nonetheless, showing us a sample of her fury. We were concerned, yes, and apprehensive about the weather, but *BOZO II* is an Albemarle—as sea-worthy a craft as has ever been built—so there was never any doubt about our safety.

The sunrise was breathtaking. Once we were through the inlet the seas were kinder and gentler. It was going to be a beautiful day; I just knew it...a real serendipity day, full of unexpected pleasures.

The next two hours were routine as we settled in at twenty-six knots to ride the fifty or so miles to our target fishing grounds. Shortly before the magic 'lines-in-the-water' hour of eight-thirty we rigged a few baits and prepared to drag them unceremoniously through the clear blue Gulf Stream waters. Such is the stuff fishing trips are made of. The next two hours were equally routine and uninteresting as the previous two. They say offshore fishing has something in common with flying airplanes—hours and hours of sheer boredom interrupted with moments of complete mayhem. They're right.

A lazy day. Gently rolling and trolling in Gabrielle's gentle swells. A weed line! Get closer. Not too close. A couple of rod tips bend and jerk, picking up small clumps of seaweed. "Crank 'em in, boys. Clean 'em up. Can't catch a dolphin with all that grass on the hook." Ziiinnng! One of the lines gets pulled a little harder. "Check that one, Stewart, 'cause it could be a small dolphin. Probably only a larger clump of seaweed, though." How many times that happened to me over the years? I can't count them.

Suddenly, about fifty yards astern it happened! First there was the crash, the splash, white water everywhere. Now I've caught a few dolphin in my day but nothing like that. "That's a billfish boys, I'll call it in. "*BOZO II* to Committee Boat, we have a hook-up, fish unknown." Captain Roberts remained unusually calm. He's done this a few times.

"Roger *BOZO*, hook-up at 10:27. Good luck gang." Stewart settled in and began cranking the reel. Now offshore fishing, if anything, is a team sport. My apologies to the old man and the sea, but not many people battle great fish single-handedly. There were six other lines in the water. Rob and I cranked like mad retrieving those lines so they would not interfere with the one hooked up. Everyone's eyes were concentrated aft, expecting to see another citation-class dolphin or perhaps a small white marlin perform some aerobatics. But Stewart was watching the line disappear from his reel.

"We'd better do something boys; half the line's gone and he's still taking it." Reverse!

"Get ready guys; we hafta back down on him." Slam, bang, crash, splash! Spray came pouring in over the transom as Carey and the Albemarle gamely tried to help Stewart recover the lost line. Crank, pump. Crank, pump. Crank, pump. We gained a hundred, then two hundred, then three hundred yards. Now the reel spool was nearly full. "We got him guys, get ready!" Then the great fish decided to give us a preview of what was in store. About thirty yards astern, the sea erupted like a blue and white volcano. What came forth, however, was not lava, but a gigantic blue marlin, half the length of the boat! What a sight!

"Did you see th-th-the size of that fish?" asked Stewart. "Good grief, that's the biggest fish I ever saw!" We all agreed it was the biggest fish any of us had ever seen and then some. "Hey, I hear some people fight these things for an hour or two, sometimes."

"Eight hours, man. Eight hours is not all that unusual and then lose the fish," I added. Twenty minutes. Thirty minutes. An hour. Crank, pull. "How're you doing, Stewart? Arms tired? I'd be hurting by now. The longest I ever fought a fish was forty-five minutes, a tuna, and my arms were tired for three days."

"No, I'm fine. I'm a young man. I can take it." His emphasis on the word young did not escape me.

"Hungry? Thirsty?"

"Nope, I'm fine." (*Cocky little kid*, I thought. *Wait another hour and we'll see how fine he is.*) Crank, pull. Crank, pull.

Two hours. Rob and I took turns relieving Carey at the helm. It's not too difficult—and mostly boring—running in reverse at 1,000 to 1,200 RPM, being towed all over Norfolk Canyon by a great fish. And he was a great one. Every so often he'd leap completely out of the water trying to shake the hook. Or was he simply playing with us? Entertaining us? Teasing us? Three hours. "Committee Boat to *BOZO*. How're you doing guys? Still got him, eh? Keep at it. We're pulling for you. Committee Boat, out." Crank, pull.

Four hours. 2:30 in the afternoon. "How're you doing Stewart? Ready to quit yet? Thirsty? Hungry? How about a cold soft drink?" Stewart drank a cold Dr. Pepper. He wasn't even sweating. How could he do it? I was aching just watching him. Crank, pull. Crank, pull. What a way to ruin our fishing trip.

Five hours. Six hours. Another leap. This time he tail-walked or grey-hounded across our stern about thirty yards aft. What a sight! Just like something you read about in Zane Grey or Ernest Hemingway, or Jack Samson.

Finally the captain, realizing that we did not want to tackle Wachapreague Inlet after dark, decided we had to tighten the drag a little, in steps, so as to either catch the fish or lose him. Actually it was a release tournament, anyway. We never actually intended to catch the fish, merely get him close enough to touch the swivel, release him, and declare ourselves the winner. The fish had other ideas. He spent the better part of the day within fifty feet to fifty yards of us, always just out of reach. We could see him down there about fifty feet below us, resting, watching us. Each time we'd tighten the drag another notch, and Stewart would crank and pull a few times, the fish decided to let us know he was still the boss. Another leap. This time he came twice his body length out of the water. There he was, after seven hours of towing us around, still leaping and shaking his head (and probably laughing at us). Crank, pump. Tighten the drag. Crank, pump.

"We got him guys. Get ready. Here he comes. I see the swivel, right there, just below the surface. He's only twenty feet away. Damn! He really IS half as big as the boat. Easy now. Get ready." We went on and on like that for another forty-five minutes. Each time we almost had him. Poor *BOZO II*'s lower unit must have gone into and out of reverse two hundred times during that last few minutes. Then, a rifle shot! Just as suddenly as he had crashed the bait at 10:27 in the morning at 6:12 that afternoon the line broke, and with one great flip of his huge tail he was gone.

How do you spell relief? Remember the old Rolaids commercial? R E L E A S E. No matter that the fish had won. He did the release. He won the battle. We lost the tournament. But the thrill of it all will be with me forever, and I'm sure we'll ask ourselves hundreds of times, "What could we have done differently?"

Nothing, probably. Savor the experience. Share it with others. Hope it happens again. But it probably won't. GREAT FISH don't come along every day.

FRECKLES

We had arrived in northern California in early fall, the first week of October in fact, and I had a very busy few months training for my new job. We had a small amount of play money, but not much time for leisure activities, other than an occasional cook-out with friends or a movie now and then. I knew there was hunting to be found in California but it was a while before I learned my way around or even had time to investigate the recreational opportunities in our adopted state. The following spring I joined a hunt club whose members were mostly blue collar workers and several retirees. The club leased thirty-thousand acres in the Sacramento River valley for 25¢ an acre. Most of the land was rice farms and the main quarry was waterfowl, but there were a few spots here and there which held some pheasants, and occasionally I saw flocks of doves in the vicinity. In a few choice spots our leased land bordered a National Wildlife Refuge. In those days, you could legally harvest six geese and six ducks a day.

My financial wizard of a wife had lived with her parents while I was in Vietnam, and she had managed to save about two thousand dollars. Our hunt club was headquartered in Colusa County, and it had a small bunk house, an old equipment shed, and an RV park with space and hookups for about thirty travel trailers. So one day we made an impulsive decision and spent our two grand on an RV, a used sixteen-foot Aristocrat camper/trailer that slept four. A few trips to the hunt club convinced us that we had found a little piece of heaven on earth. However, one afternoon while camped near an irrigation canal in early September, we discovered the true meaning of the term "swarms of mosquitoes," and it looked a lot less like heaven.

Once we moved out of an apartment in San Mateo and into a house north of the bay, it was mutually agreed that we would try to find a dog. Thus it was that we answered an ad in the Santa Rosa newspaper that read "Pups For Sale."

"Well, we only have one left, the runt, and he's a male. All our females were taken the first day of the ad," said the voice on the phone.

"I'm looking for a hunting dog," I said. "What breed is he?"

"Let's see now, the daddy's a springer and the mama is a Brittany, so he don't have no papers. But I have hunted with both parents, and they do all right. They both hunt pheasants and they retrieve too."

I was hooked. Once we saw the little thing, my wife was hooked too. We paid the $25.00 and took him home that very day. Fortunately, the backyard of our rental house was already fenced, so I did not have to undertake that project, but I did enclose a space about ten feet by ten feet. My next task was to build him a dog house. Since he was basically white and covered with little brown spots, Freckles seemed like the perfect name. Once he had proper shelter, his training became the next order of business. My father had owned several bird dogs when I was a youngster, but his time and training talents were limited, so I had seen my share of "busted" quail coveys and chewed up birds. I developed a dislike for Irish setters because we had a couple, one of which must have been the dumbest dog ever born. My biggest wish was to have a dog with more style, class, and manners than we'd ever owned before. I had read so many books on dog training that I felt reasonably capable of the task.

I must tell you this about little Freckles: we should have named him "Curiosity" or "Kitty" because he was like a little kitten with his intense fascination for butterflies, crickets, snails, and such. Within a week of his arrival, I was training him with the basic *sit, stay, come* routine, and he was making great progress. One exceptionally warm spring afternoon after a twenty-minute training session, I left him alone, free to roam the back yard while I went inside to get a Coke. I wasn't gone more than twenty minutes, and when I returned outside, I noticed that Freckles was a little wobbly as he came toward me. He sat at my feet and looked up at me with his bright little puppy eyes. I backed away a few steps and whistled. As he walked toward me he fell flat on one side. Plop! Just like that! He got up, took a couple more wobbly steps and fell again. That time he stayed down.

"No!" I shouted out loud, not at him but at whoever would listen. "No, not my new little puppy. Freckles, you can't die!"

My wife and daughter were at the mall shopping, and within two minutes, the puppy and I were in the pickup truck, headed for the vet, who was about five minutes away. Freckles just lay there on the seat, peacefully, completely unaware that I was in a panic. I raced into the vet's office holding an armful of pathetic little puppy who by now was like a limp dish towel. I described to the vet what had happened. He immediately aimed a small flashlight beam into Freckles' eyes. "Snail bait!" exclaimed the vet. "Snail bait. Have you put down any poison for snails?"

My mind raced a mile a minute as I tried to comprehend what he was asking. Then I remembered. "Yes," I replied. "Snail bait. Yes! Some small white granules along the edge of the patio, but I don't know what it is."

"Never mind." He mentioned the probable name of the poison,

but I don't remember what it was. "It's pretty deadly stuff, but I think we can save him with an IV antidote." He told me the name of the medicine, but it sounded Greek to me. I held my little pup gently on the cool stainless steel table while the doc inserted the needle into a front leg and started the flow of life-giving antidote. Then he carefully taped the syringe in place. Meanwhile Freckles showed no reaction. "Don't expect a miracle, but this usually works. By tomorrow he should be all right, but I think you should let us keep him overnight. Call us tomorrow at ten o'clock."

"Okay," I replied, "And please don't let him die." I went home a nervous wreck. Since the vet was so close, actually right on the main road at the entrance to our neighborhood, I did not bother to call. I was there promptly at ten o'clock the next day. The attendant brought Freckles to me with the small syringe still taped to his foreleg with white adhesive tape. My poor puppy looked tired, bedraggled and sad, but he was alive and that's what mattered to me.

Within two days, he was fully recovered. I scraped up and discarded all the snail bait I could find, and we resumed our training. Whenever he began to sniff and snoop along the edges of the flower beds, I promptly returned him to his kennel. As hunting season approached, Freckles was six months old. He was routinely pointing and retrieving my training pigeons, and much to my liking, he was soft-mouthed enough that he never harmed a single one of my live pigeons. I bought three pheasants from a neighbor, and we worked with them several times before they escaped and flew home. I was excited and filled with enthusiasm as opening day neared. My enthusiasm was matched by my wife's, who was not only happy about Freckles' miraculous recovery, but also very pleased with her new Charles Daly 20-gauge O/U I had purchased from Miroku in Tokyo a few months earlier.

We towed our camper to the hunt club the week before so we could get a good spot. On opening morning, I selected what I thought was a choice, birdy-looking spot, a slough between a rice field and a milo field, and off we went, already tasting our first meal of savory roasted pheasant. The rooster pheasant flushed wild about one hundred yards ahead of us, but Freckles saw it and immediately took off, running after it like a hound, only not barking. He ran at least a half mile, along a levee and across two fields, paying absolutely no attention to my whistling and shouting. I was mad, disappointed, and embarrassed; hoping none of my hunt club buddies were witnessing this terrible situation. I looked around and noticed two other hunters nearby, at the far edge of an adjacent milo field. They must have found a pheasant, too, because I heard a shot, followed by five more. I think each one fired three shots at the same bird.

As soon as Freckles heard those shots, he quit chasing his rooster and returned to me. He was limping—no, not so much limping as walking sort of stiff-legged, marching like a Nazi soldier, not bending his legs at the knees. I knelt down beside him and noticed that he was covered with cockleburs, perhaps as many as one hundred. Each of his beautiful, long silky ears contained fifteen or twenty. Under each foreleg, in the armpit area, there were another dozen or so. His hind leg feathers were two big blobs of cockleburs and matted hair and his little bob tail contained three or four. He was a pitiful sight, but I had little sympathy for his misbehaving. I could not bear to see him so uncomfortable so I began to remove the offending burrs. It was a nearly impossible task, because each time I gave a burr a little tug, Freckles would wince and yelp in pain. Each one of the burrs that I removed took with it at least a dozen hairs, and I finally admitted that I was totally unprepared for such a situation out in the field. My wife, Ginna, agreed that our best course of action was to return to the camper where we had some scissors. She carried both shotguns and I carried our champion bird dog, cradled in my arms like an infant, back to the truck which was nearly a half mile away.

It took us about an hour to remove the cockleburs. Thus ended our first California pheasant hunt. We ate hamburgers for dinner.

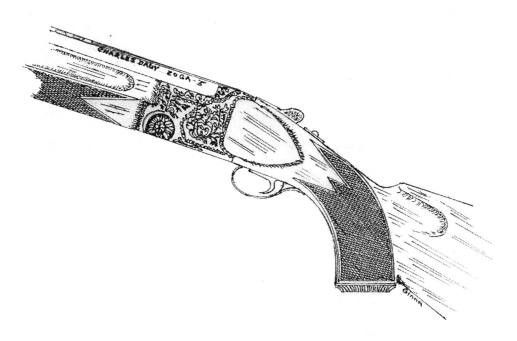

THE PURLOINED DALY

It had taken more than a year, but I finally reached the point where I enjoyed flying to and shopping in Tokyo. The first few times I flew back and forth to Japan from San Francisco, either via Honolulu or Anchorage, I was a frustrated navigator. Often I did not know exactly where the Boeing 707 was because I could not always get a satisfactory loran line or (because of the cloud cover) I could see neither the sun, the moon, nor any stars or planets in the sextant viewfinder. Much of the time we were out of range of any reliable, shore-based navigational aids, and the captain depended on me, the new guy, to keep us on course. That was often not an easy task while hurtling through the air at groundspeeds sometimes exceeding 600 knots or ten miles a minute. Sometimes, I went as long as an hour without a reliable "fix" of our position and relied on a navigation technique known as "dead reckoning" to provide air traffic control with our whereabouts. Fortunately, the Pacific corridors were sixty miles wide and vertical separation was a minimum of 2,000 feet. If we came up from Guam to Japan via South Vietnam, we occasionally had maintenance or military schedule delays causing the duty day sometimes to last more than sixteen hours, and even though the navigation was easier, I was usually exhausted by the time we reached our hotel in Tokyo. But as time wore on and I became more accustomed to navigating the Pacific, I looked forward to being in Tokyo two or three times each month.

It was not long after the 1968 Firearms Act was passed by Congress that I felt like I could afford to buy my wife a new shotgun as a Christmas present. I had shopped around in California and London and decided that she would probably like an over/under 20-gauge, most of which were too pricey for my budget. Another pilot suggested that I look in the Miroku show room in Tokyo. Miroku manufactured a beautiful over/under for Charles Daly. I had read about Dalys in magazines, and I decided it was worth checking them out, so I visited the Tokyo showroom once or twice and was impressed enough that I finally made the decision to buy one for her. On that trip, I was a crewmember on a cargo flight non-stop to San Francisco, which meant I would avoid Honolulu Customs, and thus I felt comfortable carrying the gun case inside the plane without having to worry about its security in the lower baggage compartment.

We arrived at the Cargo Customs Office in San Francisco and I proudly opened the gun case for the inspector (the fitted case itself being a work of art). I had what I considered to be all the necessary paperwork. "I'll have to confiscate the firearm, sir," said the inspector, much to my disappointment. "You'll need to have an authorized and licensed federal firearms dealer process it through customs on your behalf. You can leave it here, we'll place it in bonded storage, and your dealer can get it at his convenience. Next."

"But I don't know a federal gun dealer," I protested.

"Well, one of your pilots is one. He picks up guns here for his friends all the time. His name is Stan Roitz. You should check with him. Next."

I did not know Stan, but I made it my top priority to meet him soon. I discovered his box number in the pilot mail room next to the crew lounge, and I left him a note telling him of my predicament and asking for his help. A few days later, he called me and said he was going out on a quick turnaround pattern to Honolulu and back, and he would retrieve the gun in three days and call me back. The charge would be $20.00. I thanked him and said I would be at home when he called.

Sure enough, right on time three days later, the phone rang. "Ash, this is Stan Roitz. I have some bad news, buddy. I picked up your shotgun before I went on the trip, and while I was in Honolulu yesterday or last night, my car was stolen from the crew parking lot. Your shotgun was in it, along with a pistol I picked up for another pilot. My insurance company will cover the loss, but you'll have to buy another gun in Tokyo. Sorry."

I did not have another Tokyo trip on my schedule for November, but I would desperately try to arrange one in December. Unfortunately, I was so junior on the seniority list that all my December choices were taken by senior pilots, and I had to fly to Guam and Vietnam the whole month. At least I would be home for Christmas. I gave my wife a photo of Benjamin Franklin on a $100 bill in one of those envelopes with the little cutout window. Santa stuffed it in her stocking on Christmas Eve, and I left on another Vietnam trip on December 26th.

As luck would have it, I was rescheduled during the Guam layover and sent home via Tokyo. During that layover, I returned to the Miroku showroom and explained my problem. They had several guns on display almost exactly like the one stolen from Stan's car. The walnut stock was slightly darker, but I didn't mind, and I was sure my wife wouldn't mind either because she never saw the first one. So I purchased it and repeated my experience in San Francisco customs. I was getting good at this, and I was excited that the gun would now be available for her birthday on January 13th.

About a week later, Stan called and asked if I could meet him at the airport the next day and pick up the gun and pay him. "By the way," he remarked, "They located my car in Hunter's Point. It was on cinder blocks and burned to a crisp. No evidence of either gun, so the police have listed them as stolen. I doubt if they'll ever find either one. It's like a real ghetto down there." Hunter's Point was (and still might be) an economically depressed neighborhood, and was the scene of violent and deadly riots in 1966. I told Stan I was sorry about his car and that I would meet him the next day, which I did.

The shotgun was beautiful. Stan had made a slight addition which was to have the name of his company *PICCO* engraved on the trigger guard. He said it was required by federal law.

Pan Am reinforced the crew parking lot fence and installed a gate with a guard on duty 24/7. As far as I know the theft of crew-members' cars ceased.

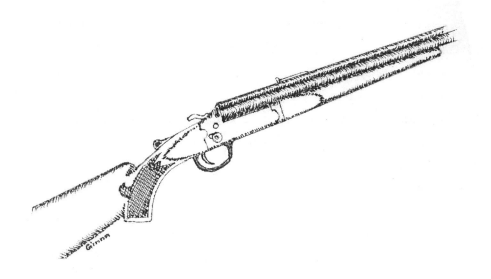

MY FIRST SHOTGUN

I visited my sister a few nights ago to deliver a couple of Christmas gifts. Her nine-year old grandson Drew was there, and within a very few minutes of my arrival, after he had helped her open my gift to her, he asked, "Gram, can I show him my gift?" As has been a custom in my family for as long as I can remember, they had allowed him to open one gift early, a few days before Christmas. Actually I think his grandpa (Poppy) was just as excited as he was about the gift, perhaps even more so. I know he had been planning it for months, asking my opinion about the matter a couple of times.

"Yes, you may," my sister replied, "But remember what we said about being careful."

"I will." With a huge grin on his little face, he happily showed me his new .22 rifle which they had given him earlier in the day.

As he stretched out his arms to offer the rifle to me, his Poppy asked, "Is the safety on?"

I heard Drew's soft reply as he clicked the safety off and then back on to reassure us. "Yes, it is."

I could tell that they had already been doing some gun safety instructing, which I was glad to observe. Not only do they both know I have a "thing" about gun safety, but they also know the main reasons for it. I still have the scars. I inspected the rifle, a cute little Savage Youth model, bolt-action with a small clip extending below the action. I opened the bolt and showed my great-nephew how similar rifles are inspected in the Army, and I told him how important it is to keep it clean. He showed me his box of ammo. Nostalgia was rapidly beginning to take hold of me and suddenly I was transported back in time to a Christmas long ago when I, too, was nine years old, and I received my very first gun.

On that Christmas morning, I acted very surprised when I opened the gift, which was the largest package under the tree. "Oh goody!" I exclaimed as I eagerly tore the tissue paper away from the little .410 after removing it from the box. "Look what Santa brought me. A shotgun. Look, Daddy! Now I can go squirrel hunting with you."

I think I was successful in concealing the fact that I had found and admired the gun about a week earlier, tucked way back under some blankets on the top shelf in their bedroom closet. I was careful not to get my oily fingers on the blankets when I returned the box to its hiding place. I did not tell my little sister I had found the gun, because I was certain she would tattle. In fact, on that same closet shelf I also discovered a gift for her, but I didn't tell her that either. I turned to face my mother. "Look, Mommy, look at my new gun."

"I see," said my mom. "But I want you to know that it is not new. Santa had a tough time finding one, and he had to settle for this one which was used for two or three years by another little boy who outgrew it. But Santa promised us that that little boy had taken very good care of it, and it is almost good as new."

"I don't mind," I replied. "I don't mind at all. Guns last for a very long time, and I'll take good care of it too. When can we go huntin', Daddy?"

"Well, maybe in a few days," he replied. "But first you have to practice with it, and learn how to handle it safely. It's not a toy, remember. Maybe tomorrow. What else did Santa bring you?" From beneath the tree, I found two or three wrapped gifts, and I opened each one slowly, savoring each delicious second. There was a new shirt, some new socks, a book, and a box which I recognized even before opening it.

"I bet I know what this is," I said gleefully. "I bet this is some gun shells." I hastily tore at the wrapping paper and discovered that I was correct. It was a box of number six .410 shells. I think they were Remington, but it was a long time ago. "These will work for both rabbits and squirrels, won't they, Daddy?" I asked. "Number six. That's the same kind you use, don't you?"

Seeing no more gifts with my name on the card, I next removed my stocking from the nail in the front edge of the mantel and found some pecans, a big Brazil nut, four quarters, a pack of chewing gum, a tangerine, and an orange nestled down inside. We had opened most of our gifts to and from each other the night before, when my extended family gathered for our Christmas Eve dinner held at our house. Christmas morning was saved for the gifts from Santa. I also noticed that the little piece of fruitcake was missing from the plate we had placed on the mantel before going to bed, and the glass of milk had been consumed. I guess my dad had taken care of them after I had gone to bed, because the fireplace was still warm, and I was fairly certain Santa could not come down the chimney onto a bed of glowing hot coals. In fact, many of my classmates at school had told me that Santa was just for kids and we nine and ten-year olds were grown up enough to know that. But however he had managed to get that shotgun into my parents' closet at least a week before Christmas, or if my parents had bought it from some friend, mattered to me not one bit. It was my shotgun now.

It was a Stevens over/under model 22-410: .22 rifle on top and .410 shotgun below. It had a brown plastic stock and fore end. It was a break-open type with an exposed hammer which took some effort for me to bring to full cock, but with practice I soon managed.

The firing pin for the top barrel was broken, but we already had another .22 rifle anyway, so I didn't mind. It was the bottom barrel, the .410 shotgun that interested me. Now I could hunt with the big guys.

During the week, I used that entire box of shells shooting at soup cans and coffee cans which Dad placed on top of the corner clothesline post. I practiced from the back porch steps, a distance of about fifteen yards. It was so tempting to practice on a real chicken, but I knew full well that as soon as I did that the gun would go back into the box for who knows how long. So I resisted that temptation. I used what little money I had the next time we went to town and bought another box of shells. I'm not one hundred percent sure, but I think a full box of twenty-five shells cost one dollar, but it was a long time ago, so forgive me if that's not the exact figure.

One cold Saturday morning in mid-January, as we were finishing breakfast, three or four of my dad's friends from work came to the farm and brought some beagle hounds. At least two of the hunters brought their dogs in dog boxes in their pickup truck beds. I think each box contained five dogs. After a few minutes of greetings and small talk about Christmas, the dogs' owners released them into our backyard. One or two of them headed straight for the fenced chicken yard, sending the fifteen or twenty laying hens scurrying away to the far side of their enclosure. The men hollered and shouted, "No!" to those dogs several times, and soon they gave up on the chickens and ran around squealing and sniffing and such so as to get to know each other. My dad released his two beagles, Bob and Lady, who joined right in. Twelve beagles is a big pack of dogs; the most I had ever seen at once being four, my dad's two and my uncle's two. I was almost beginning to feel sorry for the rabbits. After some twenty minutes of all this commotion and hullabaloo, my mom stuck her head out the kitchen door and reminded me to wear my cap and gloves, and to be careful with that shotgun.

"I will," I answered. Soon the men walked along the edge of the cotton field alongside the barnyard, calling to the dogs, a couple of which had already reached the large weed patch behind the vegetable garden. The cotton had been harvested shortly after Halloween, and the empty stalks and bolls made me remember how hard I had worked picking that cotton by hand for three cents a pound. The most I ever picked in one day was eighty pounds, but that earned me enough for two boxes of gun shells with some change. I stayed close to my dad, carrying my shotgun over my shoulder like a soldier. I had five shells in each side pocket of my jacket; figuring that was surely enough. I was finally on a real rabbit hunt with a real shotgun.

Within five minutes and within fifty yards of the house, a couple of the beagles began to bark. "Hot damn!" exclaimed one of my dad's friends. "Old Buster's done jumped us a rabbit! Y'all spread out down along that far edge of the cotton patch. He'll run down to the swamp, but them dogs will chase him back thisaway soon."

The hunters spread out in a line facing the woods with their backs to the cotton field. Dad told me to stay right here beside him at the corner, that way we would have a good view both along the field as well as along that path into the woods which led to the mill pond. The entire pack of dogs were now hot on the heels of that poor cottontail, and they were trying to let the whole world know about it. For dedicated beagle lovers, that sound was music to their ears. I knew where they were headed, and I also knew that the man was probably right—when spooked from their little hidey holes in the weed patch, the rabbits usually ran in a large circle and returned to within a few yards of their security zone. I had hunted with these men before, but without a gun.

Before long, maybe fifteen minutes, the sound of those dogs, which had grown dim then silent for a few minutes, now began to get louder. That rabbit had led them across the little branch over to the wooded area we always called cedar hill. They temporarily lost the scent in the stream, but not for long. Suddenly, *bang!* The unmistakable blast of a 12-gauge shotgun sounded off to my left, maybe a hundred yards away. Then another *bang!* The dogs continued to bark out of sight in the honeysuckle patch along the edge of the stand of sweetgum trees which separated the branch from the cotton field.

"He must have missed the rabbit," my dad whispered. "Keep a sharp lookout now. Watch that path closely, Son, 'cause that rabbit could pop up anytime. Your gun's loaded, isn't it?"

"Yes sir, should I cock it yet?"

"Not until you're ready to shoot, remember?"

"Yes sir, I remember," But I was anxious, not wanting to miss a chance if that rabbit came into view within range of my little .410. "There he is!" I shouted as I cocked that hammer and raised my shotgun to my shoulder in one practiced motion. He ran toward me along the woods path, and as soon as he saw me, he turned ninety-degrees and ran parallel to the cotton field. I aimed about six feet in front of him and squeezed the trigger, just like I had practiced at least twenty-five times. I think I closed my eyes, too. *Bang* went my little gun. I opened my eyes just as that rabbit did a summersault and fell along the edge of the field right next to the first row of cotton stalks.

"You got him!" my dad exclaimed. "Good shootin', Son. You'd better go pick him up before those beagles get him." I raced the thirty yards to where the cottontail lay. Even though I had seen dead rabbits before that day, I was sad to see that he was bloody, and saddened that I was the cause, but I bravely held him aloft for all to see, as one dog after another tried to rip him from my grasp. Soon the men calmed the beagles, my dad placed my rabbit in the game pouch within his hunting coat, and we headed down the path to another likely spot.

Several of my dad's friends congratulated me. "Way to go, young man," they said. "Nice shootin', Son. You never gave that old cottontail a chance."

One of the men said to me, "Better than I did. I missed him twice. Way to go, kid." I felt like a million bucks. I hoped my mom would be as pleased as I was.

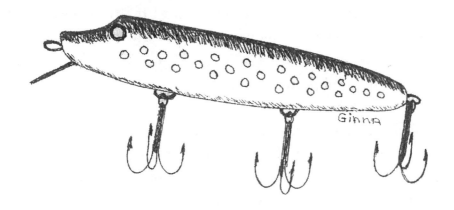

A DAY ON THE POND

When I saw the movie *Forrest Gump* for the first time, I thought of my dad, especially during the scene where Bubba described to Lt. Dan the many types of shrimp he liked. My dad loved fish. He loved to catch fish. He loved to eat fish. He loved them broiled. He loved them baked. He loved them in a stew called a fish muddle. Mostly though, he loved them battered and fried crisp in lard or peanut oil and served with hushpuppies and potato salad or coleslaw. Although I never knew his mother, I imagine that is the way she normally served them. When I was finally able to get a suitable boat, one of the first things I did was take my dad fishing. It was in the Chesapeake Bay, and the fish we caught that day were black drum, but this is a story about another fishing trip with my dad, when I was a boy of about ten.

The scene was the mill pond which adjoined our farm. That pond was the site of many of my childhood adventures and misadventures. My friend, David Blythe, tells me that he remembers several times when he and I went hunting along the banks of the pond, and I shot wood ducks which fell out beyond our reach. Not having a retriever, I stripped down to my jockey shorts and swam out to retrieve the ducks, even when it was covered with a thin sheet of ice.

The fishing trip was in July and my Unca Bill was visiting from Alabama. He also loved to catch fish, and my dad enjoyed taking him fishing in the mill pond. I begged to go along, but my dad said, "No. Maybe next time."

My Unca Bill disagreed and told Dad he thought they should take me along. I think my dad was against it because they would probably be drinking a beer or two, and I would most likely share their secret with my mom. She didn't drink, and she didn't like it when Dad drank in my presence. I don't remember if they took any beer with us that day, but the rest of the trip is still vivid in my memory, more than sixty years later.

"Okay," my dad finally agreed, "but first you'll have to dig yourself some worms for bait." I raced to dad's tool shed, grabbed a shovel, ran to the fenced chicken yard, and within ten minutes, I had secured about ten or twelve wiggly earthworms and one big, white, ugly grub. I placed them in an old blue coffee can and covered them with a couple handfuls of black loamy soil. I grabbed a cane pole and the two adults each took a casting rod and reel. My dad also took his tackle box and his boat paddle. Unca Bill carried the .22 rifle (in case we saw any cottonmouth moccasins) and I carried my can of worms. I felt like Tom Sawyer or Huckleberry Finn, off on an adventure. Our boat would be my raft.

We had to walk about three-quarters of a mile through the woods and along the bank of the pond because in summer the water level was low, and the boat was tied up at the "summer" landing, which was farther from the house than the "winter" landing. That winter landing was only about a quarter mile from the house, and we used it during squirrel season. I remember that it was hot that afternoon, and neither of us took any water to drink. We stopped a couple of times and wiped the sweat from our brows and swatted mosquitoes. "Not much farther," my dad told us.

And he was correct. Soon we reached the boat landing at a place my family always called the "Tom Hole" without ever providing any clue as to how it got that name, or if I was ever told, I forgot. It was the deepest part of the pond, it covered about ten acres, and in my seventy-four years, I have never seen it dry. In fact, that is where my dad had taught me to swim one hot afternoon a few years earlier when I was five or six. He simply tossed me overboard from the small wooden johnboat into the Tom Hole, and back paddled about six feet, just out of my reach, and said, "Paddle." So just like a dog I frantically paddled (flailed is more like it) with my arms and legs until I successfully covered the distance between us and grabbed the boat before he could back away any farther. My feet never touched bottom, so I guess it could be said that I was swimming, but the following summer my mom paid for me to take swimming lessons at the town's public pool. I was glad because they did not have snakes at the town pool, and my swimming instructor was a beautiful college girl with a nice tan. I remember her.

Dad walked through a small patch of canes, unlocked the padlocked chain from the Tupelo gum tree, pulled the bow of the boat up onto the bank, stepped into the boat, and took the stern seat. "You take the middle seat, Son," he said, "and let your Uncle Bill have the front seat."

I did as I was told, took the center seat, and placed my can of worms at my feet. Once seated, Unca Bill eased us away from the bank out toward the deepest part of the pond and that was it—we were fishing. I unfurled the monofilament line from around my cane pole, made sure the cork was where I wanted it, and put the largest worm I could find on the small brass-colored hook, which was about twelve inches below the split shot lead weight. I had done this many times before. I was ready to catch whatever fish decided he was hungry enough to attack my worm.

Meanwhile, my dad began to cast one of his painted top-water plugs out toward a clump of brushy weeds and a wild rose bush growing from an old stump next to a cypress tree. He liked that spot because it was where he had caught his nine-pound bass several years before I was born. He kept that old dried and yellowed fish head in his tool room and never failed to show it off to friends. "I know there's a ten-pounder out there somewhere," he would often say, "And one day I'm gonna catch him." The largest one I ever saw him catch weighed about four pounds. Mostly we caught perch, crappie, a few pike, and a bream once in a while. I sometimes caught a catfish with my worms. They were my favorite at the table.

Unca Bill put a lure called a daredevil—a red and white spoon—on his line and made a few casts toward the other side of the Tom Hole, away from the direction my father was fishing. Each time one of them made a back cast I watched carefully to ensure my head was down. Neither of them caught a fish. I had a couple of nibbles, but I was no more successful than they were. I think my hook was too large for the little fish that nibbled at my worm. "It's too hot. They'll probably start to bite as soon as it cools off a little," I remember my dad saying.

After about an hour, he opened his tackle box, removed a cigar-sized wooden plug painted light gray on its back, white on its belly, with a few small black spots along the sides and said, "Try this one, Bill. This is what I used when I caught that nine-pound bass a few years ago. Maybe it'll bring you luck." It was about twice the size of the lure Unca Bill had been using and it had three sets of treble hooks. I had seen Dad use it in the past, and he had caught fish with it, I knew. There was a small streak of red along its painted-on mouth, and it had two yellow and black beads as eyes. It sort of resembled a tiny pike, but it really did not look like any fish I had ever seen, but I know it must have fooled a few fish in its lifetime. I knew it had fooled at least one nine-pound bass.

Curiously I watched as Unca Bill made his back cast, thinking maybe he would catch that ten-pound bass. In what seemed like slow motion, but which probably took only a microsecond or two, that lure got bigger and bigger as it came toward me. As soon as my arms reacted in an upward motion and I closed my eyes and began to duck, that big lure hit me right smack in the nose. I screamed! My dad, who was facing away from me, looked around and said, "Good Garden Seed! What happened?"

Unca Bill was in a mild state of shock, I guess, but in his mild-mannered Alabama accent he said to me, "Oh, I'm so sorry, Ashburn. Did it hit you in the eye? Oh, I'm so sorry. Let me see."

I guess I had my hands over my face, because neither of them could see exactly where the lure was located except they both knew it was in my face. "My nose!" I shouted. "It's in my nose! And it hurts!" I forced my eyes toward the center and looked down my nose and I could see that big lure. It looked like that ten-pound bass my dad had always told me was out there somewhere. It looked huge.

My dad leaned over closer to me, took a quick look, saw that my eyes were unharmed, and immediately grabbed his needle-nose pliers from his tackle box. "No!" I screamed. "No! Don't pull it out! Nooo! It'll hurt!"

"Hush! I'm not gonna pull it out," he said calmly. "I'm just gonna cut the lure away from the hook. Only one of the trebles is caught in your nose. Hold still, now."

First he cut the line. I was trembling. "Be still. Stop shaking," he said. I tried my best to remain still but I was scared. Real scared. I was afraid one of the other hooks would get caught in my lips or in one of my eyes. Every time he wiggled it even the tiniest amount, I could feel it and see the blood ooze down my nose.

Finally, he found the right spot near the base of that treble hook, and he cut it off, holding the lure securely in his hand. He took another good look at my nose and decided that he did not want to try to remove the hook. He handed me his blue bandana, saying, "Hold this against it, Son." I think he knew I did not want to see the blood.

Then he grabbed his paddle and began to head the boat back toward the boat landing. He had already dropped his rod and reel on the boat bottom. Within three or four minutes, we were back at the landing. "I guess we'll have to take him to the emergency room," my dad said, as he took a deep bite of pond with his paddle, forcing the boat firmly against the shore.

"Of course," Unca Bill replied, "and don't worry about the cost. I'll take care of it."

"That's not what I'm worrying about," my dad commented. "It's his mama I'm worried about. She'll be a nervous wreck, and she'll give me Holy Hell."

"Well, let's just quietly walk straight to the car and not tell her anything until we get home from the hospital." That was my uncle's solution to dealing with my mom. We left the fishing tackle in the boat, not even bothering to lock the chain around that gum tree.

"We can come back here tomorrow and secure the boat," my dad remarked. I felt a little better knowing that in a few minutes the doctor would remove the hook, but I also knew it would hurt. I have a very low pain threshold. During the hike back to the house, I looked down my nose every once in a while and could not help but see that blue bandana turning dark purple.

We walked fast, even in the heat of the late July afternoon. As we got closer to the house, we took an alternate route through the backyard, on the far side of the chicken house, hoping to remain out of sight of my mom until the last minute. We almost made it. I could see her sitting in her green rocking chair on the screened back porch. "Where are y'all going in such a hurry?" she shouted as we opened the car doors.

"We're going to town for a few minutes. Don't worry, we'll be right back. We didn't catch any fish." Those were the words my dad used as he fumbled in his pants pocket for his car keys. "We'll be right back." He quickly drove out the driveway, turned down the dirt road in front of the house, and headed for the hospital, which was two miles away in the middle of town.

We reached the hospital in less than ten minutes and parked along Main Street. Instead of going straight to the emergency room, my dad decided to stop by our family doctor's office, which was on the way, along the same corridor in the small hospital. Sure enough, he was still there even though it was nearly five o'clock, I could see one patient in the waiting room as his nurse, whose name was Frances, came over to me and removed the hankie. I looked down the bridge of my nose and saw that treble hook still right where it had been the last time I had looked. "Boy, that's some nose you've got there," she remarked. "Dr. Gardner will see you in a few minutes."

It took another fifteen minutes, but eventually the nurse called for me to come to his exam room. My dad went with me, but my uncle stayed in the waiting room. Although he was not experiencing the same amount of pain I was experiencing, he was nonetheless suffering. I'm sure he felt guilty.

After thoroughly examining my nose and asking two or three questions, Dr. Gardner finally said, "That hook is rusty, so you'll need a tetanus shot. But first let me give you a little bit of pain killer." The nurse handed him a syringe which contained a pale yellow liquid, and although I'm sure it wasn't, that needle looked as big as a pencil. I focused with all my might on that needle as he stuck it right into my nose alongside that fish hook, and squeezed. It hurt—I mean it really hurt. "Give that a few minutes," said the doctor, "And then I'll be able to remove the hook, and you won't feel a thing."

He was right. It took several minutes, and when he was not looking, I reached up and gently touched the very tip of my nose with my forefinger, and sure enough, it was numb. Then he took a small pair of pliers, not too much unlike what my dad had used, except this one was shiny, and he pushed that hook farther into my nose tissue. I could see the barb come all the way through. With another small pair of pliers, he cut off the barb, then pulled the stem of the hook back out the same way it had entered. All the while I was watching and probably holding my breath. I'm sure I did not close my eyes.

"There. That's all there is to it," said the doctor. "I don't think it needs stitches, but let's put some topical antiseptic on it." He wiped it two or three times with some gauze dipped in hydrogen peroxide, dabbed some paste on it, and put a gauze bandage on it held in place with some white adhesive tape. I looked at myself in the mirror.

"It looks funny," I said, "but it doesn't hurt anymore." He told me that the pain would return in about an hour and I would probably have some swelling, but he did not think he would have to see me again unless it became infected. And then nurse Frances came over with the syringe containing the tetanus shot, wiped my arm with some alcohol on a cotton pad, and inserted that needle, which did not appear as large as the other one had.

Ten minutes later, we were back in the car headed for home. Once we got there, my mom had her say, which was not as severe as my dad and uncle had expected. She accepted the fact that it was an accident; nobody's fault, and that was that. We had fried chicken for dinner with mashed potatoes and green peas, and homemade peach ice cream for dessert.

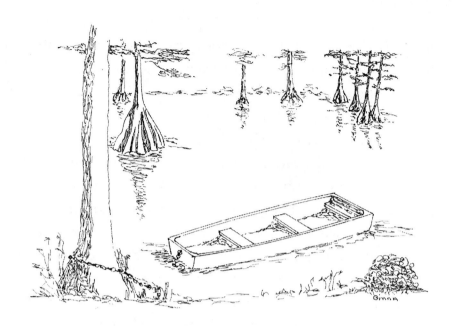

ANOTHER DAY ON THE POND

I don't mind admitting I have had a love affair with guns since I was very young. Some people may think that is a curse, some a blessing. I merely accept it as a fact. I began shooting real guns when I was about five or six years old, beginning with a BB gun, then upgrading to my dad's .22 bolt-action rifle with open sights. I don't remember the make or model…somehow my brother ended up with it. It was an old gun when I was a youngster, more than seventy years ago. Dad was always with me, of course—coaching me, teaching me, supervising me—making sure that I was not only accurate but also safe. I was not allowed to use the rifle unless he was with me. My first targets were Coca-Cola bottles, but then we switched to bottle tops placed on edge atop a clothesline post and we shot from about fifteen yards away. I was pretty good. I was also safe. "Never cock the rifle until you're ready to shoot," he always said. I would place a .22 round into the chamber, gently squeeze the trigger back, and slowly close the bolt, thereby safely releasing the firing pin forward. Whenever it was time to shoot, all I had to do was lift the bolt, which cocked the firing pin, and then re-close the bolt. Actually the rear of the bolt contained a knurled knob which was the safety, but my little fingers were not strong enough to twist it on or off without risk of releasing it prematurely. I wish I had that rifle in front of me now as I write this story, but I don't.

I shot a squirrel with it when I was about eight or nine, but I quit using it once I received my .410 for Christmas, except when we went fishing, which was in the summertime. Because of the likelihood of encountering a moccasin, we always carried that little rifle with us whenever we went fishing in the mill pond. I remember one time my dad was very glad we had it when he discovered two snapping turtles on the bank. He shot both of them. They were too large for me to carry and he could manage only one at a time, so it took us two trips to haul them to the house. He cleaned them and we ate turtle for several meals, battered and fried like chicken. I don't remember liking it, and fortunately he shared some with my Uncle Billy and another relative, one of his cousins. I have tried turtle as an adult, and I still don't like it.

I also remember one summer afternoon when I was twelve as Dad and I were returning to the boat landing after fishing in the summer "hot spot." Because of what happened that day, I don't remember if we caught any fish. As usual I was seated up front, holding the loaded but un-cocked .22 rifle alongside my leg, pointed forward, away from each of us. After he dug his last and strongest paddle thrust into the pond, the boat eased firmly up against the shore which was my signal to hop out onto dry land and help pull the boat another foot or two up onto the bank, which I did. Then I picked up the rifle and held onto it while Dad remained seated on the stern seat and used the bailing can to remove a can or two of water out of the bottom and toss it overboard. He always did this because the boat always leaked just a little. No matter that every year we turned it upside down and tarred the bottom, and we let it remain in the water between fishing trips so the seams would not dry out and open, it always leaked about a quart or more. Of course if it had rained it contained a lot more water. We had to bail it both before we went fishing and after we returned. It was a routine.

The boat had a square bow or nose about twenty-four inches wide made from one single board which was at least two inches thick. It was a firm resting place for the rifle butt, and it was my habit to stand on the shore with the rifle barrel in my right hand pointed skyward and the butt resting on the bow, safely out of the mud. I had done it dozens of times and it seemed plenty safe—after all, the firing pin was in the "safe" position—the rifle was not cocked. Gun safeties are mechanical things, and it was an old rifle. All of a sudden, the butt slipped off the bow, the rifle dropped straight down ten or twelve inches, the rear of the bolt struck the bow of the boat and *bang!* It was more of a *craaack* really—whatever—it is difficult to create accurately the sound of a rifle shot with a few letters of the alphabet.

There was no pain at first, but within a few seconds, my right hand felt like it had been stung by a dozen bees and red blood oozed from two holes: the entry wound and the exit wound. The lower fleshy part below my little finger was gray and black from the powder burn. I don't remember what my dad said (it was probably slightly profane) as the rifle fell onto the muddy bank, but I was glad that it had not fallen toward him. He was glad it had fallen vertically and not back toward me; a mere eight or ten inches and that bullet would have struck me in the chin. I do remember that he rushed forward, quickly examined me, and wrapped his red bandana around my hand. "Hold this in place," he said calmly. "We've gotta walk home and take you to the hospital."

In my mind's eye, I had a quick flashback of a similar walk home a couple of years earlier when I had that treble fish hook in my nose. This time, he took a couple of minutes and locked the boat chain around the gum tree.

Within fifteen or twenty minutes, we reached the house. My mom was upset and she insisted on going to the hospital with us; it was only ten minutes away. In her usual way, she fussed at me for being so careless. "You could have shot your dad," she remarked, "or your head."

"But it was an accident," I said. "I didn't do it on purpose." I remembered that previous ride to the hospital with that fish hook in my nose, and another time when I was seven and that car hit me. That time I rode in the ambulance. Was I accident prone?

The emergency room doctor ordered X-rays, which showed one broken bone in my hand, the one below my ring finger, but no other serious damage. Once I returned from X-ray, he cleaned the wounds, cutting away a little bit of jagged tissue and skin, being especially careful to make sure he cleaned the powder-burned area thoroughly, and then he bandaged my hand securely. I remember that he did not put a plaster cast on my hand, which surprised me. "Make sure not to use your right hand for a few days, and keep it clean. Change the bandage daily, and let Doctor Gardner see you in five days."

The wound healed nicely, with no complications, but I still have the scars. I have shown those scars to perhaps a hundred or more youngsters during my twenty-eight years as a Hunter Safety Instructor. Nothing beats a "real-life" visual aid.

GEESE DOWN UNDER

By 1967, it appeared that the war in Vietnam was never going to end, and we may as well get used to it. Even with all the anti-war demonstrations at home and waning support in Congress, Lyndon Johnson, Defense Secretary McNamara, and the Pentagon continued to pursue a path toward victory; at least that's what they told us. As more and more troops were "in-country" it became evident that Honolulu, Bangkok, and Hong Kong were not the only places US servicemen wanted to go for rest and recreation, known as "R&R." I don't remember exactly when Pan Am began operating R&R flights to Sydney, but as soon as I was senior enough to successfully bid a Sydney schedule block, I began to submit my requests. Because the route of flight to Sydney from Vietnam actually began for the flight crew in Guam, the trip was long enough that it required a layover in northwestern Australia in the city of Darwin. The airline operated two Sydney R&R flights per week, which meant that the layovers in Darwin were for either three days or four days.

After flying a trip from San Francisco and stopping overnight in Honolulu, the next leg was to Guam with another layover. On the third day, we departed Guam early in the morning, flew to Saigon or Cam Ranh Bay or Danang, disembarked our passengers, refueled, boarded 188 war-weary young troops, and set off in a southerly direction, headed for Darwin where there would be a crew change and the flight would continue overnight to Sydney. En route we flew over Borneo and several other islands. I remember on more than one occasion observing thunderstorm clouds over Borneo whose tops looked to be higher than 80,000 feet. Awesome. I also remember that one or two of our captains, possibly WW II veterans with experience in the area, would call Australian Air Traffic Control as soon as the continent appeared on our radar scope and quip, "We have the island in sight."

That comment was usually followed by an equally joking response, "Blimey, Clipper, Australia ain't an island, it's a bloody continent." It was fun to tease them.

After a good night's sleep on my very first night in Darwin, my first mission the next morning was to visit the closest police station and discover the requirements for importing a firearm. I wanted to hunt some of the local wild game, maybe wild pigs or whatever it might be, instead of lounging around a swimming pool for three days or shopping. Hong Kong and Tokyo were for shopping; I was more interested in a safari. I had grown up reading Ernest Hemingway and Robert Ruark and marveling at their exciting African adventures, and I imagined I would never be able to afford an African safari. Australia seemed like the next best thing, especially since I could fly there for free. The police station was within walking distance of our crew hotel, and I arrived mid-morning. The constable on duty was named Kevin—I'm sorry to say I have forgotten his last name—and he was a kindly young man about my own age, 26. "Heck, mate, you don't need to bring a firearm here. I have plenty of them. I have a bolt action .303 Enfield rifle and a Browning 12-gauge shotgun. You're welcome to use 'em anytime you're here."

I was overwhelmed at his generosity; he had only known me for five minutes. I had once owned a .303 Enfield, and I actually had a Belgian Browning Gold Trigger 12-gauge at the time. In 2012, I gave it to my grandson Trey.

Kevin continued, "Heck mate, one of my best friends has a cattle station a few miles out of town and I'm sure he'd love to let you hunt out there." Once again this situation and Kevin's offers were quite a surprise, and all I could think of to say was "Thanks." I mean, how lucky can a guy get?

Kevin invited me to accompany him the next day to visit his rancher friend. Actually I did the driving because the airline provided each flight crew with a couple of little jeep-type vehicles called mini-mokes or something like that, one for the cockpit crew and one for the flight attendants. The captain authorized me to use one that afternoon. No one else wanted to go, so Kevin and I set off for the ranch, which was only about 45 minutes away by mini-moke. He introduced me to his rancher friend and told him what I wanted to do, which was to go hunting, perhaps for wild pigs or whatever. "We don't have any pigs," he said, "but we have plenty of wallabies. Shoot all of them you want to." I knew that wallabies were small kangaroos, and I had no desire to shoot them. I guess he discerned my lack of interest by the look on my face, and then he said, "We also have geese. Are you interested in geese?"

"Geese? Great!" I replied. "That's great. Where are they?"

"They roost down along the river, about five miles east of here," he replied. "Every morning shortly after daybreak they fly off the river, go out to feed on some of my pastures for a couple of hours, and return about ten o'clock. There are some trees along the river bank where you can hide, and you should be able to get off a few shots as they come and go. How about tomorrow?"

"Well, pickup is at six o'clock tomorrow night, so, sure, I can come in the morning, assuming I can get the moke. I'll have to ask the captain. By the way, how large is your ranch? How many acres?" I was curious.

"We have fifty-six squares," he replied. I must have looked puzzled. "That's fifty-six square miles, or about 36,000 acres. It takes a lot of ground out here to feed one cow. Well, I've gotta get back to work. See you tomorrow morning. My daughter and son can show you where to hunt."

Man, oh man, oh man have I ever more stumbled into something fantastic. This was all I could think. I soon learned that instead of measuring the carrying capacity of the ranch in cow/calf units per acre, because of the scarcity of suitable grasses and the dry weather, they measure the capacity in acres per cow/calf unit. Strange to me, but practical.

I drove Kevin back to his house in the moke, whereupon he gave me his Browning autoloader and a box of shells. He had known me for only about 36 hours! With the captain's permission to use the mini-moke, I was up before dawn the next day, but I waited until daylight to depart the hotel because I did not want to get lost in the dark. The family was just finishing breakfast when I arrived, and five or six youngsters rushed out of the house to greet me. The teenage daughter, perhaps thirteen, an adorable little blonde, and one of her younger brothers were assigned to be my guides. She was in charge. I was reluctant to let her drive the moke, but she insisted that she had been driving for about five years, and besides, she knew the way to the geese and I didn't.

So off we went towards the river. I held on to the moke because she showed no mercy as we sped along a dirt track. (They don't call them paths.) Within about fifteen minutes, I was hiding in a small grove of eucalyptus trees along the river bank, and the kids drove a couple of hundred yards away and hid in another clump at the base of a small hill.

After things quieted down, I soon began to hear the faint honks of geese as they commenced to fly up from the water, not visible to me because of a bend in the river. However, soon the sky was full of geese heading straight for me and only about twenty yards above the far bank. The river (actually a large stream) was only about fifty yards wide where I was hiding, and the geese were overhead in a few seconds. I selected one and fired. It fell almost at my feet as the Browning semi-auto recycled. I missed with my second shot, and that flock was gone, out of sight behind me. As soon as I inserted two more shells into the magazine, another flock of about a dozen geese came into view, headed straight for me, not even giving me enough time to retrieve the first goose. This time I missed my first shot, but was successful with both the second and third. Not thirty minutes had passed and I had three geese. Was I dreaming or what?

But that was it. We saw no more geese. After fifteen or twenty minutes, I motioned the kids to return with the moke, and we drove back to the ranch house with my three geese. I decided to be a generous guest, and offered the geese to them, but they preferred that I keep them. I learned that they were called Magpie Geese because of their black and white coloring. For a minute I pondered exactly what I would do with them, and then I decided to offer them to Kevin. And that is what I did as soon as I drove back to town. He only wanted one. He was at work, and said I was welcome to clean them at his house when I returned his gun. So that's what I did. I cleaned his shotgun, breasted the three geese, and put two breast filets in his fridge. His wife returned the gun to its storage spot in the closet, gave me a plastic bag for my four breast filets, and bid me goodbye. "Will you be returning next month?" she inquired.

"I think so; I hope so," I answered. I returned to the hotel, filled my room sink with ice from the icemaker down the hall, nestled my bag of goose breast filets securely down in the bed of ice, took a shower, and then went to bed. It was about two o'clock in the afternoon, and I had four hours before pickup if the flight from Sydney was on time. It was.

That night on the crew bus to the airport, I told the captain about my hunting success and asked if he was interested in goose for dinner. I think he said yes. I had flown with one of the Los Angeles-based flight attendants a couple of times in the past. Her name was Susan, and on the bus to the airport, she told me her assignment was to work the aft galley, which I knew included heating about half the frozen meals in the aft galley ovens for the troops. I brought my bag of chilled goose filets aboard, found a little spot to store them beneath the navigator's table at the rear of the flight deck, and headed straight for the aft galley before the passengers re-boarded. "What's for dinner, Susan?" I asked her.

She removed a frozen entrée package from the cold storage compartment and wiped the condensation from the label. "Looks like chicken breast with some kind of sauce," she replied. She lifted one corner of the foil top and sniffed. "Smells fruity, kinda like pineapple." I told her about my goose breasts, and asked her if she liked wild game. She said she had never eaten any, but was willing to give it a try. She told me that she would skim a little sauce off the top of several passenger meals, save it in a couple of empty plastic cups, and after they finished the passenger meal service, she would cook my goose and bring it to the cockpit. And that is exactly what she did.

While flying at thirty-one thousand feet over the South Pacific, about two hours north of Darwin, Australia, en route to Saigon, Susan joined the other pilots and me in the cockpit, and we feasted on fresh baked goose breasts with special tropical fruit sauce, mixed vegetables, and rice. I drank a Coke, and everyone else had coffee. As my good friend John often says, "It just don't get no better than that!"

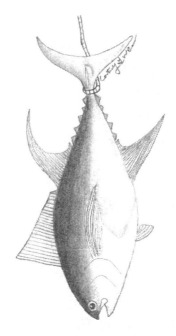

PACIFIC YELLOWFIN

During the late nineteen sixties and up until I was transferred to New York in 1971, I spent many layovers in Agana, Guam because so many of our flights passed through there. Sometimes we had as many as six or eight San Francisco or Los Angeles flight crews spending twenty-four or more hours in Guam between flights. Because airline crews seem to have a knack for ferreting out the best places to eat and the best beaches for sunbathing, we got to know the place fairly well. A US Navy officer's club was a favorite. Taxis were rare and expensive, so fortunately Pan Am provided each layover crew with a car, and because Guam is a US territory, our driver's licenses were valid. The cars were cheap, low-end, four-door sedans perhaps five years old, but they ran. I remember my friend Jerry and I drove to a beach and he tried to teach me how to snorkel, but I was not very good at it. I mainly remember stepping on some kind of thorny little sea critter. Jerry was experienced enough to wear sneakers. I was not.

My most memorable layover in Agana was one day when I joined three other crewmembers and the boat owner on an offshore fishing trip. We were on a cargo flight which arrived from Honolulu, and we had a crew change with a twenty-four-hour layover before proceeding to Cam Ranh Bay the next day on a similar flight. Many times we carried thirteen cargo pallets (a full load) each one packed full of ammunition, usually hand grenades or other explosives. We did not receive hazardous duty pay.

On a previous layover, this particular captain had met (at a local hangout) an American civilian named Dave who worked for the US Navy and who owned a small cabin cruiser. While sharing a couple of beers, they discovered that both had a passion for deep sea fishing, and they arranged to go fishing the next time the captain was in Guam. I was fortunate enough to be with that same captain when we arrived in Guam from Hawaii in the middle of the night. When he asked if any of us would like to go fishing the next day, all three of us replied, "Sure, how much does it cost?"

"All we have to do is pay for the fuel, which will probably be less than $100, so if we split the cost it's about $25 each, plus or minus. The hotel will provide us with box lunches for five bucks each. We can go tomorrow morning after we get some sleep. Meet me in the crew lounge at ten o'clock. I'll call my friend Dave and tell him it's a go."

After six or seven hours of sleep I arose, grabbed a quick breakfast, picked up my box lunch, got two Pepsis from the vending machine, and met the other guys in the crew lounge. We drove to the marina, met the boat owner, made some small talk as we loaded our meager meals aboard, and were underway by about eleven o'clock or shortly thereafter. Except for my twenty-three day voyage to Vietnam aboard a troop ship, I had only been offshore a couple of times to go salmon fishing out of Fisherman's Wharf in San Francisco, so I was a greenhorn on this trip. My father had gone fishing a few times out of Hatteras, North Carolina when I was a youngster, but always with some of his co-workers. He usually returned home with a washtub half full of dolphin (mahi-mahi) which I eagerly helped him clean. He also had a dark pink, sunburned face and arms and he smelled of beer, so I knew they had a good time. In those days, the road to Hatteras from Oregon Inlet was made of perforated steel planks.

Because Guam is a volcanic island with a steep drop off, we reached the fishing grounds within ten minutes of departing the marina. My flight captain, who was obviously an experienced boat-man, took the helm while Dave, the boat captain, lowered the out-riggers, attached the lures to the lines, and set the rods in place. "You just head for that point straight ahead," he told the helms-man, "and don't worry about running aground; the bottom is a thousand feet below us."

I watched him carefully because I wanted to learn how to do this, never before having fished this way. He let two lines run straight behind the stern, and he attached the outboard fishing lines to the outrigger lines with a hefty toothpick and a rubber band. "Watch those 'rigger lines," he instructed us, "that's where we're most likely to get a strike." He took over at the helm while his four clients (or guests) sat and watched and anxiously waited.

We trolled back and forth and back and forth in a large race track pattern, always staying within about a mile or two of shore, and always near the base of that mountain peak he called "the point." I dozed awhile on a bunk inside the cabin, and then ate my ham and cheese sandwich at about three o'clock. The other three pilots seemed to be enjoying the boat ride as they swapped turns sitting in the small fighting chair, but I was getting bored as the sun began to drop toward that mountain cliff.

All at once the starboard outrigger toothpick snapped, released the trolling line, and the reel started to screech. "Fish on!" shouted the boat captain (who was also the mate). "Grab that line."

One of the other pilots—perhaps the captain, I don't remem-ber—grabbed the rod and sat down in the chair. "You guys reel in those other lines," Dave commanded. We each took a rod and began to crank in the remaining three lines when he said, "Never mind, fish off." I looked astern and sure enough I could see that the captain's line was slack and his rod no longer bent. Fish off, indeed.

Once again, I watched carefully as Dave cranked in the line which had contained the fish, inspected the shiny artificial lure, re-attached the line to the outrigger, and then turned the boat around to head back toward the spot where the fish had attacked the lure. My captain said to me, "Why don't you sit in the fighting chair, Ash, since you've never caught a big fish." I complied, hoping that we'd soon have another strike. The sun was setting and I barely could see a small flock of seagulls off that point of land which seemed to be our reference point. The flock of birds was circling ahead and off to the port side as the boat continued toward the point.

Suddenly I heard *bzzzzzzzzz* sound as the port outrigger fishing line began to stream off the reel. Someone grabbed the rod and placed it in my hands: "Here you go, Ash, he's all yours." I began to crank. I made no progress because line was streaming off faster than I was able to reel it in. "Don't touch that drag!" someone cautioned, so I continued to crank. "Pump the rod up and down. Lift the rod and crank as you lower it."

My arms were already getting tired but I continued to follow the instructions of the other guys, all of whom seemed to know more about this sport than I did, but they all hollered at me at the same time. Soon it was almost too dark to see anything but that mountain silhouetted against the gray and tangerine sunset.

I continued to crank and reel, crank and reel for what seemed like an hour but was probably less than half that. I was slowly gaining line. Dave showed me how to guide the line evenly across the reel spool so that it did not pile up in one narrow space. I don't know how much line was still between me and the fish, but the reel was barely half full. I was making slow progress. Finally, Dave reached over and tightened the drag ever so slightly, something he had told me not to do. "That should help. Probably a shark. If we don't get him soon, we'll have to quit, it's getting late." Even though we had not seen the fish, it must have acted like a shark. I couldn't tell because I was new at this; I just continued to pump and reel.

"Yeah," said my flight crew captain, "We have pickup at midnight, and it's a long way to Vietnam and then on to Tokyo. We need to get a short nap at the hotel." Soon it was decided by the majority that I had fifteen minutes to catch this fish or we were going to cut the line. Hoping that no one noticed, I tightened the drag just a little bit more. Then some more. As if by magic I began to fill the spool with line. Within five or ten minutes, the reel spool was nearly full, and the boat captain grabbed his gaff and peered over the stern of the boat.

"I see him," he shouted. "Looks like a tuna. Here comes the leader. Keep cranking, Ash and hold the rod up straight."

With his left hand, he grabbed the leader, and simultaneously plunged his gaff over the stern. "Got him!" he said. "Got him! But I need some help."

I could not see what was going on down at the water level, but I was excited. The flight captain and the first officer leaned over the stern, one grabbed the leader and the other helped with the gaff and together they hauled the fish aboard. "Yellowfin. Nice one. Good job, Ash." I don't remember who said that, but I was relieved that the fish was aboard and I no longer had to crank and pump. I ached all over. The three other fishing lines were already aboard and stowed. While one or two of the other fishermen put the fish in the fish box, Dave steered toward the marina. He seemed to know his way around in the dark, and within about fifteen minutes, we were once again in his boat slip.

A small crowd was gathered on the dock, which must have been a routine event, and someone attached a rope to the fish's tail and hauled it up to the weighing scale. "Eighty-three pounds," I heard someone say. "Eighty-three pounds. Nice fish."

Because we had no way of keeping it or anywhere to put it, Dave suggested that we give it to the small crowd of onlookers, maybe a dozen local Guamanians. And that is what we did. They exclaimed their thanks over and over again. We paid the boat owner for the gas, thanked him for a super trip, and vowed to try it again soon. That day remains one of the highlights of my time spent on the west coast. And to this very day, that tuna remains the largest fish I ever caught—except maybe that Mako shark I caught out near Diamond Shoals tower which I did not weigh.

ROBERT E. LEE

"Hold the light steady, Ash. I can't do this in the dark," Jerry said with a strong tone of impatience mingled with pure frustration. It was after midnight, and I was cold. We were somewhere in the middle of Eldorado National Forest, not very far from Lake Tahoe.

"Well, let's do it in front of the truck, then, dammit, and use the headlights. I can't hold both the dog and the flashlight," I replied as I replayed in my mind over and over again the events that led up to this situation.

It had begun with a phone call one morning about three months earlier, not long after we had moved into the first home we had ever bought, having lived in rentals for the first six years of our marriage. It was located in Bennett Valley, out past the fire station. We also rented an eight-acre pasture which the owner had offered with the house, but because we could not afford the entire package, we settled for one acre with the intention of buying the remainder after my next pay raise. The southern boundary of the pasture was Matanzas Creek. On the phone, Jerry began with, "I know you have a kennel for your bird dog. Is it large enough to hold another dog for awhile? I have a problem here in Sacramento; more dogs than my wife wants and also so many that I need a kennel license. I can bring a dog house. Help!"

"Well, I guess so. Tell me more," I replied.

"Don't have much time right now. I'll explain when I get there. See you later today. Thanks." Depending on which way he decided to come, the drive from Sacramento could take from two to four hours. I truly did not know exactly what to expect. I had hunted pheasants with Jerry once with his two pointers and I knew he had another dog or two, but I had no idea he had exceeded the city's legal limit. What I did not know, or if I knew I had forgotten, but learned later that day, was that his female Plott hound, Sadie, had given birth to six pups who were now about five months old, giving him a total of ten dogs. A neighbor (or maybe even his wife) reported him to the authorities, and he had to dispose of a few dogs or else buy an expensive kennel license for up to twenty dogs. He expected to sell some or all of the pups soon, but he needed to act today or face legal problems with the city. I was one of several friends he called asking for help.

He arrived mid-afternoon with a blue plastic barrel in the bed of his pickup and a brown dog asleep on the seat beside him. He drove past the garage and stopped at my back fence adjacent to the pasture and beside the small tack shed where I stored my dog food. We did not yet have horses, but soon it would also store my saddle, bridle, and the like. In a few weeks, a former neighbor, Maria, who was heading off to college, would be bringing her horse named Lady to stay with us.

Jerry attached a leash to his dog and led him over to where I was standing beside the dog kennel. "Ash, this is Robert E. Lee, one of my Plott hounds. Just call him Lee. I got his parents from my cousin in North Carolina. I think Lee shows more promise than his litter mates. We need to train him to hunt mountain lions."

"Hey, wait a minute!" I exclaimed. "Look, I agreed to keep him for awhile, maybe a month or two, but I don't know anything about training a mountain lion dog."

"No problem," he replied. "I can show how you in fifteen minutes." He produced a plastic freezer bag which contained about twenty small, cut-up pieces of calves' liver. "Here, you hold the leash."

Next, he opened the gate to my pasture, dropped a liver tidbit on the ground, walked about ten paces and dropped another. He proceeded around the perimeter of the pasture, dropping a little piece of liver every few steps, gradually increasing the distance between each piece. "Okay, give me the dog," he said as he returned to where I was standing beside the gate. He knelt beside his dog. "Come on, Lee," he said in a loud whisper as he took the leash from my hand. He led the dog toward the first little liver bit, stopping just out of reach. I could see that Lee smelled the food as he strained against the leash. Jerry unsnapped the buckle and the dog immediately ran to the food, swallowed it in one gulp and took off in pursuit of the next piece. Within five minutes Lee had run the course around the pasture, not missing a single bit of liver, and returned to Jerry, sniffing at his blue jeans pocket. I was impressed, and I said so.

"Surely that's not all there is to it," I remarked, fairly certain that I was about to bite off a bigger chunk of hound training than I wanted to chew.

"Well, you also need this." From the floorboard in front of the passenger seat, he produced a one-quart mason jar which contained a dirty gray rag that looked like a terrycloth dish towel. "This will help." He slowly unscrewed the jar lid and held the opened jar toward my nose.

"Damn!" I exclaimed. "That's awful! It smells like cat piss."

"Good nose, buddy. That's exactly what it is. What you do is after about a week of making a trail with the liver pieces, you introduce Lee to the lion scent. He's already trailed it a couple of times in my back yard, but there isn't enough space there to do a good job. He can see all the liver pieces at once. Out here, you can space them far enough apart that he won't be able to see from one piece to the other. After you place all the pieces in your pasture, then you drag this scent rag along the trail. Pretty soon you won't need but a couple of liver bits, one at each end of the trail. Oh, and be sure to wear rubber gloves. Now help me put this barrel in your kennel."

Within two hours, we had introduced his dog, Lee, to my springer, Freckles, stretched some fence wire down the middle of the kennel, fabricated another gate, and placed the blue barrel with one end cut out on a couple of boards. Freckles was wary of other male dogs ever since John's black Lab had bitten a hole in one of his ears, but he did not seem to mind that his kennel had just been cut in half. He and Lee growled at each other a couple of times; then they settled down as neighbors. Jerry gave me another bag of liver, two stainless steel bowls, a twenty-dollar bill to buy some more liver, and a half bag of Purina dog chow. Always in a hurry, he jumped into his truck cab. "Thanks, Ash. Maybe we can go lion hunting in a couple of months. I have to fly to Honolulu tonight. I'll call you next week." He backed his truck out the path and then he was gone.

My wife and I watched both dogs for awhile and decided that we'd have no trouble with them, and went inside for dinner. Early next morning, we both went outside. I repeated the liver trail routine in my pasture, waited about ten minutes, and released Lee. Like magic, he ran the circuit, ate each little treat, and returned to my side. I led him to his half of the kennel, fed both dogs some dry dog food, and returned to the house.

"I've got a trip tomorrow," I said. "Can you handle this?" She liked dogs, she liked to hunt, and she had no problem with helping a friend in need.

"I think so. It might be fun. But I'm not messing with that stinking jar until you get home. That's your job. You're the one who agreed to teach the dog how to trail that rag. I'll feed him and do the liver thing a couple of times, but that's all. And you'd better not get re-scheduled this time."

Airline crew schedule changes had become more and more of a problem since we moved nearly two hours north of San Francisco airport. Sometimes I went away expecting to be home in three or four days, only to return after eight or ten days. The previous month it had been twelve days. After such a long trip, usually in Southeast Asia or other Pacific stations, I often returned with a darker tan, and she accused me of lying around a swimming pool all day surrounded by bikini-clad flight attendants, which was sometimes the case. She had grown tired of driving to San Francisco to pick me up several times only to learn that I'd he home the next day or the next after that. So we had used all our savings a few months earlier and spent it on a used Chevy six-cylinder pickup truck which became my commute vehicle. It also towed our RV trailer reasonably well.

After I mended the pasture fence in a couple of places, we told Maria that we were ready for her horse. Because the horse did not like being trailered, Maria rode her all the way from Rincon Valley to our house early the next morning, a distance of about four miles. We assured her that we would take good care of her mare, and that we would try to ride her at least three or four times each week, as she had requested.

Within a month, Robert E. Lee was following the scent lure everywhere I dragged it, even with only one or two liver tidbits along the trail. It took the horse several days to accept the stinking dish towel, however, but soon I began to ride her around my pasture, across the paved road to a neighbor's larger pasture, and then through a small woodlot near the fire station, dragging the scented rag about thirty feet behind us. It took me about forty-five minutes to complete the circuit, and then I placed a small chunk of liver within a few feet of the beginning of the trail. After watering the horse and taking a short break, I released Lee, remounted the horse, and off we went. Occasionally Lee would let out a howl, but for the most part, he silently followed the trail all the way to the end. We rarely saw any traffic along the road and I felt that it was safe for all of us.

Once or twice, I ran into Jerry in Guam or Tokyo and assured him that his dog's training was probably complete, and that he could come and get him any time. "I've got a better idea," he said. "How much time do you have off next month and when?"

"Well, I have a six-day block of days off in early November, and another few days off closer to Thanksgiving. I'm going goose hunting then, but I'm free during the first week."

"Me too. You bring Lee to my house and I'll drive us up to Echo Lake, and we'll go lion hunting with him and his parents. We'll have fun. Dress warmly. You won't need a gun."

So, that is how it happened that we were on that lonely service road in the Eldorado National Forest that cold night in November. I had arrived at Jerry's house around four o'clock in the afternoon, planning to spend the night and go hunting the next day. But to my surprise we immediately loaded Lee, his mama, Sadie, and his father, Tiger, into the back of Jerry's pickup, which contained a camper shell. We made some ham sandwiches and threw a bag of dog food behind the seat; Jerry grabbed his .44 magnum revolver, a couple of flashlights, and off we went, on our very own lion hunting safari. At sunset.

Within three hours or maybe four, we arrived at his "hot spot" along a mountain trail overlooking a broad valley in the Sierras. I could tell that some of the valley was heavily forested, but it also contained some clear cuts. I had no idea exactly where we were, but Jerry assured me that it was okay to be there, and this is where he had seen a mountain lion two or three times earlier in the year. He showed me his dog-eared topographic map, and pointed out two or three prominent features: a creek and a couple of mountain peaks in the distance. He drove slowly along the trail and then suddenly stopped, saying, "I think this is a good place to let the dogs out."

We opened the camper shell door and out they came, each one scrambling over the other in order to be the first out. They nosed and sniffed about all around the truck, Lee and Tiger each watering a truck tire while Sadie soon disappeared over the edge of the trail, down the hillside. Within a minute or two, she let out a mournful howl. Tiger and Lee followed her, and suddenly Jerry and I were alone on the mountain side on a cold and dark November night. "Hot damn!" exclaimed Jerry. "They're on a lion track. Ain't that a pretty sound?"

I had hunted rabbits with my dad and some of his friends and their beagles when I was younger, and yes, I thought it was a pretty sound. We heard the dogs howl once or twice more, each time fainter than the other. Finally, he said, "They must be headed down to Wolf Creek." (Or Bear Creek. I don't remember).

There was a long period of silence as we listened more intently but heard nothing. Finally, after maybe another hour or slightly longer, he shined his flashlight onto the map and said, "Let's drive down there to that bridge." Placing a finger on the map, he pointed out the spot which was down a twisting, winding mountain trail that led to a small blue line, a creek. "We can probably hear them better down there."

I ate a ham sandwich and drank a Coke while we slowly descended the mountain trail toward our proposed rendezvous with the dogs and perhaps a mountain lion also. We stopped a couple of times, shut off the engine, and listened. Not a sound. I referred to the map, trying to keep up with our progress along the trail.

Suddenly, as we neared the bridge, a big mule deer buck crossed the trail about fifty yards in front of us. We stopped and listened, curious about the situation, but we heard nothing. Within a couple of minutes, Sadie appeared and ambled over to us with her tongue hanging out. Then came Tiger, who looked tired and ready to call it a night. Jerry gave both of them some water from a bowl and then attached them to their leashes, one on each side of the truck so they wouldn't get tangled. "I guess they were running that deer all along and not a mountain lion," he remarked, sounding disappointed. "Where's Lee? Have you seen Lee? Do you hear anything?"

"I don't hear a thing," I replied. Then we heard what sounded like a yelp, then another, not the same barking or howling sound as if following a trail or a bark as if something had been treed, but more like a dog in distress.

Jerry shined his flashlight beam back up the hill in the direction of the sound and called out, "Here, Lee. Come, boy. Here, Lee."

I whistled a couple of chirps. Then we saw him. He came running up to Jerry, whining and whimpering as if in terrible pain. Then we saw the quills.

"Porcupine!" said Jerry. "Damn! He's gotten into a porcupine. What a mess." He firmly grasped Lee's collar and attached a leash. "Here, Ash, you hold him while I get my needle-nose pliers. This will take a while." Fortunately, Lee was not aggressive and he seemed comfortable with me, since we had spent several months together. I shined my flashlight onto his sad, brown face. I had never seen a porcupine and definitely had never seen a dog with about a dozen white quills protruding from his lips. He even had a couple in his tongue. What a pathetic miserable-looking spectacle he was, indeed. It was well after midnight and we were hours from a vet. Jerry acted as if he had done this before, as he said, "This won't be easy."

He returned from the truck with his pliers. I sat down on the cold ground and held Lee as close as I could with one arm while shining the light in his face. Jerry managed to remove about five of the largest quills, while Lee twisted and squirmed against my restraint. I tried very hard not to brush against his face, but Jerry was right—it wasn't easy. I dropped my flashlight. That is when Jerry scolded me and I told him we should use the truck headlights and then I could hold Lee with both hands. So that is what we did, and it worked. It took about an hour, and I got colder and colder as the night wore on. Finally, all the quills were removed and Jerry applied some kind of antiseptic paste to Lee's swollen lips, which he promptly pawed at. I guess it stung.

About four hours later, just as the sun was coming up over the Sierras behind us, we drove into Jerry's driveway in Sacramento. I was tired and hungry, not at all enthusiastic about the evening I had just endured, and I was pleased that by that time, Jerry had been able to reduce the number of dogs to the legal limit. I slept on his sofa for about three hours and then drove home to Santa Rosa, leaving Lee behind.

It was then that I decided I was not a mountain lion hunter. Give me birds any day.

Ginna

SAMMY AND THE BLACK DUCK

For whatever reason, sometimes it is difficult for newcomers to touch base with the local populace and feel welcome. One of the few places in America where I observed that this phenomenon is usually not a problem is California. Many folks we met in California were from somewhere else anyway so there weren't many native sons and daughters in the places we lived. Being from somewhere else gave us at least one thing in common with many of our neighbors. Before long, we also met dozens of natives who were friendly, too, and who made us feel at home. I'll always remember John Steinbeck's little poem about California natives, "The miners came in forty-nine, the whores in fifty-one and when they got together they made the native son." I think he was a native, born in Salinas.

That situation is not the case in many parts of the east and of the eight or nine places I've lived, the distinction between newcomer and native is nowhere more evident than on Virginia's Eastern Shore. Born-heres and come-heres are the local terms. I suppose there is a strong case to be made for the born-heres to be suspicious of new arrivals for several reasons. I don't know all the reasons nor do I let them bother me—I just try to fit in if I can and go about my business if I can't. When a newcomer buys several acres and a large house near a small village with small lots and even smaller houses, I suspect the natives think the newcomer is probably another rich, uppity, come-here who will look down his nose at the locals. Some do. Others don't. Having come from humble beginnings myself, I never felt like I had any reason to be uppity or to look down my nose at anyone. My long love affair with hunting and fishing gave me ample reason to think I had at least those two traits in common with the born-heres.

It wasn't very long before we became reasonably good friends with several of our neighbors on the neck, some of whom were descendants of the first European arrivals in the 1600s and some of whom were recent come-heres, as we were. I started trying to shoot a few ducks over decoys, but it wasn't long before I noticed that the ducks were routinely flying to several areas without decoys. A few days later, while I was chatting with a born-here neighbor in his kitchen, negotiating a fair price for a bushel of oysters, I mentioned my poor success with the ducks. After looking first one way and then the other to make sure we were alone (even in his own kitchen) he whispered, "Bait. Probably corn. Them ducks you see pitchin' where they ain't no decoys—they're bein' fed. How do you expect to kill any ducks if you ain't usin' bait?"

I must confess that I had shot a few mallards and some wood ducks in a harvested corn field when I was a teen, and my hunt club in California leased thirty thousand acres of rice fields, but the truth is I didn't think I had ever knowingly shot over bait. I didn't tell him these things but even so, I really didn't know how to react to his comment. I'm certain he saw the look of surprise on my face when I replied, "I...uh...I...uh...I...always just set up my decoys and waited. It worked in California."

"Sonny, this ain't California. This ain't no National Wildlife Refuge. 'Round here if you don't bait, you don't shoot. Come here, lemme show you something." He walked across the kitchen, put his hand on the refrigerator door handle, and paused. "Don't you say nothin' to nobody about this, now, but looka here." He opened the door and showed me the contents of his fridge, which was mostly filled with ducks, about fifteen or so, nicely dressed and ready for the roasting pan. "Black ducks," he said. "You ever eat a black duck? They ain't but two dollars apiece. You want a couple?"

The year was 1973, if I remember correctly, and market gunning had been outlawed for several decades yet here was a man trying to sell me freshly killed wild ducks right in his own kitchen. "No thanks, I don't think so. You keep 'em." I responded. "Maybe I can get some if I hunt in the right place.

"They ain't no good 'less they been eatin' corn," he offered. "You might get a shot at some out by Back Way Gut." Well, I had leased some three hundred acres of marsh out near Long Ridge from a banker in Norfolk, and I had built three blinds in September, but so far the only excitement I had had was getting caught on a mud flat as the tide was ebbing out. Nevertheless, I decided to take his advice and try the area again, but without the corn.

A few days went by before I had the opportunity, and my regular shooting partner could not accompany me so I went alone. I was there before sunup, the tide was right, the wind was right, and I set out twelve decoys. It was cold, but it was beautiful on the marsh at sunrise, as it almost always is. Even the mud smelled good. I observed several small flocks of ducks trading back and forth over the marsh and across the creek on the far shore, some mere specks against the horizon. A few pitched into likely looking feeding spots hundreds of yards from me, and I was getting discouraged, to say the least. Four hooded mergansers zipped by behind my blind, and I gave them a wave. A few bufflehead splashed down in a little cove, well out of range. Several thoughts mingled in my mind, not the least of which was the possibility that my oyster-selling, black-duck-selling neighbor might be right. I may not get any shooting without bait.

Finally, I heard one short *quaaack* off to my left, and I turned my head in that direction. There, at my nine o'clock position, about thirty yards away and silhouetted against the pale, beige and orange dawn, came one lone black duck, wings set, boring straight for my "deeks" (decoys.) It was not quite like shooting ducks in a barrel, but almost. I quickly stood up and fired, just as he was lowering his landing gear. He tumbled into the shallow water, and I made a quick retrieve, expecting a few more to show up. But I was mistaken. He must have been the only stupid duck in my area that morning, but at least it was a black duck, and I had been assured by my neighbor that they are good table fare.

I quit about nine o'clock, took up the deeks, and eased my boat out of the gut and into the main creek before the receding tide caught me on another mud flat. The wind was kicking up a little chop, but there were no white caps, and the twenty-minute boat ride home was pleasant enough. I flushed a few little knots of bufflehead as I rounded the last point of land before reaching my dock. Throughout the ride home I was excited about my first Eastern Shore black duck, and what a treat it would be for dinner.

That night we feasted upon it, accompanied by large portions of rice and other vegetables since it was, after all, only one duck and there were two of us plus the two children. I think they preferred hot dogs, which we always kept on hand in case they were picky about some of our wild selections. It did not taste as good as we had imagined and, in fact, it was a culinary disappointment compared to several years of rice-fed mallards, widgeon, teal, and geese in the Sacramento Valley. I guess in my haste or naiveté or both, I forgot one important ingredient of the recipe and that was a diet of grain.

"It was okay, I guess, but I'm not terribly impressed," said my wife as we finished the Cabernet and started clearing the table. She had grown up eating wildfowl, more so than I, and she is not finicky. Her evaluation was accurate. I noticed a few scraps of duck flesh left on each of our plates, evidence that we were both unimpressed.

We had two dogs at the time, one of whom was an adorable little black mutt named Sammy, a hybrid cock-a-poo mix, which some Sonoma County neighbors, a nice young couple with no kids, had given us before we left California. (We learned a couple of years later that they were arrested for possession with intent to distribute.) Meanwhile, back to the dogs. Whereas my springer, Freckles, was an outdoor dog, Sammy had complete run of the house and he especially liked to hang around the kitchen after meal time, looking for handouts. My efficient wife had even trained him to come running at the tappity-tap-tap of her toe whenever she dropped a small scrap which Sammy had not seen fall.

As it so happened, Sammy was not in the kitchen when the small scrap of black duck accidentally slid from a plate and hit the floor, and so she whistled and gave her best little toe tappity-tap-tap. Sammy, who was as efficient as the best dust buster, came running from the den, slid to a halt on the vinyl floor, cocked his head to one side, and looked at that little piece of duck meat. He walked all the way around to the other side of it and then leaned forward and took a sniff. I started to laugh because he looked kind of funny as he picked it up daintily between his front teeth with his lips curled back. Then, much to our shock and disbelief, he dropped it, lowered his shoulder, and rolled in it! "Look!" my wife shrieked. "Can you believe that? We just made a meal off that black duck and Sammy won't even eat it. Don't you ever bring another one into this house!"

And I didn't.

TUMP JUSTIS

It was a beautiful, sunny, Sunday morning in late February, with the weather being unseasonably springlike. As I looked out the kitchen window, I could see the red maple buds which were about ready to pop at the edges. The wind was calm and the creek looked like the proverbial sheet of glass—the locals call it *Slick Cam*. I had been up for a couple of hours, first walking to the mailbox with my dog, Freckles, and then reading the Sunday funnies. I glanced at the clock. It was 9:05 and my wife and two girls were still upstairs getting dressed for church. I was already dressed and preparing breakfast for the four of us. If they didn't hurry and come downstairs soon, we'd be late. A typical Sunday morning.

"Y'all come on down to breakfast; French toast is getting cold!" I shouted from the bottom of the stairwell. No sooner had I said those words than I heard the shots, first three in rapid succession, followed by two more at longer intervals. I raced to the back porch just in time to see several ducks zip past the pecan trees, cup their wings, and glide onto our freshwater pond. I heard a couple more shots about a half mile or less, up the creek, and then silence. I saw no more ducks.

Within five or six minutes, the phone rang. It was my next door neighbor who said, "Don't bother to stop by to give us a ride to church 'cause we're not going. About eight of my ducks just flew onto the pond, some crippled pretty badly." He sounded out of breath. "Did you hear all that shooting across the creek?"

"Yeah," I answered, "Some of my ducks flew through the yard but they looked healthy to me."

"Well, not so with mine. I think two or three of 'em are nearly dead right now. I saw someone in a skiff picking up some dead ducks on the far shore, so I called the game warden. I told him not to come to my house, but to go to the old Custis place across the creek. I think old Tump Justis is gunnin' out of season again, and this time he shot my tame mallards. We're gonna catch that crook one of these days, maybe today. Stop by after church." He hung up without another word.

We had been neighbors for five years, sharing a common boundary between our two small farms. Each of us had a small pond about a half-acre in size, which we created with some financial assistance from the Soil Conservation Service. We both had raised a few mallards from eggs we hatched under our laying chickens, and they spent about an equal amount of time on each of our freshwater ponds, and they also flew up and down the tidal creek as well. It's hard to say which ducks went with which farm, but between us we had twenty or so, maybe a few more. In late February and early March, long after duck season was over, and as mating season approached, they pretty much had the place to themselves. It was interesting to watch their courtship rituals as the drakes, usually more than one, noisily splashed across the water in hot pursuit of a hen. Several hens nested near the marsh or in our weed patches or quail cover. The previous spring, one hen mallard built her nest under a small azalea shrub in our front yard, a short fifteen feet from the front door. Her brood lasted only one day, however, because some predator got all the ducklings their second night. We think it was a raccoon, but we never found out for sure.

Raising ducks was fun. Even though we both hunted waterfowl, we also enjoyed having a few tame barnyard ducks around. My neighbor had quite a reputation as a wood carver, mostly miniature waterfowl, and he always said he liked to use live models. The truth is, he was so talented he probably could have carved them from memory with his eyes closed.

Each of us also had some geese; mine were domestic, white Emdens, and our neighbors' were Canadas, descendants of a small flock whose wings had been pinioned or clipped not long after hatching, several generations ago. They never migrated but stayed within a mile or two of their birthplace year round. Many people don't realize it, but geese make very good watch dogs, honking noisily when strangers approach. One undesirable characteristic they have, however, is that they can make a terrible mess with their droppings. That trait is what makes them so unpopular when they take a liking to a golf course. If I were a golfer I'd probably find them a nuisance, too. Instead of playing golf, I spend some of my spare time planting a few acres of corn every year. It encourages the doves to hang around, and the geese and ducks make a meal from it now and then also. I enjoy watching geese feeding in a field of corn stubble.

Church lasted the usual sixty minutes and we left immediately. After swinging by the supermarket for a couple of items and grabbing some hamburgers at the McDonald's drive-thru, we headed for home. "Don't forget to stop by Chet's and find out how the ducks are doing," my wife reminded me as we neared the turnoff to our neck of the woods. About a mile out of town we met the game warden going in the opposite direction, and we took for granted that he had not caught the poacher who shot Chet's ducks. A few minutes later we drove into his front yard, told the girls to stay in the car a few minutes and finish their burgers, and we walked past the end of his house toward his barnyard. Chet was in his tool room, removing the last few feathers from a fat drake mallard.

His tool room and workshop were in their usual state with wood shavings an inch thick on the floor. "Hello, neighbors. Watch your step," he said welcoming us with his usual greeting. "I'd shake your hands but mine are a little messy. Isn't this the damndest thing you've ever seen? I know what you're thinking, I shoot ducks too, and so do you, but not somebody's pets, and surely not more than a month after the season has closed."

"Yeah, I know what you mean. We just met the warden heading out the neck. What'd he say?"

"He caught the SOB red-handed. Old Tump was in his pickup heading out that old logging path from the Custis place and the warden stopped him. He had three ducks in a burlap sack behind his truck seat. Warden said he wrote him a ticket for trespassing, another one for shooting ducks outta season, and a third one for hunting on Sunday. He also confiscated his shotgun. Said Old Tump didn't do much talking. He also said he'd need me as a witness in court because I saw him in the boat and because they were my ducks he shot."

"When do you reckon court will be? I'd like to go."

"Not sure, but I'll let you know. Man, that Tump, he's a piece of work, you know. I've been living here for fifteen years and I've met a lotta locals, but he's the lowest, most worthless skunk around. Do you know him?"

"Not really," I replied. "I mean I recognize him when I see him, once in a while out on the creek, and sometimes in the little country store, but I wouldn't say I really know him. The only time we ever carried on a conversation I had trouble understanding him. He came by the house one Saturday morning last year and tried to sell me a bluefish. I was having a heck of a time trying to get the lawnmower started when he drove into the yard and leaned out of his truck window. He said something like, 'Dal tells me he's heerd that yew loike bluefish. Oi done cort one in m' gill net, and Oim tellin' yew he dang neer tore it up. Yew can have him for three dollers. Oi ain't never ate neither one. Cort 'em in m' crab pots many toimes, and th' dang crabs won't even eat 'em. Oi reckin Oi ain't about to eat neither fish the crabs won't eat. Yew wornt him, yew kin have him for three dollers.'

"It looked to me like that fish had been out of the water for several hours, probably down in the bottom of his scow, and I told him I only liked them fresh. 'How's about two dollers then?' he continued. I said, 'No thanks' and he drove away, disappointed I suppose, and now when I see him he just sorta nods and doesn't say anything."

"Well," Chet replied, "I heard he used to sell bootleg whiskey in his younger days, and he was one of the most successful market gunners around here. He must be pushing seventy-five or maybe more. Old man Poole told me Tump never got caught, but that's hard to believe. Never got caught until today, that is. I guess most of the locals just got used to him, and he didn't care if he shot the last duck."

That tendency to mind your own business and not stick your nose where it doesn't belong is okay up to a point, but I never could understand the mindset of most people whose livelihoods depend on hunting and gathering. On one hand, they depend on the resource, whether it's crabs or clams or ducks or whatever other critter God put on this earth for them to harvest. And yet, without so much as a care, so it appears, they seem willing to deplete that same resource or turn a blind eye as a neighbor depletes it. One local crabber told me that a single she-crab lays a million eggs, and crabs will eat anything (except maybe a bluefish) so there's no way we'll ever run out of crabs. What he fails to realize, as he traps 'em in the spring, traps 'em in the summer, dredges 'em out of the mud in the winter, and sells under-sized ones, is that nearly every critter in the water likes to eat crabs. Most of the shorebirds like to eat crabs. Many fish love 'em, especially when they're soft right after they shed. Humans like to eat crabs. By the time a year rolls around, those million eggs are probably down to only two crabs again in time to start the cycle all over. Same with wild ducks.

Some folks think there's an endless supply of them up in Canada or on the moon or somewhere.

I guess a month or more went by before Chet called and said he had to go to court the following Tuesday to testify at Tump's trial. I was scheduled to be at home so I decided to go, too. Come Tuesday, Chet and I went to Accomac, driving separately because we had different places to go afterward. There were not many spectators that day; a few family members of several defendants in the cases that preceded Tump's case. By the time his case came up, there were only three or four of us remaining, and I didn't recognize any of the others.

I sat alone on the back row as the game warden answered the prosecuting attorney's questions about that Sunday back in February. It was fairly straight forward. The warden referred to his notes, told the judge about receiving the phone call, rushing to the scene of the alleged offense, and upon arriving finding the ducks in the sack in Tump's truck. He said he had probable cause to search the truck, based on the information he'd been given. "I asked the defendant if he realized the charges against him, Your Honor, and he said 'Yes' so I filled out the citations for the three charges. I also took his shotgun and the bag of ducks. I reminded him that in some states I could also have taken his truck, but not in Virginia."

Next, my neighbor Chet testified about hearing the shots, about seeing several of his pet ducks crippled, splash down onto his pond, and about seeing a man in a small boat across the creek picking up several dead ducks. Continuing he said, "Yes, Your Honor, I used my binoculars. No sir, I am not absolutely positive of the man's identity, but I'm sure they were my ducks. And Your Honor, Mr. Justis might have had only three ducks when the game warden caught him, but he shot more than that. At least two died that morning in my barnyard and three more suffered a broken leg. No telling how many died that we don't even know about."

The judge listened intently. Having no more witnesses, the prosecuting attorney concluded with a brief summary of the charges:

trespassing, shooting ducks out of season, and hunting on a Sunday. The judge, himself a duck hunter, looked down at old Tump Justis, sitting alone at a table in the courtroom. "Does the defendant have legal counsel?" he asked Tump.

Tump stood up. "No sir, Your Honor, Oi ain't got neither loryer. Oi didn't figure 'twood do me no good. It's just me."

"Well, Mr. Justis, I've heard the charges against you. I've heard the testimony of two witnesses, and I've seen the photographs of the evidence. These are serious charges, and I'm inclined to find you guilty on all three counts. Do you have anything to say in your defense?"

"Yes sir, Your Honor, Oi do. Oi do have somethin' to say. All Oi can say is that this seems like a whole lotta fuss over nothin'. After all, Oi only got three ducks."

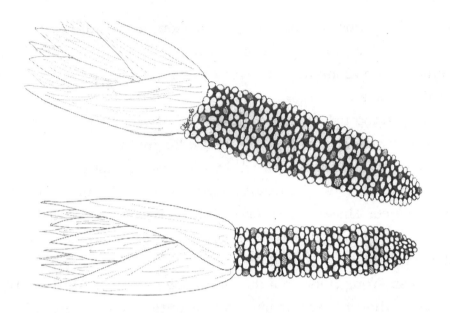

SPREADIN' A LITTLE CORN

Author's Note: This hunting story was first published in the October/November, 1990 issue of Shooting Sportsman *magazine.*

Old habits die hard, I guess, and when a habit is passed down for three or four generations it almost takes on the character of an inherited trait. I have observed this phenomenon on more than one occasion, and in all corners of the world, but it is especially evident along the shores of the Chesapeake Bay.

It was while I was hurriedly setting out the goose decoys the other morning that I first noticed the corn. Dawn was breaking and I was running late. It had been dark as I placed the first three or four dozen around in what I hoped would be a realistic-looking and tempting arrangement, and I had to use a flashlight. Then as daybreak neared and I suddenly realized the flashlight was no longer necessary, I discovered that what had at first appeared to be clods of dirt or firm cornstalks underfoot all of a sudden materialized into full, firm-bodied, genuine ears of *Pioneer 3369* or some similar yellow hybrid. I had been out of town for about a week and had not hunted that particular field for at least that long. But I had left my decoys in the farmer's barn and I had given his teenage son permission to use them during my absence. My three dozen and his two dozen made a nice spread.

The corn had been harvested at least four months earlier and now there was a nice green crop of winter wheat in the field. "What's this yellow stuff all over the ground?" I asked the boy. We were hunting the wheat field together that morning since it was Saturday and there was no school. I could not convince the farmer to join me, but his son had been going with me occasionally and he seemed to be enjoying the sport. In fact, he had asked for and received his twenty-four shell decoys as a Christmas gift from his dad.

He looked at me with a bit of a grin between his rosy cheeks, which I could barely see in the dim twilight. "Jes a little corn I spread around," he answered. "Dad says it keeps the geese comin' in."

"Keeps the game warden comin' in too," I added. "Boy, they'll put us under the jail if they catch us shootin' over bait. Your daddy gonna pay our fine? When did you do this anyway?"

"About a week ago. Jes' after that big rain. Place was full of geese th' whole time you were gone. Dad and I got two." He grinned again.

"That's great," I said. "I'm glad you got some geese, but we can't shoot over bait, man, it's just too risky." My senses told me that the smartest thing we could do would be to take up the decoys and move to a different location, or else call it a day. But it was already legal shooting time and it would take at least an hour to move. Scratch that idea. And after all, I rationalized, I had not been able to hunt at all for at least a week and the season would be over soon and the game warden seldom checks field shooters. He is kept busy enough with the water blind hunters. (Those boys use corn all the time.)

So I decided to stay. "Help me cover this stuff," I said to the boy as I hastily began to stomp the ears into the ground and cover them with mud or corn stubble and other debris. Many of the cobs were empty, hard evidence that the geese had, indeed, been dining on this tempting treat. He silently helped me cover the most obvious ears but we missed many.

What would the judge say? I thought to myself. Depends on the judge, I suppose. It hadn't been very long ago that one of the local judges and another prominent attorney had been caught 'spreadin' a little corn' themselves. Not long afterward that particular game warden was transferred to another region. A coincidence, I suppose.

The boy and I quickly scrambled under our flimsy blinds of wire and weeds and reeds as the birds began to fly. First a few ducks showed up, not even bothering to circle, just boring right in like we had 'em tied to a string. I sat up and raised my gun to shoot at a nice big drake mallard. Click!. In my haste I had forgotten to load. Poetic justice? The boy was still fumbling with his gun and his shells and had not been ready either. *Just as well,* I thought. *We shouldn't even be here. It's stupid of me to be his accomplice and to reinforce and add validity to his outlaw tactics.*

I watched in silent disgust as the ducks flew away. Not disgust at the ducks, but disgust at our situation. *Can't blame the boy,* I thought. I mean, he knows you aren't supposed to bait. He heard the lecture on ethics at the Hunter Education Course, and he's been hunting with me for two seasons now (with no corn) and even though he has not yet shot a goose while with me he seems to be having a good time. But it was accepted for so long as THE way to hunt waterfowl. His daddy did it and his granddaddy did it, and who knows how far back in their family's history the tradition of 'spreadin' a little corn' goes. When will we ever break the cycle? Will we? We must.

As I lay there staring at the empty sky I remembered the only time I ever hunted with the boy's daddy. It was a few years ago, say mid-seventies. I had met him at a party. I was new in the Chesapeake Bay area, having lived most recently in California for a few years. During the party the subject of hunting came up and before the evening was over he invited me to join him and his father the next morning to go duckin'. They own two big grain farms which straddle an old millpond. The mill is gone but the dam remains and the pond has been used for irrigation during the past seventy-five years.

I arrived at six o'clock in the morning as instructed. After some brief socializing over coffee and doughnuts we drove a few hundred yards from the farmhouse to the woods near the pond. We walked single file down a narrow path, recently cleared, through some scrub pines, wild cherry trees, and heavy underbrush to the edge of the pond. There under a big pine tree was a well-built duck blind made of material resembling the surrounding underbrush, probably the stuff cleared from the path. Inside the blind were two folding stools and an upturned green plastic bucket; a few empty red high-brass shotshell cases, and an empty cardboard shell box, but no decoys. I looked around on the bank outside the blind and also at the pond. Nothing.

"Where are your decoys?" I asked naively.

"Don't need 'em," was the reply.

"But how will the ducks...?" I surprised myself, I stopped so abruptly. He smiled a weak smile and then put his finger in front of his lips.

"Shhh!" he whispered. "Here come some ducks." The three of us quickly scrambled to our seats (I got the bucket) and put our heads down as about six ducks whistled by. I peeked out under my hat brim and looked over the edge of the blind and saw them splash down out near the center of the pond perhaps fifty yards in front of us. Six or eight more glided in right behind them and with no hesitation whatever the twelve or fourteen ducks swam straight toward us. I watched nervously as the farmer and his father reached for their shotguns which were leaning against the blind. "Get ready," he whispered. "When I say 'shoot', shoot." The ducks kept coming.

There was no more time for any more conversation. When this tiny raft of birds was about twenty, maybe only fifteen yards in front of us a few of them tipped their tails up and began feeding. Then I knew. What I had suspected must be true—corn! I had a firm grip on my shotgun but I was trying to decide what to do.

"Okay, shoot," he whispered. "Take 'em...now!" He and his father each fired at the small knot of feeding ducks. I stood and fired at two ducks as they flew, pumping their wings, frantically grabbing for altitude. I got them both. I missed with my third shot as five or six ducks flew away. I counted. On the water in front of us were eight dead ducks. I felt strange, like a highwayman who might have ambushed a stagecoach, or perhaps an infantryman who had trapped an enemy patrol in a deadly cross-fire. Was this hunting? Certainly not as I knew it.

The young farmer produced a small aluminum johnboat from beneath a nearby brush pile and he paddled out to retrieve our ducks. "Whatchew think of that, young feller?" his father asked me. "Did yew have duck shootin' like this in California?"

"Well, ahhh, not exactly," I replied. "I normally used about a dozen or so decoys, and, ahhh, shot mostly widgeon and a few mallards and teal." I was nearly speechless but I was an invited guest and I didn't want to be rude, but I didn't know what to do or say, so I just tried to fill the empty spaces with some conversation. "What kind of ducks are these, anyway? I don't recognize them."

"Hell, I don't know. Just ducks. Good eatin'. Nice and fat." I don't doubt it I thought to myself, what with their steady diet of corn. I resisted the urge to lecture the old man. After all, I was a guest. But when does the fun start? I asked myself. This just doesn't seem like sport. I remembered the expression 'like shooting a sitting duck' and now I knew, truly knew, what it meant. Somehow, by killing these ducks this way, and by that I mean unfairly and without any respect for my quarry, the ducks had been robbed of their dignity and so had I.

"That was some fancy shootin' guys," the young farmer said as he nosed the boat onto the bank and tossed the ducks into a pile beside the blind.

"Hell! That weren't nothin'," said his father." I've seen shoots like this when we'd get thirty ducks. Weren't that long ago, neither."

"C'mon now, Pop, don't exaggerate. Not thirty. Not lately, any-way." The son seemed to be poking fun at the old man. I picked up one of the ducks to examine it in an attempt to identify it. I knew I didn't want any fish duck.

"Why don't chew take 'em home, young feller...we got plenty ducks in th' freezer."

"No thank you," I replied. "I only shot two. You boys got most of the ducks. Why don't you keep them?" I guess I was attempting to whitewash my guilt by refusing any of the birds. But they were in-sistent that we at least split them, so I took four and they took four.

We returned to the house in silence. I thanked them for the hospitality, told them what a nice piece of property they had, and I prepared to leave. "Come on back anytime," the old man said. "Lot-sa game here; deer and quail. You deer hunt?"

"Well, I've shot a few, not many, but I have a bird dog at home just itching for a place to hunt."

"Bring him over here, Son, and help yourself. We got three other farms 'bout like this one. You hunt 'em all you want." Even though I knew we had different hunting styles, I was grateful for the gen-erous offer.

"Thank you sir. I just might do that. Thanks again for the ducks." I left with the four ducks. The first thing I did at home was to thumb through my duck identification book. I discovered that we had bagged ring-necked ducks. First (and only) time I ever saw any. We ate two for dinner that night. They were good; the old man was right, but I had eaten duck just as good before, and enjoyed it more, perhaps because of the sport involved. Who knows?

I continued to hunt those farms over the years, taking a few quail and doves each year. I saw lots of deer tracks, and a few deer, but I never shot any. I never did duck hunt with them again, however. But two years ago I showed up to quail hunt one afternoon and the farm by the pond was full of geese. "Been hanging around here since Thanksgiving," the farmer said. "They're ruinin' the wheat. Why don't you shoot some?" So I started goose hunting the wheat fields, taking the youngster with me a few times. That's how we happened...

"Geese!" said the boy in a loud whisper, loud enough to arouse me from my daydream. "Geese at three o'clock. High." He was right. They were very high, and flying by with a tail wind, definitely headed for some other field across the county. The sky was clear as a bell as the bright sun climbed higher. It looked like it was going to be one of those bluebird days. We stayed another hour, saw a few more flocks fly by, but none of them indicated even the faintest interest in our spread. I am still puzzled by that.

"Looks like we're wasting our time," I finally said. "Let's pack 'em outta here. Maybe our corn brought us bad luck." Secretly I was somewhat relieved that we had not done any shooting to attract any attention from passersby, in case any passerby happened to be the game warden wanting to check us more thoroughly. We disassembled the decoy spread, packing the nested shells into feed bags, and hauled our gear to the barn. By the time we finished the second round trip I was cursing my down parka because it had, indeed, become a bluebird day.

But a few days later a cold front swept down over the Great Lakes, across Pennsylvania, and headed for the Chesapeake. I called the boy. "Looks like we might get a little snow," I told him. "Geese been around?"

"I've seen a few pitch into the fields," he replied. "Yesterday they were there all day, but nobody's been huntin' 'em."

"Why don't we remedy that?" I suggested. "See you around 5:30 tomorrow morning." I nearly hung up the phone, but suddenly I remembered to ask, "Oh, nobody's been spreadin' any corn around have they?"

"No sir."

I was there bright and early at five-thirty. Plenty early, but not bright at all. It was one of those days duck hunters dream about... overcast skies, low scuddy clouds, a light misty drizzle, poor visibility, and the smell of snow in the air. I selected the back field, the one on the OTHER side of the pond from where the corn had been. I didn't want to take any chances. The place was full of fresh goose sign. We took our time setting the decoys out, trying to make certain each one was in just the right position. We finished just after daybreak and we had a few minutes to chat, certain the geese weren't flying yet. We sat on our plastic tarps beside our portable blinds, about thirty feet from one another. "I left here in a bit of a huff last week," I said. "But that business about the corn really upset me. I hope you understand. Nothing personal."

"Yes sir. I... I think I understand." He paused. "I'm not sure my daddy and my granddaddy would understand, though. They think we're crazy comin' out here in these muddy fields layin' on our backs, jes' to shoot a goose. They've never done it."

"I thought you said you and your dad got two last week."

"We did, but we, ahh, we got 'em with a rifle. Sneaked through th' woods over there by th' ditch."

"Damn! That's no way to shoot geese. Rifles are for deer. And I know you know it's illegal."

"Yes sir, but Dad says..." He stopped in mid sentence. "Listen! Is that geese?" Before either of us could answer they were upon us, appearing from the northwest with the wind at their backs. They were already crossing the road near the barn; no more than three hundred yards from us and less than a hundred yards up. About thirty, and they were coming fast. We quickly pulled our blinds into place and the boy started honking on his call. I was pleased to observe that he was as excited as I was. Perhaps this culture clash he found himself in would resolve itself. I hoped so.

The geese made one low half-circle pass, losing half their altitude in the turn, and descended upon us like manna falling from heaven. They were hungry. The lead goose was no more than twenty yards in front of me, and maybe shoulder high when I sat up and dropped him. They flared immediately, turned tail to the wind, and climbed. I aimed at another, but didn't lead him enough and missed clean. Just as suddenly as they appeared they were gone, vanishing into the misty sky to the southeast. "Why'd you shoot so soon?" he asked.

"Whaddaya mean, soon, that one was almost on top of me." I stood up and walked toward my goose.

"But why didn't you wait for them to land? I didn't even get a shot!" His disappointment was obvious and he seemed angry at me. ME!

"Heck, there were geese all over us. Musta been thirty. You should have shot. I didn't realize you were waiting for me to tell you when. I'm sorry." I tried to soothe his hurt. I'm pushing fifty, but I remember what it was like to be a kid of fourteen with an empty game bag.

"I thought you waited 'til they landed. I've never shot at one in the air before." All of a sudden it hit me like a freight train. No one in this family had ever bothered to teach the boy anything about wing shooting. I took it for granted that he knew what to do. Stupid of me, especially after the duck hunt a few years back, while he was still in diapers. What could I say?

"No, Son, you gotta give the geese a chance. We don't shoot them on the ground and we don't use rifles, and we don't shoot ducks on the water. That's just not how it's done." I was trying to say what my father might have said had he been there. I hoped I was getting through. I laid my goose on the ground with his neck outstretched as if feeding...one more decoy in the spread. "Tell you what. Let me try to explain. We're lying out here with our backs to the wind, right?"

"Yes sir."

"Now the geese want to land into the wind, you see, so they should be coming right toward us, like that last bunch was. The next geese that come by, YOU decide when one is about to sit right on top of you…it'll be farther away than you think, 'cause they're so big…but you decide when to shoot. I'll lie here and talk to them. When you sit up they'll start climbing fast. You aim right at his head and just before you pull the trigger raise your gun a little bit and cover his head with your barrel. Nothing to it." I knew I was making it sound a lot simpler than it was, but I didn't know what else to say. Did he understand? "Got it?"

"I think so." We waited another twenty or thirty minutes. It began to snow. My feet were cold and I suspected his were, too. "Geese!" he said. His young ears are better than mine. I honked a few times on my call, hoping I was talking their language. There were six. They circled once, maybe seventy-five yards out and that far up. They circled a second time, not really getting any closer. I hoped the boy was ready. If he waited too long I would have to shoot. They were forty yards away and closing. I turned my attention back toward the geese on my side of the flock, tossing my blind aside, also. I was about to shoot when I saw the lead bird crumple. Then I heard the boy's gunshot. I fired at a bird out on the edge, hit him, but he didn't fall. He folded in mid-air with my second shot.

"I got him!! I got him!!" he shouted. He was on his feet and running across the field before my bird hit the ground. He came running back to me, carrying his goose, and this time the grin was literally from ear to ear. "I got one! I got one in the air! I did jes' like you said and I got him. Wow! Wait 'til Dad hears about this!"

"Isn't this fun?" I said. "This is what goose hunting's all about. See, we didn't need the corn." The snow fell harder. It grew silent all around us; that eerie silence that sets in when it starts to really snow. We saw no more geese that day. But if I never see another goose, I'll always remember the look of satisfaction on the boy's face when thirty minutes later he proudly displayed his trophy to his father.

"Look Dad, look! I got one flying!"

SELWAY-BITTERROOT

I knew Jerry liked to hunt big game, especially mule deer and elk, because he talked about it a lot. He worshipped Jack O'Connor, and I believe he read everything O'Connor ever wrote. I had joined Jerry on a mule deer hunt once or twice when I still lived in California, and not long after I moved to Virginia, he invited me to join him and our friend, John Blum, on an Idaho elk hunt. On our second deer hunt I had taken a shotgun and hunted grouse while he hunted mule deer. I figured I should accept this invitation or he would not ask again. Once I accepted and we began to plan the event, he said, "You can't smoke. It'll drive away every elk within five miles. We won't see one."

I had been smoking cigarettes for seventeen years, half my life, and I had even quit once for six weeks, but took it up again when I missed a flight to New York and had to wait in Baltimore for two hours, nervous that I would be late for check-in. Living in Virginia was nice, but sometimes the commute to JFK, New York's Kennedy airport, was exasperating. I finally joined a few other pilots and rented a commute pad in Kew Gardens, a neighborhood in Queens.

"Okay," I replied. "Okay, I'll quit. Just stop bugging me about it."

"I'm serious. No smoking." I never did get up the nerve to ask him how cigarette smoke would scare away every elk within five miles but campfire smoke or sizzling bacon did not bother them. I guess that is one of hunting's mysteries. Actually, I was looking forward to the chance to hide away up in the mountains, far from a store, and far away from a cigarette. With help, encouragement, and support from him and John, I was sure I could quit for good this time.

Ginna was excited that I would be using the trip to quit smoking, but she tired of my incessant planning and she let me know about it. "I have to be careful because of the weight," I told her. "I can carry only thirty-six pounds plus my rifle and the clothes on my back."

Jerry was specific about the weight we could pack into camp because this would be a self-guided hunt using his four horses. Every time I thought I had it down to within a pound or two, something else which seemed vital came up. I decided to take one of my home-cured hams which weighed twelve pounds, one third of my allotted weight. After I mentioned the ham to Jerry, he allowed as how we could consider it a food item, and it would not count against my personal thirty-six-pound limit. Finally, after four or five months of planning, studying topographic maps until I had them nearly memorized, packing and re-packing, I was ready.

I flew to New York from Norfolk and caught a Pan Am freighter to San Francisco. I had been cutting down on my cigarette consumption all summer long and was down to six Marlboros a day, a drastic reduction from two packs of Camels. It was September 16, 1976. I remember smoking one on the flight to San Francisco, and I saved the last one until the last minute, stomping it out on the ground at our cargo terminal at one o'clock in the morning as Jerry's truck came into view.

"I thought I told you no smoking," he said as he saw me.

"That was the last one," I answered. "The last one. I've been down to six a day for two months. I brought along twenty packs of chewing gum to satisfy my craving. I brought that ham I told you about. Where's John?"

"He's waiting for us at his house. Let's go."

Here I was off on another safari of sorts. After picking John up and loading all our personal gear, we drove up to Placerville, arriving at sunup. Jerry had to shoe one horse which he did while John and I began to load hay, oats, pack saddles, bridles, halters, and other assorted gear into the horse trailer. Soon we loaded the four horses and got underway on our long drive from California to Idaho. I was already tired and miserable, and I had not had a cigarette in nearly twelve hours.

We reached Elko, Nevada sometime after dark and camped out at the rodeo grounds which had a nice corral for the horses. At daybreak we resumed our drive, and I believe we made it to Salmon, Idaho after a long day's drive. I was allowed to drive the pickup in the flatlands while Jerry napped, but he took over in the hills. I was glad. About half my Doublemint gum was gone by the time we reached a little store in Darby, Montana, along the Bitterroot River south of Hamilton. We knew a Pan Am captain who lived in Hamilton, but we decided we did not have time to visit. Elk season opened in two days, and we still had a long drive up through the Nez-Perce Pass to Magruder Campground on the Selway River where we would park the truck and begin our fourteen mile hike up to our chosen camp site leading the horses. "I have to get some more chewing gum," I insisted, so we stopped briefly in Darby where I bought twenty-four additional packs of Doublemint. "Thanks, guys. Let's go."

I had not had a cigarette in three days. If I remember correctly it took several hours to drive to the campground, most of it in the dark. *What have I gotten myself into?* I thought, but I didn't say anything.

At the campground, we saw one other truck parked, but no people were in sight. As soon as we unloaded the horses Jerry began to moan and groan. I won't repeat what he said, but he discovered that his newest horse had foundered. I knew that foundering was some kind of foot problem, but that was the limit of my knowledge, having read a couple of paragraphs about it in my wife's horse-manship book. "Dammit! Dammit to Hell," Jerry exclaimed in disgust. "She's not gonna be able to go with us. I'll have to take her to Hamilton and see if Jack can keep her." Jack Mahr was our pilot friend who lived up there on a small ranch he bought after moving to Montana from New England. "Let's unload the gear. I'll help pack two of the horses, and you guys get started toward camp. I'll catch up with you."

It took three or four hours to pack most of our gear on two horses. I was new at this, but I had read extensively about it, and even though I was slow, I was thorough. I had learned the most from a wonderful little book called *Horses, Hitches, and Rocky Trails* by Joe Back, a gifted writer and wonderful illustrator. Jerry hobbled his main horse, Dancer, who grazed while we packed my horse, Ol' Tom, and the one John would use whose name I forget. We had brought two dozen eggs which we placed two per bag in small ziploc bags, and nestled them down in the oats in one pack box.

Satisfied that our packing job was as good as we could do it, at about two o'clock in the afternoon, John and I were ready to begin our hike, which we knew we would not complete by dark. We called it a Hudson Bay start which is a technique used by pioneers, fur trappers, and mountain men whereby they began a trip in the afternoon, travelled two or three miles before dark, set up camp, and if they discovered any important items were missing they sent their fastest rider back to obtain the missing gear. Jerry loaded Dancer and the sick horse into his trailer promising to catch up with us within twenty-four hours.

By four o'clock John and I had hiked perhaps six miles, climbed two thousand feet, and I was pooped; too many cigarettes and too much weight around the mid-section. Ol' Tom had stepped on my left boot, and we had to stop while I lashed the rubber heel back in place with a leather shoe lace. I always carried some spares. I made a mental note to include some rubber cement next time.

"There's a little stream about fifty yards over there," said John, pointing to a small clearing in the woods slightly downhill from the trail. "Let's check it out."

We did, and upon discovering that it seemed suitable for the night, we unloaded the horses, fed them a small amount of grain, hobbled them, and set up a spike camp for the night, heating some beans right in the can and roasting a couple of hot dogs. We hated to have to re-pack the horses the next morning, but we knew no other way. We were not about to continue our hike in the dark along a trail neither of us had ever seen. We slept off and on until sunrise, when we heard a familiar voice.

"Hey, wake up, guys. You gonna sleep all day?" It was Jerry, bent nearly double, leading his horse. "I'm in pain, guys. My gut feels like it's about to bust wide open. Musta been that water I drank back there down the trail. Y'all haven't seen a bear, have you? I think one must have pooped in that branch." He admitted that he had gotten thirsty at about midnight and bent down and sipped some water from a little stream. Within four or five hours, he was suffering from acute stomach cramps, but he knew we were only a mile or two ahead of him so he continued, in the dark. He chewed some pink Pepto Bismol tablets and sat around on the ground while John and I re-packed our horses. We had cold cereal and orange juice for breakfast while trying to decide whether to continue our hunt or return to the campground and take Jerry to a doctor in Hamilton.

"I'll be fine," he said. "Just give me a few more minutes and I'll be fine." He was. Within an hour he seemed like his old self, and the three of us resumed our hike.

By noon, we found what we thought was a really nice place to camp for the rest of our remaining seven days. It was sheltered from the north wind, had a cool stream nearby, and was within one hundred yards of an alpine meadow where the horses could graze. It seemed perfect. We spent much of the afternoon setting up camp, and once satisfied that it would serve our needs, we spent an hour perched on a rocky outcropping and used our binoculars to search a broad valley one mile east of us in search of elk. We saw none. We also noticed that the weather seemed unseasonably warm for mid-September in the Rocky Mountains. We were prepared for snow. That night we ate some pan-fried ham slices and hash browns. I drank one of the six Cokes I had stashed in the cool stream. My supply of chewing gum was holding steady, and thankfully, my companions tolerated my grouchy mood. Withdrawal.

Each day was warmer than the previous one, and after hunting together for three days without seeing or hearing an elk, we decided to split up so we could cover more territory. After cinching the wooden pack saddle on Ol' Tom and covering it with a blanket and my down jacket, then improvising some stirrups with rope, I tried riding the horse, but it was very uncomfortable so I walked and led him along the narrow, rocky trails.

One or two miles north of our camp, I intersected another trail coming up from the southwest, and after locating it on my topo map, I followed it for a short distance soon discovering that it contained two different sets of boot prints plus a small horse or pony track, unshod. As I rounded a sharp turn along the trail, I smelled the distinctive and unmistakable smell of wood smoke. Searching a small valley below me with my binoculars I discovered the source of the smoke and followed the trail which led to it. There I found two young men and their burro in their camp which contained a small pop-up tent. The men were shirtless. "Good morning," I shouted from fifty yards away. "Sorry to interrupt, but I was curious about your fire. Having any luck?"

"We got an elk two days ago," one of them said as he pointed to the northeast, "on the other side of that ridge. Nice six-by-six," he continued, pointing this time to the elk antlers leaning against a tree. I had not noticed the antlers. "But it's so warm, we lost most of the meat except the backstrap which we ate. The rest spoiled.

The rack is all I could save."

"Yeah, I know what you mean about the heat," I replied. "I'm so sweaty I figure every elk in Idaho can smell me. Three of us are camped about five miles southeast of here. We hiked in from Magruder Campground."

"We crossed your path yesterday," one of them said, "You have three shod horses, right?"

"That's right. That's us. We have not seen or heard an elk. Don't know where they're hiding. I think it's too warm."

"Yeah, we're pulling up camp and going home tomorrow. We see no reason to stay in this heat. Even if we get another elk, we have no way to keep the meat cool."

"Have a safe journey," I told them. "I reckon you'll pack that rack out on your little burro, right?"

"Yep. Everything else we'll put on our backs the same as we did coming in. Good luck."

I bid them goodbye and began my hike back to our camp, discouraged and tired. On the way I saw a male spruce grouse standing in the trail, and as I approached to within ten yards of him, he trotted behind a tree. Believe it or not, I picked up a rock about the size of a baseball, crept slowly to the tree, peeked around it, saw him on the other side, staring at me, and threw the rock at him. That rock struck him squarely. Before he could fly or run away I had him firmly in my grasp. *Dinner!* I thought. No one was in camp when I returned, so I cleaned the grouse, wrapped it and some carrots and onions in aluminum foil with some butter, placed it in a bed of coals, and peeled three potatoes. Later, Jerry cooked them in his skillet. That night we had roast grouse for dinner.

After telling Jerry and John about my encounter with the two backpackers and the burro, I informed them that I would not be hunting tomorrow. Using my binoculars I had seen a little alpine meadow and a small lake within two miles northeast of our camp. "I'm going up there and take a bath," I told them. "I'm gonna build a small fire, heat some water, shave my face, and wash my body. I can't stand myself I smell so bad. I don't care if my camp fire scares every elk to Montana, I need a bath! If I can't have a cigarette, at least I can get clean." I had an extra pair of jeans, which were back in the pickup, but I had a clean shirt, socks, and underwear with me.

Next morning after breakfast, I did as I had promised. I led Ol' Tom to my little private pond and spent two hours heating water, shaving my face, stripping down to my birthday suit, bathing my body, and putting on clean clothes (except for jeans). I did not have a thermometer, but I estimated the air temperature was at least sixty. There were several elk wallows along the edge of the little pond, but they were old and dried out. The water was clear. I figured no elk had been anywhere near the place for at least a week.

I will not bore the reader with details about the next two days as they passed uneventfully except that one day I shot another spruce grouse (a hen) with Jerry's pistol, using a snake load of very small #12 lead pellets. Some people call these bullets "rat shot." She tasted as good as the first one had. I might not be an elk hunter, but if there were birds around, I could sure get one or two. Some folks call them "fool hens," and they do not seem to be afraid of humans, but they're passable table fare.

Having not seen or heard an elk, we finally decided, one day ahead of schedule, to call it quits and head home. No way they could blame it on me; I had not smoked a cigarette...didn't have any. We didn't talk much along the trail back to the truck except to complain about the heat. When we reached the campground, we saw a guide leading a string of pack horses and mules. He, too, was calling it quits because his clients had become discouraged. He said the temperature was 75° and the bull elk had quit bugling. "First time I've ever seen it this warm in September," he told us.

On our way back to California, we took a slightly different route and stopped for dinner in Ketchum, Idaho, near Sun Valley. I had chicken-fried steak and a cold beer. The Sawtooth Mountains are awesome. I could easily see why the area appealed to Ernest Hemingway. We drove hard the next day, spent another night at the rodeo grounds in Elko, then we returned Jerry's horses to their pasture in Placerville. He left the sick horse in Hamilton, Montana, returning in October to check on her. Sadly, she had not recovered and had to be put down.

In my whole life I had never worked so hard at having fun and I was happily ready to return to Virginia. In those days, airplanes had smoking and non-smoking sections. I had been two weeks without a cigarette, and one of the proudest moments in my adult life—except for saying "I do" at my wedding—was when the American Airlines agent at the check-in counter asked me where I wanted to sit, and I replied, "Non-smoking."

I slept all the way to New York. Elk hunting is hard work.

SPANISH MACKEREL

Ibelieve it was the second summer after I returned from Vietnam, and the first real vacation I had earned after completing my probationary period with the airline. We flew to New York from San Francisco and then on to Norfolk to visit both our families for two weeks, one week of which was spent down on the Outer Banks of North Carolina at my in-laws' cottage in Kill Devil Hills. Both my wife and I had visited the beach separately as teenagers, either staying with relatives or in rental units. Her parents had recently purchased a cottage not far from Avalon fishing pier, and we were excited about the opportunity to play in the surf with our young daughter and also do a bit of surf casting for bluefish. One tradition that we discovered both our families shared was that sometime during the week we made at least one trip out onto the pier, either to fish or simply to look around and observe the other tourists. All the North Carolina piers were once privately owned and they charged a small fee to fish, but in those days if you brought no tackle along, you could walk out onto the pier for free. Because people abused that privilege, they now charge admission just to go out and look around. It was fun to observe both novices and experienced pier fishermen (and women) as they cast spinning rods out beyond the surf or simply lowered a bottom rig for catching spot.

We had had moderate success fishing in the surf. Nothing to brag about, but we'd caught enough fish—a mixed bag—for a nice meal the second night: fried fish, coleslaw, and hushpuppies. One mid-week morning, we were completely skunked so after a lunch of pimento cheese sandwiches, my father-in-law, Bobby, suggested that we hike to the pier and see what success those folks were having. Using his binoculars, he had observed some activity, and he wanted to get a closer look. The girls decided to stay close to the cottage and wade and splash around in the surf.

The tide was out so we could walk along the hard-packed sand near the water's edge instead of trudging through the softer sand higher up the beach. We reached the pier in about ten minutes. As we leisurely strolled along the pier, we saw several people catching fish, a few with spot or croakers in the shallower water up near the beach, and out closer to the end of the pier, two or three people were landing small bluefish, less than a pound in size, nothing very impressive. Suddenly, one man with his small spinning rod bent nearly double was cranking up something a little larger. He brought his catch up over the rail and plunked it down on the deck, telling his wife to run to the car and get the cooler. He unhooked his fish, turned around, and cast his shiny lure back into the ocean. I did not recognize what species it was, but my father-in-law knew. "Spanish mackerel," he said. "Good eating. I wish we could catch some. But they have razor-sharp teeth."

Concentrating on reeling in his lure, the successful fisherman was not paying any attention to his catch which was flopping around on the deck. My father-in-law continued to walk out to the far end of the pier, maybe another twenty yards, but being curious, I approached the beautiful fish to get a closer look. It was perhaps two pounds in size and it gleamed in the sunlight, but it was still very much alive as it flipped and flopped ever closer to the edge of the pier. "Hey mister!" I said, "You'd better do something with your fish or he's gonna go over the edge."

I noted that he had not brought a cooler with him because I had heard him tell his wife to go fetch theirs. The man seemed to have his rod and reel and a lure, a small plastic tackle box, but no other gear or tackle, except a knife in a leather sheath on his belt.

"What should I do with him?" he inquired. "My wife's gone to get our cooler."

I quickly answered him as I gently kicked his fish closer to the center of the wooden pier, farther from the edge. "If it were mine, I'd kill it."

"How?" By now I was pretty sure he was a city-slicker tourist and not an experienced fisherman.

"I'd use that knife you have there and cut off his head." He handed me his rod, and then immediately did as I suggested, neatly severing the fish's head from the body. *Perhaps he was a surgeon*, I thought. Ever more curious about the mackerel, especially the still brightly colored head and large eyes, I reached toward its mouth to get a closer look at the teeth. Bobby had mentioned that they are sharp.

Suddenly and as quick as a lightning flash, the severed head opened its mouth and snapped shut on my left forefinger, grasping it securely with a mouthful of razors. I simply could not believe what had happened as I noticed a very small trickle of my own blood ooze along my entrapped finger. Now I was the one who looked like a dumb tourist. I had been around enough bluefish to know that the last thing I wanted to do was grasp the head with my right hand and pull my finger out. That was a surefire way to shred the caught digit. So, while holding the head (or while the head was holding me) I very carefully eased my right forefinger close to the fish head's top lip so as to pry it open and release my trapped finger from this devil's grasp. I knew it would possibly be painful, but I was willing to take that risk.

Just as Bobby walked up to observe my predicament and possibly offer some help, that devil fish head opened its mouth once again and seized my right forefinger in its grasp clamping down like a steel trap on both fingers. "I don't know you," Bobby remarked as he backed away from me, certain, I'm sure, that he had been right a few years ago when he thought his daughter had married a klutz. "I don't know you," he repeated.

I can't remember a time when I felt more stupid or embarrassed, except maybe that time when I was twelve and my dad took me to the hospital with that self-inflicted gunshot wound in my right hand. It was an accident.

By this time, the lady had returned, and as her husband picked the fish off the deck and placed it into the cooler, I heard her say to him, "Honey, can't you help that man? He has both hands caught in your fish's mouth." Aware of the delicate situation, the man gently inserted his knife blade into that devil monster's mouth, careful to keep the sharp edge away from my fingers. Once he was satisfied that the knife was in the proper position he twisted the blade ninety degrees and pried that terrible mouth open enough for me to extract my fingers without any further damage.

"Thanks," I said. "By the way, are you a doctor?"

"No," he replied, "I'm a school teacher from Cincinnati. Sorry 'bout your fingers. Thanks for your help with my fish. I'd have lost him for sure if you hadn't said something."

"Thank you for saving my fingers," I commented. "The way you handled that knife I was sure you were a surgeon." He turned away and once again cast his lure into the Atlantic. Relieved that I was no longer the main object of ridicule along the pier, I joined my father-in-law (who by now condescended to walk beside me) and we went back to the cottage.

I have never caught a Spanish mackerel, but I'll never forget the one that caught me.

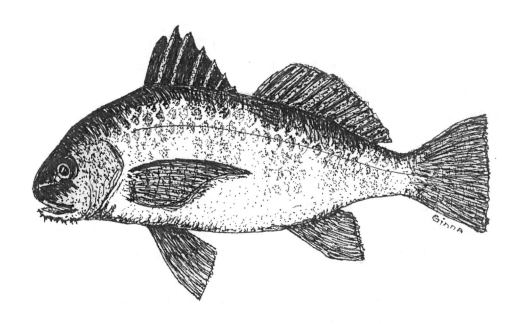

BLACK DRUM

Not long after we finally spent our savings and bought a suitable fishing boat, our Mako, we continued to fish in the bountiful waters of the Chesapeake Bay, a pursuit we had begun when my father-in-law gave us his old Wolverine wooden ski boat. I subscribed to several fishing magazines, my favorite being Saltwater Sportsman. I particularly enjoyed the Tred Barta columns, but I also relished reading articles about fishing gear, lures, methods, and bait. And boats. I guess nearly every boat owner is always on the lookout for his next boat, the one that's a bit larger or a bit faster than his current one. For five or six years in a row, I didn't miss a boat show in New York or Virginia Beach. I remember my father-in-law told me more than once that he was going to use the money I saved him on wedding expenses (we eloped) and buy a bigger boat. He never did.

Although we loved to catch bluefish, our main target in those early days was the gray trout (*Cynoscion regalis*) a species which frequented the mid bay around Pocomoke Sound. Actually a member of the drum family and also called weakfish, their food of choice in our area was the "peeler crab" which is a blue crab in its final hard stage before molting (shedding) and becoming soft. I finally decided that nearly every fish in the bay likes to eat crabs.

The creek-side boundary of our small farm was 1,600 feet, or more than a quarter mile, of tidal marsh, and not long after we moved in, one of our waterman neighbors asked if he could place two or three peeler traps along our waterfront. The previous owners had not allowed it. I told him he could, as long as they were not right in front of the house. Many mornings in May and June (and sometimes even into July) around sunrise we could hear him and his partner fishing their peeler traps, emptying the crabs into their wooden scow. Later in the morning, they transferred the peelers into little wooden cages or pens they called "floats" which they checked every hour or so and removed the crabs immediately after they shed their old shells. Over the years they captured many peelers along our creek frontage. As a result of our agreement, whenever I was able to go gray trout fishing, I would visit his crab shedding house in the nearby village to obtain some peelers to use as bait. I usually got a dozen or so. "How much do I owe you?" I would always ask.

"Not a thing, but if you catch more trout than you need, I'd love to have one." So we had a bartering arrangement—he trapped peelers on my property in exchange for the bait I needed—an arrangement which lasted for the entire twenty-seven years we were neighbors.

I remember one morning I went down to his place of business to get some peelers. I had recently read a magazine article about cobia, another fish which visits the bay. The article said that cobia like eels, and live ones are good cobia bait. As I stood on his dock waiting for him to put some peelers into my little styrofoam cooler, I noticed an eel attempting to enter one of his crab floats through one of the narrow gaps between the side slats. I asked the closest waterman, a man known as "Bumps" what they did with eels.

"We hate 'em," he replied. "They tries to eat our crabs."

"Well, there's one right there. I see him, right there, outside that float," I said, pointing to the eel, which was about twelve inches long and slightly larger in diameter than a hot dog. "Can I have him? I read that cobia like them. I'd like to try him as bait."

"Sure, you can have him. Let me getcha a net." I remembered my early days in flight school when I would nervously grip the control stick way too tightly and my instructor cured me of the habit by making me hold a pencil on the back (or top) of my middle finger held in place with the index and ring fingers. The tighter I tried to squeeze the control column, the more pain I exerted on my middle finger with that pencil, and after a couple of sessions I soon began to grip the control stick more gently. I also learned that I have a very powerful grip. I also knew that eels are slippery.

"I don't need your net," I told him as I thrust my right hand into the water, aiming about two inches behind that eel's head, and holding my fingers in such a position that if I caught it, I could grasp it the same way my flight instructor made me hold that pencil—my super grip. In a flash and a splash, I came up with that eel firmly secured in my super grip with his body wriggling and twisting and trying to wrap itself around my wrist.

"Well, I'll be damned!" said Bumps Savage to his companions inside the crab shack. "Y'all come out here! Come see what that airplane boy done. He done caught a eel with his bare hand. Damndest thing I ever seen!" I think he was impressed and nearly every time I saw him after that day he reminded me of the time I caught that eel.

Unfortunately, I did not know enough about the fine art of using an eel as bait. I hooked it in the lip instead of the tail, and within a few minutes, instead of an appealing live bait swimming naturally, it was one big ball of eel which had tied itself into a knot, something no self-respecting cobia would try to eat.

The next time my father came to visit, accompanying my sister, Ann, her husband, George, and their son and daughter, Greg and Beth, we decided to go fishing for gray trout. This trip would be my father's first outing on my Mako. I obtained some peeler crabs from my source, and after loading our tackle and ice into the boat and bidding farewell to the girls, we headed down the creek toward one of my favorite fishing spots known as "Crammyhack," a sandy ridge near a buoy along a drop-off at the edge of the channel in Pocomoke Sound which leads to Saxis. It is east of Watt's Island and north of Onancock Creek. When we arrived, we couldn't help but notice several boats on the other side of the channel at a place the locals called Stone Rock. I recognized one of the boats belonging to a friend, and I called him on the CB radio. "Whatcha doing?" I asked.

"Drowning crabs," he replied. "We've been here about an hour, but we haven't caught anything. Some folks caught some black drum here yesterday. I reckon things will get better soon as the tide turns. Come on over." So instead of dropping anchor where we were, we motored across the channel and anchored near eight or ten other boats. It was nearly slack tide. I had to watch the tide closely because our creek was not very deep, and at the lowest of the ebb, I had difficulty making it back to my dock. The tide soon turned, the boats began a slow swing, each one pivoting on its anchor, drifting with the tide, and all of us anxiously awaiting the "bite."

We had each baited our hooks with a chunk of peeler crab and lowered them to the bottom using three-ounce lead sinkers. It wasn't very long before the radio chatter picked up and four or five boats reported hookups. We had never caught a drum before, and we did not know what to expect. With ten or so boats over Stone Rock, each boat containing three or four people, I reckon there must have been thirty or forty chunks of crab floating a few inches off the bottom over six or eight acres of fishing grounds. It happened quickly as if a school of drum had suddenly located our delicious offering of tempting crab.

"I got a bite!" said Greg.

"Me, too," said his dad.

Line began to peel rapidly off each Penn reel as the fish tried to escape.

"Tighten your drag ever so slightly," I urged them, "but not too much." They cranked and pumped the rods, slowly gaining on their catches. "Watch your rod, Greg. Don't let it rest on the gunwale; it might break."

"But he's heavy!" responded my nephew. "Must be a big one."

We heard several other folks commenting on the CB that they had boated large black drum. Soon both Greg and his dad brought their fish to the surface having overcome the unexpected weight of the drum. "Look, Granddaddy, he's huge!" my nephew exclaimed as we lifted his large fish into the boat and dropped it unceremoniously into the fish box. It nearly filled the box.

"Must weigh a hundred pounds!" said Greg.

"Mine too," said his dad George, as he pulled his drum over the gunwale. "Hold that lid up so I can put him in the fish box." The two drum, each weighing about thirty-five pounds, occupied enough space in the built-in fish box that there would be no room for another.

"If we catch another one, we'll have to put it in the front box," I told my crew. "Good job, guys."

As I finished that sentence, the fiberglass rod I was holding bent and line began streaming off the spool. I had not felt a nibble. Having just seen their efforts, I too, tightened the drag slightly, just enough to stop losing monofilament line which was rated at thirty-pound test. Even though he had not caught a fish, Granddaddy was excited over our action.

Before I could get my fish into the boat, my father exclaimed, "I got a bite! I felt it!" He lifted his rod slightly, just as the fish must have inhaled his peeler crab, biting that sharp hook. "There he is! I got him," he shouted as line began to peel off the reel. Zzzzzz!

"Hang onto him, Granddaddy," Greg exclaimed. "I bet he's not as big as mine." My dad cranked and pumped and cranked and pumped his rod for a few minutes in the warm afternoon sun.

"I need a drink of water, Son, this fish is heavy." I held a cup of water up to his lips and he took several sips. Soon he began to tire; his seventy-five years (fifty-eight of them smoking cigarettes) began to show. He continued to crank and pump the rod, but he soon quit pumping. Then he quit cranking.

"Lift your rod, Granddaddy," said George to his father-in-law. "Lift your rod up off the gunwale, or it might break. Come on, Granddaddy, you can do it. Keep cranking." George offered his encouragement as best he could, but we could see the old man weakening.

"Good Garden Seed!" he exclaimed. "I never hooked a fish this big. If I hook another one, one of you guys will have to take the rod." All three of us noticed that his rod was once again resting on the boat.

"You can do it. You can do it. I know you can," said his grandson, Greg. "Keep cranking, I'll help you hold the rod off the boat." Greg stood beside his grandfather and gently lifted the rod a few inches above the side of the boat with one hand and with the other hand he patted his grandfather on the back. "I'll help you."

I think those actions and words of encouragement were all my dad needed. He did not want to let his grandson down, and he began to crank with renewed strength. The fish was slowly losing the battle. Meanwhile, as Greg assisted his grandfather, George and I brought my fish aboard and placed it in the front fish box which was built into the center console. We didn't have enough ice for both boxes, so we would have to head home soon.

Finally, we saw Dad's fish come to the surface alongside the boat. It was spent, just as tired as my dad, if not more so. We hoisted it into the boat, placing it alongside my fish in the front box. "Good fathers! That's a lot of fish," my dad exclaimed.

"It sure is," said George. "Now we have to go home and clean them." None of the four of us had ever caught (or cleaned) a big black drum. As George hauled in the anchor, I started the engine and got on the CB and called my friend, "C Boy" Lewis, who had just pulled away from Stone Rock in his boat.

"How do you clean these things?" I asked. The scales are as big as a silver dollar."

"What I do," he responded, "is nail the tail to a big board and scrape the scales off with a hoe. That's the only way I know. They're good eating. See you later. Oh! How many did you catch?"

"We have four, about thirty-five pounds each. Thanks for the help."

Immediately I increased the throttle and headed my boat in the direction of home, comfortable that I would beat the low tide and be able to reach my dock with ease. I was right. The girls met us and were thrilled with our catch, but uncertain as to what we could do with all that fish.

"I don't even know how to cook it," my wife informed us. She had never seen one either. "Call Mr. Russell. He or Gladys will know." They were neighbors who helped us at hog-killing time. Gladys knew how to cook just about everything, and she told Ginna to beat up an egg or two, dip the drum pieces into the mixture, then dredge them in flour, fry them in hot vegetable oil, and place the cooked fish on paper towels before serving. Gladys also liked to eat. I remember on more than one occasion several of us would be seated around the dining table, enjoying our meal (especially fresh pork tenderloin) and Gladys would remark, "There's a whole lot of hummin' in this meal. I mean, just listen to y'all. Everybody's saying 'Hmmmm Hmmmm.' Now that's a whole lot of hummin'."

Meanwhile, after George and I nailed the tail of the largest fish to a heavy two-by-eight board, we scraped those huge scales off with a garden hoe. It was not easy; so difficult in fact that we decided one fish was all we wanted to clean. I let George finish the cleaning and filleting job while Greg helped me load the other three fish into my pickup bed. We drove to a nearby neighborhood of modest homes known as White Rabbit, along the road to Greenbush, and offered the fish to our neighbors who gladly accepted them, offering to pay for them. I think I took one dollar each to help pay for the gas.

We enjoyed the fish for dinner with hushpuppies, coleslaw, and iced tea. Except for my sister, who eats only flounder and maybe a shrimp now and then—she is not a big fan of seafood. A few days later, my wife and I returned to Stone Rock. She hooked a big black drum and fought it for about ten minutes before her line went slack. When she reeled it in we discovered that the hook had been straightened. Cheap hook or very strong fish; we never did learn which.

As the summer slipped by, we returned to the area several times, but never caught another black drum. I also never caught a cobia or another eel with my bare hands.

DROWNIN' BEARS

Author's Note: This story first appeared in the March, 1992 issue of Gray's Sporting Journal, *in their Yarnspin section. It was told to me by the bear hunter while we shared a dinner meal in Frankfurt, Germany. The action took place in Alberta, Canada. I try to tell the story as if I'm sitting around a campfire, spinning a yarn.*

Seems that after huntin' bears for twenty years in Pennsylvania and never even gettin' a shot at one, my friend Eugene decided to go on a real Canadian bear hunt, you know, the kind with outfitters and guides and such, way up in the wilderness of Alberta. "Lotsa big bears up there," he told me.

Now I never hunted bears and I probably never will. I don't particularly like the idea of huntin' somethin' that might end up huntin' me before the day is over. I remember that Robert Redford movie a few years back where this crusty old mountain man asked, "Do you skin Griz, Pilgrim?" whereupon a big bear followed him into the tent and the mountain man continued, "Well here's one, skin him!" or somethin' like that. I leave bear huntin' and shark fishin' to hardier souls than I am.

Anyway, back to Eugene and Alberta. Seems that every spring this particular outfitter buses about twenty hunters and ten guides up a loggin' road deep into the boondocks miles and miles from civilization where they proceed to hunt bears just comin' outta hibernation. They hunt them over bait. Now I won't make any social or political comments about that method except to say that in my part of the country bait huntin' has always been associated with puttin' out a little corn for ducks or fruit for the deer, and the game wardens take a dim view of the practice. Takin' unfair advantage of hungry critters, they say.

But I know it is common practice to hunt bears over bait, and anyway, if you don't take advantage of the bears they might end up takin' advantage of you. Seems like half the covers of outdoor magazines these days have someone runnin' from a grizzly or gettin' mauled by a grizzly. I myself have observed huge Brown Bears feedin' on salmon up at Brooks Falls in Alaska, and believe me, I let them have all the salmon they wanted. Our friend and host made us release most of the fish we caught in Alaska so we wouldn't have bear bait hangin' from our belts. It makes my neck hairs stand up just thinkin' about it.

Seems these guides up in Alberta use a bait with a pungent aroma and they place a few fish in the cache to make it more appealin'. They cover the whole thing with some tree branches and they visit the site daily until they notice evidence of a bear's visit. Then they station a hunter at the site. Eugene's huntin' partner had already bagged a nice bear the first or second day of the hunt, so when one of their sites attracted a bear, Eugene was selected to be the next lucky hunter.

It was a good location. There was this borrow pit and some beavers had dammed a portion of it, thereby creatin' a little pond. The bait station was near the dam, and Eugene the bear hunter chose a hidin' place nearby which gave him a good view of the bait as well as the bear's most likely approach path. He sat there for a couple of hours tryin' to decide if he was havin' fun. Sure enough, along came this bear hungry for some fish for breakfast. Just as he got abeam Eugene's hidin' place he kinda slowed down, then he stopped to sniff the air, checkin' for who knows what! Now the way Eugene tells it, he hadn't had a bath for a few days, and so he started to thinkin' while he was sittin' there watchin' his bear that maybe, just maybe, he might smell like a more appetizin' meal than that pile of dead fish. Remember what I said about the hunter becomin' the hunted?

Well ol' Eugene looked real hard at that big bear and decided he didn't want to give the bear too much time to decide whether he wanted fish or Eugene for breakfast. Just as he was takin' aim, the bear started movin' again closer to the bait. Eugene decided to wait just a little bit longer, knowin' the risks of shootin' at a movin' target. The bear stopped again, sniffed and snorted once more. He looked first toward the bait and then toward Eugene and he couldn't seem to make up his mind what to do. His indecision was a costly mistake.

Eugene could already visualize that nice rug in front of his fireplace in the Poconos. He held his breath, took careful aim, and put a 200 grain .30 caliber bullet right behind the bear's shoulder. But much to his surprise, instead of fallin' that bear stood up full height, slapped his shoulder with a big paw as if he was swattin' a bee, and looked around. "Whoof!" he snorted. Eugene froze! The hundred yards which separated them seemed to shrink to five. He surveyed the pond, which was between him and the bear and he tried to calculate how long it would take the bear, with a bullet in his shoulder, to run around one end or the other, or else to swim straight across to get him. That pond kept lookin' smaller and smaller.

But twenty years of practicin' so to speak, paid off, and Eugene got hold of himself. He chambered another round and put another shot in the same place. This time the bear fell and, would you believe it, he did a somersault right into the pond, completely disappearin' with a splash and a big 'glub, glub.' Eugene watched in silent disbelief as his trophy sank outta sight.

Now the guide had told him not to go chasin' after a wounded bear, but he never told him what to do in a situation like this. So Eugene the brave decided to wait a while before goin' to fetch his trophy. Surely that ol' bear can't get outta this predicament, thought the mighty hunter. He waited nearly an hour. Over in the next draw the guide heard the shots and he carefully worked his way to Eugene's hidin' place whereupon he discovered Eugene standin' there, shakin' his head and lookin' down at his bear lyin' on the bottom of the pond. Figurin' for sure he was dead, they fetched a rope from the truck in order to tow it across the pond to the edge near the trail where it would be easier to load into the truck.

They waded into the pond and tied the rope to a hind leg which was just below the surface 'cause the pond wasn't really all that deep. Soon as they put a little tension on that rope and started tuggin' at it the bear rolled over and burped. Yessir! A big bubble of air that musta been trapped in his lungs escaped and came rushin' out with a loud groan and a whoosh, and both those fellers, Eugene and his guide, took off a runnin' 'cause they figured that a bear that could burp must still be alive. They didn't stop runnin' until they were about fifty yards away and then the guide looked over his shoulder and saw that the bear was not followin' them and they stopped and laughed so hard they nearly cried. After they finished laughin' at themselves they towed that ol' bear around to the other side of the pond where they decided to leave it 'til they got some other fellers to help lift him into the truck.

Now Eugene is a proud sorta guy, an accomplished sportsman and a veteran hunter. He knew his bear was a trophy, rightfully earned, even though ambushed on his way to breakfast. But at the same time, so he told me later, he knew he'd been spooked by that burp, and he was a little uneasy about that—especially since his guide also knew about it. The two of 'em had shared an experience which they'd just as soon forget—fear. Fright. Stark terror. They stood there, caught up in the emotion of the moment, kinda starin' at each other with a look which said, without sayin' it... "Boy! He sure fooled us." Each one knew that he was probably thinkin' the same thing as the other one, that is to say, how can we keep this our own little secret? They discussed the matter and decided they couldn't.

So that night in camp they each took turns tellin' the others about the incident at the pond with the two of 'em, both grown men with fifty years huntin' experience between 'em, runnin' from a dead bear that burped. And bein' dead for an hour anyway—first shot and then drowned and pretty near hog tied.

MARSH HENS

During the time we lived in Accomack County on Virginia's Eastern Shore from 1971 until 1997, nearly twenty-seven years, I was able to observe a gradual decline in the bobwhite quail population. I suspected several reasons, not the least of which were feral cats, hawks (especially Cooper's hawks) and possibly insecticides. I remember on more than one occasion seeing in June or early July a family of quail—the babies being only one or two days old, little fluff balls—in the soybean fields and then a crop duster would fly over, spraying for loopers or caterpillars or armyworms or other pests. Many little critters love soybean leaves.

Within a few days whenever I flushed quail in the same vicinity, only a pair flew up, the adults. I think the baby quail ate the dead insects and died. I also observed a Cooper's hawk perch in a sweetgum tree near my pond every January and stay for about two weeks. What quail that survived the insecticides usually disappeared during that time. I read in a magazine that such hawks typically eat one quail a day. I even wrote an article about the hawk population and the devastating effect they were having on our quail. I submitted the article to Virginia Wildlife magazine, but the editor at the time told me that if she published my story it would cause hunters to begin shooting every hawk they saw. Of course I also knew that habitat loss was a factor, but I read in a magazine about a research project two biologists did in North Carolina where they legally shot several hawks and found quail inside.

I do not think I contributed very much to the decline of the quail population, but I must confess that I did harvest a few every year for many years. I was fortunate enough to have good dogs and several landowner friends who allowed me access to their farms. One of my most memorable quail hunts was the day my pointer, Bogey, stopped dead in his tracks along some honeysuckle at the edge of a recently harvested soybean field behind three abandoned broiler houses not far from Lee Johnson's air strip. When the covey flushed, I shot quickly firing all three shells. Much to my surprise as I was putting the third bird in my game vest, Bogey brought me a fourth bird. That is the only time I ever got four birds on a covey rise.

Of course, quail were not the only game in town. What we were blessed with were hundreds of mourning doves. They roosted there during the summer and each pair raised one or two clutches of young, and then in late August during corn harvest, some northern doves began to arrive. September was dove shooting time. Either my neighbor or I grew corn nearly every year. We also had several farmer friends who allowed us to shoot doves on their properties. I remember that another friend, Dave Tyler, lived not far from a very productive dove spot over on the seaside along Folly Creek. We had permission to shoot on that farm, and those years when cucumbers were the crop of choice, our dove shoots were very successful. Often my friend and fellow pilot, Jerry, would be able to join us for those shoots along the cedar trees which bordered the cucumber fields. One of the most disappointing days in my life was the day I drove over to check out that farm in August and discovered three or four homes under construction in my favorite dove field. We never hunted the cedars again.

Not only did Jerry like to shoot doves, but he also liked to eat soft shell crabs, especially the way my wife lightly dredges them in flour and fries them slowly in enough butter to keep them from sticking to the skillet. All of us, including Jerry, also liked clams, and whenever he would visit, we always tried to have at least one meal of steamed clams as an appetizer followed by soft crabs and coleslaw and spoonbread. One time I was having difficulty locating some clams, trying all my neighbors in the seafood business without any success. Finally, Woody Zember, a crabber, said he thought one man he knew down in Quinby might have some clams. I commented that Quinby was a long way to go for clams. His reply was, "Not for a friend." Without realizing it, he shamed me into making the forty-mile round trip, and I bought four or five dozen clams. They were yummy.

One Saturday in September, during our dinner of doves, Dave Tyler asked me if I had ever hunted rails, also called marsh hens. I replied that I had not—didn't know much about it. "Well, the tide should be right the next couple of days. Come on over to my shop Monday about noon and I'll take you rail hunting. Bring your shotgun."

I had not yet purchased my little 20-gauge Browning side-by-side so my bird gun of choice was my 12-gauge Browning auto-loader. Because I did not want to be late, I arrived at Dave's place of business in Wachapreague at about eleven o'clock. He owned a marine railway and boat repair business. We had been friends for several years. In fact, I took his oldest teenage son duck hunting and deer hunting a few times and told him stories now and then about some of my flying experiences. I do not want to take credit for it, but after graduating Virginia Military Institute, young David became a Navy helicopter pilot, eventually reaching the rank of captain and commanding a squadron of submarine chasers.

First, Dave gave me a tour of his machine shop. Then he and I departed his marina and motored out into the vast marshes between Wachapreague and Cedar Island during the highest tide I had ever seen. Dave occupied the stern and told me to sit up front in the wooden scow. He followed the channel markers, but nearly the whole area was flooded. He headed for a grassy area still visible above the high tide, shut the engine down, began to push the boat forward with a long wooden pole, and said, "Get ready, Ash, there should be some birds in that grass."

He was right. About twenty-five yards ahead of me, a rail flushed and I dropped it, an easy shot. Then another. Same result. We hastily retrieved the small brown birds and proceeded to another likely-looking spot. One or two marsh hens flushed from nearly every grassy area. They were hiding on the few remaining spots of dry land they could find as the tide reached its maximum flood stage.

After I shot eight or ten birds, we switched places and Dave shot a few birds. I must admit I did not find it very challenging—the shooting that is; I think I missed three and dropped eight—but poling that scow was not easy, especially if the wind was not at my back. Dave had done it many times in the past, and he was accustomed to daily work much harder than flying airplanes so he had less difficulty than I did. It was not very long, maybe an hour, no more than two, before the tide began to ebb, exposing more and more grassy areas, and soon I could make out the channel with which I was more familiar.

"That's it," said Dave. "We might as well go home. They have too many places to hide now. But we have enough for dinner."

"Are they good eatin'?" I asked.

"You'll find out soon enough."

When we reached his house, I helped clean our birds, while Dave's wife, Dolores, called my wife and invited her to dinner. We ate the fried rails. I must admit that I did not find them to be very appetizing. It was not her cooking, I hastily add—I had consumed many fine meals at the Tylers'—it was the birds. They were tough. They were stringy. There was not very much meat on their bones.

Although it might have originated with old-time wooden fences, I think I discovered the origin of that saying "skinny as a rail." I never hunted rails again.

WEST VIRGINIA TUNA

For several years it has been our policy that whenever we go offshore fishing in my 22-foot Mako Center Console boat that if we are not back home or at least back at the marina by dark, then we have a problem. A couple of times in the past we had cut it very close, but we usually were safely inside Oregon Inlet by sundown, and more likely already back at the cottage by dark. If we departed the marina before sunrise and fished until about one or two o'clock at the latest, we could usually have the boat back on the trailer by four or five, maybe six o'clock in the evening. More often than not, one or two family members met us at the marina. It had become a tradition, I guess you could say, and the tired fishermen looked forward to the greeting. Not only did they enjoy greeting us, but while waiting, they also enjoyed seeing the marlin flags waving in the stiff breeze, watching the big charter boats back into their slips with such ease and confidence, and watching the mates toss their catches up onto the dock before going to the fuel pumps.

All of us can remember a few years back when many of the clients had more fish than they knew what to do with and would share a dolphin or two with an eager bystander. All you had to do was ask. But by the 1970s, those extra fish found their way into the retail store inside the marina for sale at the market price. No more freebies.

We had been at the beach for ten days of our two-week vacation, weary of staying in the cottage most of that time watching the high surf pound the beach and listening to the weather reports calling for more of the same each morrow. Ten days and the boat stayed on the trailer—not the most satisfying vacation for people who loved to fish as much as we do. As much as we enjoy playing Scrabble, we were beginning to tire of the game. Finally on the eleventh day, things looked promising ... at least promising enough to launch the boat, which we did at five o'clock in the morning—except Ginna and Nancy, who decided not to go—"Too soon after all that wind," they declared.

The weather was almost always unpredictable in the summer, but one thing was certain, it would be windy by noon and the ride home from twenty or thirty miles offshore would be rough in my little boat, often taking three or more hours. That is one reason the charter boat fleet consists mainly of sleek, sturdy, and seaworthy fifty-foot and sixty-foot sport fishing vessels, often manufactured right in the local area around Manteo or Wanchese. They are not only seaworthy but beautiful. On many occasions during the ride home I would be able to follow one of those big vessels up close and ride the slack water right behind his wake all the way to the inlet (with the captain's permission, of course). It was tedious and demanding work, requiring almost constant jockeying of my throttle in order to maintain just the right RPM to stay in the flat water, but it made for a smoother ride. Of course if the big boat had twin engines, as most of them do, I could not keep up with them for very long, and had to back off, slow down, and struggle against the oncoming seas and the spray all alone. My guests often hunkered down under the vinyl doghouse cover in front of the center console to avoid the spray coming over the bow every few minutes. Standing at the helm I had to meet it face on.

If our day had been successful, with several fish in the box, the rough ride home was worth it. We did not always have success, and once in a while we returned with an empty fish box. On that particular day, which followed ten days of high winds, Jerry and I had tried every trick in our book of fishing skills to hook up. We trolled a ragged weed line, weed patches really, for several miles and finally decided that other boats south of us had already caught whatever fish that may have once lurked beneath. We circled one of the Navy towers a few times, far enough away to avoid amberjacks but hopefully close enough to attract something else. We trolled artificial lures of all types. We rigged a fresh ballyhoo every so often. We even cut up a couple of ballyhoo and made a chum line, then stopped and jigged while drifting with the wind. We trolled close enough to other boats a couple of times to observe that they were having no better luck than we were. Shortly before noon we heard some chatter on the radio that indicated some of the charter boats were catching marlin down at the point, maybe twenty-five miles south of us, but by that time we had used enough fuel that we could not make it down there and still have enough remaining to make it back to port safely. It was after several trips such as this one that I decided to increase my fuel capacity.

We finally admitted defeat and gave up. "Maybe we'll have better luck tomorrow," I said, trying to offer my crew some encouragement. It is hard to leave the fishing grounds when you have been skunked, thinking that it won't be long before you get a strike. I hate to disappoint my guests, but I have enough experience outside Oregon Inlet to know that eventually I would have to face the rough ride home and then navigate the inlet which can be treacherous, especially if the tide and the wind are opposing each other. I usually try to follow one or two of the charter boats because they know the subtle changes in the channel, navigating it almost daily whereas I am lucky if I get more than five or six chances a year. After nearly three hours of meeting that southwest wind head on, we made our way through the inlet and under the bridge into the calmer water of the Albemarle Sound. We'd be at the ramp in another thirty minutes.

We did not have to jockey for position at the boat ramp because mine was the only small boat which needed to be hauled out; no others were in view. The parking lot contained five or six empty trailers, so I knew there were probably five or six small boats still at sea or fishing in the sound. Right on schedule and much to our delight we saw the girls waving at us as we approached the dock. "I hate to tell them of our bad luck," Jerry remarked.

"Yeah me too, but they'll be glad to hear that they avoided those rough seas." I eased into the upwind side of the calm water of the launch ramp, and let the boat drift the short distance and come to rest against the dock. Jerry tossed a line to one of the girls and then he jumped up onto the dock. I grabbed a post and held the stern in place up against the dock and then tossed him another line. They would hold the boat secure while I fetched the truck and backed the trailer down the ramp. I had been doing it for ten years and I was fairly good at it.

"Catch any fish?" Nancy inquired. "I see that you're not flying any flags." Sometimes we flew a dish towel to signify getting skunked, but today we had not bothered.

"Nah, we didn't catch a thing," I replied. "Too soon after all that wind, I guess." Both girls, my wife Ginna and Jerry's sister Nancy, began to giggle like two pre-teen girls.

"Well, we did!" one of them said. "We did! We can have tuna for dinner." They jumped up and down like excited teenagers at a rock concert. Without waiting for me to retrieve the boat trailer, they began to tell this story, each one taking turns relating the events.

One of them said, "We came down here early enough to see the charter fleet come in. Many of them had no fish. A couple were flying marlin flags upside down (indicating catch and release), and one or two had some small dolphin. We saw one mate toss four yellowfin up onto the dock, while their clients backed a panel truck up close. Soon they loaded the four tuna into the truck and drove off. We noticed the license plate was from West Virginia, thinking the three men were probably way too tired for a long drive home, but we gave it no more thought. We continued to the end of the marina and saw a few more fish. Finally, after thirty or forty minutes, we drove the car around to this side of the parking lot to wait for you guys. That's when we saw that panel truck again, the one from West Virginia, over by the dumpster."

"Yeah, they had placed a half sheet of plywood on the ground and put one of the fish onto the board. The wind was blowing enough that we could see the fish was already getting sandy. One of the guys was sitting on a bucket beside the van drinking a beer. One was sitting on the ground drinking a beer. The third man was just standing there, holding something in his right hand, looking down at their catch. We parked nearby and slowly walked over to them. We commented that it looked like they had had a successful day. I noticed that the knife in the one guy's hand was an unopened Swiss Army Knife with a red handle. We told them that the marina has a fish cleaning service.

"The guy said, 'Yeah. The mate told us about it, but we thought it was too expensive. There's no place to clean the fish at our hotel, so we decided to give it a try here.' "

"Do you have another knife?" asked Nancy, as she peeked into the van.

"Nope, this is it. I guess we shoulda brung some from home." (Although I was not there to witness it, I had known each of the ladies for about fifteen years, and I'm certain that at this point, if one listened closely, one could hear the wheels and gears turning in both girls' heads.) They both know how to clean a tuna.

"Well, just stay right here while I go back to our car," Nancy told them. "I think we can help you. We just happen to have a couple of sharp filet knives." One girl retrieved the two knives while the other one told the men to stand aside. Within about fifteen minutes they had successfully reduced a forty-pound tuna to four nice filets, while these three men watched in amazement. After placing the fresh tuna filets into a cooler, and tossing the carcasses into the dumpster, the men placed another tuna onto the board. Both girls tackled it and the next one with the ease and skill of a plastic surgeon.

One of the men said, "Hey, let me try the next one." So the girls relinquished one of the knives and offered enough guidance that soon the man from West Virginia, the one who appeared to have consumed the fewest beers during the day had cleaned and filleted fish number four. They thanked the girls, who began to walk away.

"No sweat," said the girls. "Glad to help. We have to go meet our guys at the boat ramp now."

"Hey, wait a minute. You ain't gonna get away that easy. Here, take a couple of these filets for your trouble. We'd have been here all night if you hadn't come along. You got a cooler, don't cha?"

"Yessir, we sure do!"

And that's how our girls caught half a tuna without ever setting foot on the boat that day, while Jerry, Arnold (Jerry's dad), and I struggled all day on that rough ocean and came home empty-handed. Dinner was terrific. Grilled fresh tuna always is.

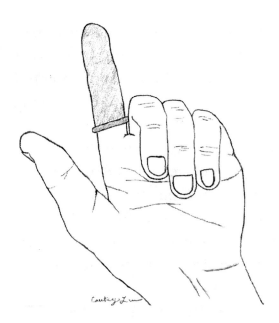

THE CUT FINGER

I went to my dentist the other day because I had been up to my usual tricks of eating too much sugar and failing to floss regularly. He was up to his usual trick of asking me a question and then sticking his fingers in my mouth before I had a chance to answer. "Been fishing lately?" he asked as he grabbed my chin with one hand and shoved it downward while poking one of his pointy-end steel stickers in my mouth. Both of us belonged to the Marlin club and we fished together on separate boats one or two weekends each summer.

"Oomph, humph, ahh, mmmm, aaagk," I tried to answer without biting his fingers, which he removed for a few seconds. I looked cross-eyed down past the tip of my nose, noticing that he wore a little rubber finger glove on his left index finger. I had seen him wear gloves before but never a glove with four fingers missing. It looked kinda like a miniature condom and I felt strange looking down my nose at it. "What's that little finger glove for?" I asked him before he started to drill.

"I cut my finger pretty bad sharpening a knife," he replied. "I was down at the marina doing a few last-minute chores getting the boat ready for the tournament next weekend. After I finished working on the engine and organizing my tackle and such I had a few minutes to spare and I noticed that my bait-rigging knife looked a little grungy so I decided to touch up the edge a bit. I have one of those sharpeners that you pull the blade across between two small sharpening wheels and it puts on a pretty good edge after only five or six strokes. I was nearly finished when I heard a shout, 'Doc! Hey Doc! Come quick!' I looked up just before beginning that last, long, firm, stroke of the blade across the sharpener and I missed... and I sliced clean down to the bone.

"It was so quick and smooth that I didn't feel a thing until it was over and I stood there looking down at the blood flow and I looked up at old Rudy standing there on the dock. 'Come quick!' he said, huffing and puffing after running about two hundred yards. 'Come quick, doc. Old Ezra down to th' clam house done passed out and we think he done had a heart attack!'

"But I'm a dentist," I explained and I took out my handkerchief and wrapped it around my finger as best I could, trying to stop the blood with pressure until I could get to my office and suture it back together.

"Yes suh, Doc. Yes suh, I know that. We done called th' ambulance an' it's on th' way, but can't you come see 'bout Ezra anyway, pleeese. I mean, you're th' only doctor we got.'

"So I climbed up onto the dock, not worrying about my blood, which was already starting to dry all over the cockpit and I trotted the three blocks down the street to the clam house, CPR techniques running through my mind. With every step I took my heart started to beat faster, and by the time I reached Ezra that makeshift handkerchief pressure bandage I had wrapped around my finger was saturated.

"No pulse. I began CPR on Ezra and while I was pressing down on his chest my bandage slipped off and every time I pressed down on Ezra my pulse would beat faster and the blood would spurt out all over Ezra and me and the floor and on a few bystanders. What a mess!

"A few minutes later the EMT boys from the firehouse arrived and took over from me and started working on Ezra right away and they looked around at the mess we'd made and one of them asked me what happened. 'Looks like old Ezra's got a problem with his heart,' I replied."

"What happened!" he asked. "Did it explode?"

"I waved my cut finger at him. 'No, the blood is mine. If you boys have everything under control here I think I'll go sew my finger back together.' So I came back here to the office and put five stitches in it and I think it'll be fine in a few days.

"Open wide, now."

Author's Note: After consulting with my dentist (who requested not to be named) it was mutually agreed that I embellished this story. He remembers telling me about cutting his finger earlier in the week and wearing the little finger glove during my visit, but he insists that I fabricated the rest of the story about Ezra and his heart. Perhaps I did. It was many years ago. I have to accept his version of events, but what you have just read is MY story, and I'm sticking to it.

Diamond Shoals

I wrote in the preface that a boat is a hole in the water into which one pours money. Oh, 'tis true, 'tis true. Actually, after spending twenty-three days aboard a troop ship crossing the Pacific from Oakland, California to Vietnam, I was pretty sure that I did not really want to own a boat. However, once we moved from California and were firmly settled along a tidal creek on Virginia's Eastern Shore, I developed a different mindset.

My wife's father passed along a sixteen-foot wooden boat, a Wagemaker Wolverine, with a 35 HP Evinrude that proved less than desirable and dependable. They had used it for water skiing in the 1950s, and it was at least twenty-five years old, spending most of the time on the trailer in his yard. A secondhand replacement Evinrude engine was no better. I remember the day I drove in the driveway with that second engine. Looking down at me from the den window, Ginna exclaimed, "Oh no! There goes my new sofa."

That boat had never before had a name, but it soon became *Sofa Two*. We fished in the Chesapeake Bay a few times with it, and I used it to get to my duck blinds, but we soon longed for something a little larger. We began to go together to boat shows in Norfolk and Virginia Beach, and I attended a few shows in New York. After inspecting several dozen boats and deciding we simply could not afford what we wanted, new, we began to look at used boats, drawn to Grady Whites and Makos. We visited the Grady White factory in Greenville, North Carolina and I even spent an afternoon at the Mako plant in Opa Locka, Florida during a Miami layover. Both products are well-made and impressive. We continued our search, finally settling on a used Mako 22-foot center console with a 125 HP Evinrude. It was four years old.

At first we named it *Flying Fish,* but a few years later, after discovering at least two other boats with that name, one in Chincoteague and one in North Carolina, we decided on *Jetstream,* since that is where I spent a good portion of my life. We first fished in the Bay, and within a week of buying it we came upon a large school of bluefish south of Onancock Creek. I had not brought the outriggers so we were trolling two flat lines pulling Hopkins No-Equal spoons with treble hooks. Ginna was at the helm while I spent most of my time removing those treble hooks from the fish our daughters were catching, fast and furious. I soon discovered that single hooks worked fine so I switched, making it much easier to remove them from those mouths with the razor-sharp teeth. We were using thirty-inch steel leaders ahead of the lures, attached to the mono line with a snap swivel. Two or three times a fish attacked a swivel, cutting the mono and we lost both the leader and the lure. In her excitement my wife once remarked, "They're over there," pointing to starboard, followed immediately by, "they're over there," pointing to port. Then, "Oh damn, they're everywhere!" We quit when the fish box was full, counting forty-four blues, most about two or three pounds. We easily had one hundred pounds of fish.

We always had a policy that the girls had to help once we were back at home, either clean the boat or help clean the fish. We had fresh broiled bluefish for dinner and we gave some away to our friends, the Tylers. We discovered that most of our friends did not think bluefish were suitable table fare, leaving us with more than we knew what to do with. They do not freeze well, we knew, so I decided to smoke them. Following a technique used in Alaska, one I had seen on a TV show, I filleted both sides, leaving the two fillets attached at the tail. I brined them overnight, patted them dry with paper towels, hung them in my smoke house on two-by-twos, and smoked them all day over hickory firewood, maintaining a temperature as close to 105° F as I could. It worked. We used them as appetizers, served on a Ritz cracker. Once smoked, it freezes well.

It wasn't long before I overheated the engine, and my brother helped me overhaul it, replacing one piston and all the rings and bearings. Then I blew another piston and a friend came and towed me to the ramp in Chesconnex from about three miles away out near a spot we called Crammyhack. Completely fed up with the 125 and vowing never again to buy a used outboard, I began looking at new outboard motors, finally settling on a new 200 HP Evinrude V-6. It was beautiful. I began to think "seaside" and maybe even "offshore." After all, it had three carburetors, each cylinder had its own independent coil, and I had two marine batteries and a CB radio. It seemed as safe as a multi-engine airplane.

My friend Jerry, who had his own 41-foot Hatteras sport fisherman in Ft. Lauderdale, convinced me that my boat, with its new engine, was indeed, suitable for offshore fishing. He joined me and we trailered it to Hatteras, spending the night in my Suburban in the parking lot at Teach's Lair Marina. I had prepared the car for such events, making wooden inserts with screen wire which fit into the lowered windows, and my wife had made curtains which fit into a track I screwed into the ceiling. We could sleep in peace and with privacy. Shortly after sunrise the next morning, supplied with two dozen frozen bally-hoo, plenty of ice, lunch, suitable rods, reels, other tackle, and a full tank of gas (fifty gallons) we cruised out of the marina, down the channel, and out through Hatteras Inlet, headed for the area around Diamond Shoals light.

Within an hour, we were catching king mackerel two at a time, but losing about one for every one we caught. The ones we lost were biting the bally-hoo (which were rigged with a single hook under the chin in the gill plate area) in half, attacking them behind the hook. We tried a second hook, aft, known as a stinger rig, and started losing fewer fish. Once, and this is where the day began its slow progression into one of those misadventures, while I was at the helm Jerry was reeling in a king which rushed the boat faster than he could crank the reel, getting under the propeller. Before I could shift the engine into neutral, the steel leader snapped and he lost the fish. I immediately shut the engine off, concerned that perhaps some of the leader wire had become entangled around the prop shaft. We could see the Diamond Shoals tower, confident that we were far enough outside the shallow water that we would not run aground, and we decided to raise the engine and inspect the prop. Even then, I was not satisfied and I suggested that we should remove the prop to inspect the shaft more closely.

My dad had a saying, "Slow procedure, ain't it, boy?" He would have felt right at home with me that day. Having no spare propeller, I carefully secured a rope around it before unscrewing the prop nut, which had a small hole in it. Just before removing the nut, I carefully inserted some leader wire into the hole, safely securing the prop nut to the boat. I even secured my wrenches with braided fishing line. After about an hour or maybe even two, of slow methodical work, hanging out over the transom, I was able to satisfy myself that there was no wire around the shaft and no damage to the prop. All of a sudden I looked down and about six feet from me was a hammerhead shark as large as I am. I weighed 250 at the time and was six foot two.

"Damn!" I shouted as I quickly slid away from the transom. "Look at that! Do you see that shark?"

"He won't hurt you," Jerry laughed. "Just don't fall overboard."

After deciding that we were not a meal, the shark disappeared in a few minutes, and I returned to my chore of replacing the propeller, carefully securing it with the brass nut, and reminding myself to get an extra nut and prop, and to drill holes in all my boat wrenches. In perhaps another thirty minutes, I was satisfied that the engine was ready to be re-started, but before I could do it, a huge container ship appeared in our view, perhaps a mile south of us and headed directly toward us.

"Please, God, let this engine start," I prayed as I lowered it into the water with the switch on the console. "Please." It fired up and I eased it into gear, turned ninety degrees from the ship's path, and pushed the throttle forward. The word EVERGREEN looked as big as a house as that ship grew ever larger.

"He's not gonna hit us," Jerry remarked, "but his wake will be huge, so get as far away as you can."

I did. Within ten minutes he had passed us, heading north, and we both commented that he likely never saw us. We were safe.

After allowing him to get a mile or so away from us, we began to fish again, but by now we had lost sight of the tower. We continued fishing another hour or two, following a weed line. We caught one bull dolphin (mahi-mahi) and lost a couple of fish we never saw. It was early afternoon, maybe two o'clock, and I decided that we should probably head back to Hatteras Inlet.

All of a sudden an outrigger clip snapped, a rod bent, and the reel screamed *bzzzzzzz!*

"You take him, Ash, I'll drive," Jerry exclaimed. I grabbed the rod and plunked the handle end into the gimbaled rod holder on my seat. It was not a real fighting chair, but it would do. Jerry reeled in the remaining three lines as I continued to crank. Once we saw the fish jump, a good 150 yards astern, so far away that we could not identify it. "It might be a small marlin, or a sailfish," Jerry said, trying to reassure me that the fight would be worth it, "or maybe another dolphin."

I kept fighting against the fish's steady pull. It was touch and go for maybe twenty minutes, but soon I began to fill the reel spool with line, then the leader came into view. Jerry put the engine in neutral, the boat stopped, and water began to splash over the transom. Not much, but enough that it worried me, this being the first time I had been offshore in this boat. I worried that it would find its way below deck where the batteries were stored. Jerry grabbed the leader and we both managed to pull the fish against the transom beside the outboard. We could see that it was a shark. Not a hammerhead like I'd come face to face with earlier in the day, but a Mako, namesake of my boat. I did not want a live shark in the boat with us, especially one that looked to weigh at least a hundred pounds, and I was anxious to get back to shore before the seas got any rougher. Not knowing any better, I grabbed my sharp knife and slit that shark's belly open, cut the hook out of its mouth, and let him slide back into the ocean. "Let's get out of here," I said as I took control of the helm and turned the boat toward what I thought was Hatteras Inlet.

We were aware that we had most likely drifted north with the Gulf Stream the entire time we had been working on the prop, as well as when we avoided that container ship and fought the Mako, but how fast and how far we could only guess. I had a portable radio with a weather channel and an AM broadcast band, which I was sure I could tune to a shore radio station and get a bearing. We did it all the time on airplanes. But we were only a few feet above the water and far enough offshore that I could not receive a clear station, only static. All we could do was head in a westerly direction, knowing that the shoreline had to come into view before long. *Where was that tower? How much gas did I have remaining? Is the gauge accurate? What am I doing here?* We didn't talk much, just stared ahead and watched the needle on the fuel gauge.

In about one hour we saw what appeared to be some landmarks way, far away in front of us and the depth finder indicated that the water was getting shallower, so we were reasonably confident that we were headed to the beach, but because we had no visible north/ south reference, we were uncertain if we were headed for Hatteras or Oregon Inlet. Consulting my printed chart did not help, so we just kept heading toward land. Finally, we could make out a radio tower, but I still could get no signal or bearing reference. "I think I see the beach!" Jerry shouted. "Yes, it's the beach." He grabbed the binoculars and began to scan the beach, looking for anything recognizable.

Knowing that Diamond Shoals covers a large area, I was now worried that if I wasn't careful I would get caught up in the surf and run aground. I definitely did not want to become another wreck in the graveyard of the Atlantic. "I see somebody! He's surf casting," exclaimed Jerry. "I don't see a vehicle...no, wait, there's one up by the dunes."

Hoping that the fisherman had a radio in his Jeep, I got on my CB radio and started talking. "Does anyone read the *Flying Fish*, off the beach?" I asked. (At the time we had not yet changed the name of the boat to *Jetstream*.) "This is vessel *Flying Fish*, about 300 yards off the beach. Does anybody read me? Over."

We could see the man run to his vehicle, and soon we heard, "Yes, I see you." Relief. He must have kept the volume full up on his CB, for which I was grateful.

"This is *Flying Fish*. Our compass is acting funny," I replied. "Can you tell us exactly where you are? We're supposed to be going to Hatteras, and we're low on fuel."

"Well, I suggest you forget about Hatteras," he said. "It's thirty-five miles south. You're off Rodanthe, and it's only fifteen miles to Oregon Inlet."

I turned the boat north and a little away from the beach as Jerry searched for Rodanthe on our chart.

"He's right. He's right. We'll never make it to Hatteras."

"I know that, dammit! I just wonder if we can make it to Oregon Inlet, but it's our only shot." I stayed just far enough outside the surf, within about a half mile of the beach as the sun dropped lower toward the horizon. Fortunately, the wind had slacked off and I was able to maintain about 4,000 RPM which gave me enough speed to stay on plane with the boat, saving precious fuel.

It wasn't long before we could make out the arch of Bonner

Bridge and the Bodie Island lighthouse. Jerry gave me a thumbs up. *Only a few more miles*, I thought, as the sky grew grayer and grayer. Soon I could make out the lights of the Corps of Engineers dredge which seemed to be constantly on duty in the channel, sucking up mud and depositing it out the side discharge pipe into the outgoing tide. If I could not make it to the bridge, I would head directly to that dredge, but that Evinrude engine kept purring along. *Please don't quit*, I said to myself, hoping that God was listening.

Soon we passed beneath the bridge and followed the channel lights to the Oregon Inlet Fishing Center and the safety of the boat ramp, hoping to make it before dark if we made it at all. We did.

As we eased toward the ramp dock, Jerry said, "Damn, that looks like Roger Anderson. You know Roger, don't you?" I could see a man standing in his boat—a few feet longer than my boat—which was tied up to the dock. "Hey! Roger! Is that you, Roger? It's me, Jerry," my fishing partner shouted over the idle of my engine. I killed the ignition as Jerry tossed a line to Roger and we drifted alongside his boat. I had not met Roger, but I knew he was also a Pan Am pilot. I soon learned that he also lived in Virginia.

"Hey Jerry. Whatcha doin?"

"It's a long story, buddy. This is my friend, Ash. We've been fishing all day, but we need some help. Do you have a car? We need a ride to Hatteras to get the boat trailer."

"Yeah, I have a car. I cruised my boat down here last week, off shore. Gonna leave it here a couple of months. My wife drove down to get me and I went home and drove my car back down here yesterday. Sure, I'll take you to Hatteras. Let's go."

I happily got in beside Roger and we departed at sunset. Jerry decided to stay with the boat, wash it down with fresh water, and also clean our fish. It's fifty miles one way by road from Oregon Inlet to the marina in Hatteras, and I spent a good portion of the trip explaining our day to Roger. He said he understood, but I think he silently thought to himself, *what a couple of losers.*

By the time he dropped me off at my Suburban and I returned

to my boat, three hours had passed. I found Jerry asleep, curled up beneath the vinyl doghouse cover. The two of them helped me load the boat onto my trailer and then the three of us each sipped a beer, glad that the day had ended safely. Roger slept aboard his boat. Jerry joined me in the Suburban and we happily went to sleep, dog tired.

The next morning, I put forty-nine gallons of gas into my fifty-gallon fuel tank. I made a promise to myself to get better radios, including a proper RDF (radio direction finder) and figure out how to increase my fuel capacity.

God takes care of fools and poor navigators.

OUTSIDE OREGON INLET

When most people think of the term shifting sands, the usual image that comes to mind is a desert, but for many of us who fish off North Carolina's coast, the typical image is Oregon Inlet, which is famous for many things, one of which is uncertainty. I fished there for about ten years, during the 1980s, and passed through the inlet three or four times each year. I can truthfully say I do not remember ever taking the exact same route in or out more than once or twice. My memory bank contains several stored images of that side-cast dredge discharging millions and millions of gallons (or cubic yards) of slushy gray mud and sand onto each outgoing tide as it attempted to keep the channel open for the trawlers whose access to Wanchese and Manteo is so critical for the state's seafood commerce. I was sport fishing, of course, and my livelihood did not depend on the channel, unlike hundreds of other fishermen and women. My memory bank also contains haunting images of partially sunken trawlers forever trapped in the shifting sands outside the Bonner Bridge, their outriggers and pilot houses barely visible above the crashing waves ... reminders of the inlet's treachery.

Not long after Jerry and I had that unforgettable incident in which we were lucky to find Oregon Inlet with enough gas to get home, I invited Roger Anderson to join us on another offshore fishing trip. All three of us happened to have vacations at the same time, and Roger had taken his boat back to Gloucester, Virginia (Jerry's was in Eleuthera) so the default vessel was my Mako. All three of us also happened to be qualified flight navigators as well as Pan Am pilots based at JFK and we loved to catch tuna and dolphin. To improve my navigation capabilities, I had recently purchased a portable AM/FM radio with RDF (radio direction finding) capabilities. I also had a marine communications radio and I still had my CB.

As often happens during the summer months, a storm had passed several hundred miles east of the Outer Banks a couple of days before we arrived, keeping us in port the first half of the week. As soon as we thought it safe enough, we ventured forth, passing under the Bonner Bridge at sunrise and heading east through a moderately rough inlet. The water was rough enough that I had to go slower than I liked to go, unable to remain comfortably on plane.

Several times during our first hour I heard Roger make the statement, "The seas are confused." Roger had been a Navy pilot and had spent a couple of tours at sea aboard aircraft carriers, so I acknowledged that he was the more experienced sailor of the three of us. After hearing that statement two or three times I asked him exactly what he meant by "confused seas."

His reply was, "Well, see for yourself. Look. The major swells are from the east, coming from that big storm out by Bermuda, but there are also smaller waves from the southwest, caused by the local wind conditions, and they are meeting the larger swells at an angle. See how chaotic and choppy the surface is, with no symmetry or consistency? Things should improve as we get into deeper water."

He was right. Although the conditions never did get calm, as we got closer to the Gulf Stream it was tolerable, and we decided to put our fishing lines overboard. We had seen a few charter boats depart the marina ahead of us, but once they cleared the inlet they headed southeast, toward "the point" outside Diamond Shoals, beyond my safe fuel range unless I simply went there and immediately turned around and came home. Nobody does that.

I had mounted a rod holder on the aft wall of the built-in fish box so we could troll five lines, which we did, using bally-hoo baits rigged with single hooks and dressed with plastic skirts. I steered toward a flock of birds four or five hundred yards east of us, thinking they might be over a school of tuna. Before I reached the birds, both outrigger clips released with a loud pop and two of the three flat lines began to scream zzzzzz!

"Lines down!" Jerry and Roger both shouted at the same time. "We've got four hookups, guys!" Chaos! Action-packed, confusing, exciting, fun-filled chaos! I grabbed the center flat line rod, which had no strike, and began cranking as fast as I could to get it out of the way. Once I stowed it, I grabbed one of the other rods and began to crank. I noticed Jerry and Roger switching positions to keep from tangling their lines. The fourth line went unattended and soon went slack, indicating that fish was gone. Roger began to crank that reel and bring that line aboard while at the same time keeping tension on his fish. Miraculously he accomplished that task, stowing the rod safely out of our way. Now we had three fish on, one for each of us, and I had my hands full trying to steer the boat and reel my line in while my two companions managed to keep our lines from tangling. We swapped rods more than once as those three fish crisscrossed behind the boat. Within twenty or thirty minutes we successfully boarded three nice yellowfin tuna about forty pounds each.

"Boy! That was fun!" I think we said simultaneously.

"Where'd those birds go?" I asked.

We scanned the horizon in all directions, but the birds had vanished—gone missing, to use the currently accepted, official term.

Also gone missing was the Navy tower which we had passed shortly before those fish crashed our baits. *Not to worry*, I thought, *I have my RDF.*

So we put five baited lines back in the water and continued to fish...for several hours. We ate our lunch. We changed baits. We tried artificial lures. We swapped turns at the helm, all the while searching for our lost tower.

As time went by, we caught three or four dolphin near a barnacle-encrusted wooden pallet which was drifting along in the Gulf Stream, but no more tuna. I tried to troll in a large, long oval pattern, oriented on a north/south axis, knowing that before long we would surely see our tower, our safe visual reference point. If I remember correctly there are four towers located some twenty or twenty-five miles east of Oregon Inlet, labeled A, B, C, and D, which the U.S. Navy uses for pilot navigation aids during aerial combat training and simulated air-to-sea bombing practice (and possible contact with outer space for all I know.) I have also often used them to identify my location, especially important as a known starting point before heading back to the inlet. Knowing that departure time was getting close and my fuel quantity was getting low, I shifted my trolling pattern closer to shore, still scanning the horizon in all directions searching for a tower. We paused at idle engine speed for a few minutes and emptied my two six-gallon portable gas tanks into the main fuel tank.

Finally we saw, south of us, what appeared to us to be a tower, barely visible on the horizon. Referring to our paper chart, we estimated that it was either the most southern of the Navy towers, or else Diamond Shoals lighthouse, and in either case I decided our remaining fuel would not allow us to get close enough to it for a positive identification; it was not in the direction of the inlet. If it were indeed Diamond Shoals, we did not have enough fuel to make it there and then back to Oregon Inlet. So the three hardy fishermen and federally licensed navigators, each of whom had successfully navigated vast stretches of both the Atlantic Ocean and the

Pacific Ocean many times aboard 707s and military planes, made what we always called a "WAG" (also known as a *wild ass guess*) pointing to a spot on the chart and agreeing that we are *probably here* and home is *thataway,* pointing to the western horizon.

I turned to a compass heading which I estimated would take us to the inlet while Jerry stowed our fishing tackle and Roger began using the RDF. I should point out that the area we were fishing has known and verified erratic magnetic variation up to 12 degrees, anomalies which can affect a compass. Those facts are plainly stated on the charts. If we were thirty miles offshore we could be as many as six miles from our assumed position, and the compass accuracy was not guaranteed. We knew these things, but we trusted our RDF. At this point, our exciting day of fishing became another one of those misadventures.

I maintained the heading we had agreed upon, nervously watching the fuel gauge. "Come on, Roger, what do you say? Are we headed to the inlet or should I change course slightly?"

"I can't get a positive ID on a radio station. I don't think we're close enough to shore yet. Are you sure about that tower we saw?"

"Hell no, I'm not sure. All I'm sure of is that if we don't see land soon, this old Evinrude is gonna get awful quiet. Jerry, do you see anything on shore yet? Any towers?" I asked him, as he searched the western horizon with the binoculars.

"Not yet, but I'm sure we'll see something soon." He was right, because within another twenty minutes we could make out a very faint radio tower looming dead ahead. We still could see no identifiable land marks and somehow I thought that radio tower should be farther north of us.

"What about the lighthouse? Do you see the Bodie Island lighthouse? It should be close to twelve o'clock, in front of us. Do you see it?" I asked as I tried to swallow the lump in my throat.

"Nope, just that radio tower."

Then I asked, "What about the RDF, Roger? Try WOBR—I think it's 1530 AM—Can you get anything?"

"Yes, I have a station coming in, but the pointer doesn't agree. It's pointing way too far southwest. Let me check again." Roger continued manipulating the RDF radio tuner and rotating its heading indicator, desperately trying to establish a reliable course line for us to follow.

Then the engine coughed. *Sput, sputter, sputter, sput.*

I could tell we were nearly running on fumes but before I could say anything to my crew, it quit completely. You could have cut the silence with a knife. We stared at each other in disbelief: no land in sight, daylight about to disappear, no radio contact, and out of fuel. I turned the ignition switch two or three times; the engine cranked, but would not start. I decided I would not waste any more battery power.

"Okay, guys, the depth finder shows 240 feet, so we can't be too far from shore. Let's put the anchor over and see what happens." My anchor line was only 150 feet long, but we tied all the mooring lines together which added another 100 feet, and we let the anchor slip over the side. It went straight down, running out of line but not hitting bottom.

Roger spoke up, "We might as well get ready to spend the night out here. We have food and water and raincoats, and the fish are well iced. As soon as the boat drifts closer to shore, the anchor will hit bottom and we'll be fine until morning." He attached some parachute cord to a five-gallon bucket and tossed it overboard as a sea anchor. His demeanor did not seem to address the knot in my stomach or my blood pressure.

"Yeah, but what about the girls? It'll be dark soon. They'll be nervous wrecks when we don't arrive by dark." I tried to sound calm as I grabbed the binoculars and searched the western horizon. I could see that radio tower, but it was not where it should have been. I called the Coast Guard. No reply. I was beyond radio range.

We did a little more housekeeping, stowing rods and coolers, and such and prepared to take turns on watch; two resting while one stayed alert, me first, since I was the captain of the vessel. Just before daylight completely faded, while I ate my last peanut butter and jelly sandwich, I saw something on the northwest horizon. It looked like a boat. Grabbing the binoculars once again, I searched in that direction, and sure enough I could see a boat. It was heading south, and would pass between us and the shore.

"Hey guys, look alive; a boat at eleven o'clock, just off the port bow."

Handing the binoculars to Jerry, I retrieved my searchlight from the storage compartment beneath the center console and plugged it into the cigarette lighter receptacle. "Here goes guys," I said. "I'll signal him an SOS."

I aimed the light directly at the boat, which was just barely visible, maybe five or six miles away, and clicked the light switch on and off—three short flashes, three long flashes, three shorts: S-O-S. We waited. I repeated my signal about a minute later, hoping that someone aboard that vessel was looking. Jerry was staring at it through the binoculars.

"She's turning! She's turning toward us! Here, you look, Roger. She's changing course isn't she?" Jerry exclaimed as he gave the binoculars to Roger.

Then we heard, "Vessel off Kitty Hawk, this is vessel ——. We see you. Are you in distress?" As I write this story thirty years later, I am embarrassed to admit that I have forgotten the name of our rescuer. Shame on me.

"This is *Flying Fish*. We're dead in the water, engine quit, and we're adrift. Our anchor won't hold," I replied. "Can you call the Coast Guard for us; they haven't answered me."

"Hold tight, we'll be right there," was his reply as the boat began to come closer.

"We're gonna be okay, guys," said Roger with a sigh of relief. "We'll be home soon."

It took about forty-five minutes for that boat to reach us, and the sun had set, but it finally came alongside, downwind of us. We hastily hauled our anchor aboard, and drifted quickly against the larger boat, slamming harder than I would have liked. "Hold that bumper steady, Roger."

"I'm doing the best I can." We bounced up and down, scraping against its side, as one of the crew tossed us a line which Jerry attached to our bow cleat. Then we hastily climbed aboard with help from two crewmembers, as my boat drifted along his side toward his stern. Soon it was directly behind his boat, under tow. It looked so helpless, my little Mako, rolling and swaying and tossing in the swells, but it was secure, and we were headed home.

His Loran showed that we were nearly seventeen miles north of Oregon Inlet. "I can't take you to the inlet," the captain said, but I can tow you abeam and give you some gas; you'll have to get home on your own."

"May I use your radio to call the Coast Guard?" I asked. "We need to let them know we're okay. My wife has probably already contacted them." I did. They answered that three ladies had already been to see them, just after dark, leaving a phone number before returning to the cottage. The Guard promised they'd call and notify them of our safety.

Our rescue vessel was an old WW II wooden-hulled boat, formerly a mine-sweeper. It was based in the Bahamas, under contract with the Navy, one of its main tasks being to help train sonar operators on nuclear submarines. It had departed Norfolk after damaging one of its two prop shafts, and was heading to Jacksonville where a suitable marine railway was available to haul it out for repairs. The captain was staying close to shore, avoiding the north current of the Gulf Stream, and making only about eight knots on one engine.

Because his boat, *Unicorn*, was often in the Bahamas, at Eleuthera, Jerry and the captain occupied themselves with conversation during the nearly two hours it took for us to arrive outside Oregon Inlet. As we came within a mile of the sea buoy (visible on his radar) we hauled my little boat up to the larger vessel and retrieved our two gas cans. The wind had subsided, making it easier to transfer my crew. The captain gave us ten gallons from his generator supply tank in return for ten dollars and a fifteen-pound dolphin. As soon as I indicated that my engine was running normally, we released the tow line and with a hearty thanks, bid them farewell. By now the sea was nearly calm, and Bonner Bridge loomed ahead in the moonlight shimmering on the waters outside the inlet.

"Coast Guard Station Oregon Inlet, this is vessel *Flying Fish*. We have the bridge in sight, and we should be there within the hour. Thanks for your help," I reported.

"Roger, *Flying Fish*. Welcome home. Be advised another vessel with the same name is also in the area. We spoke with her earlier today."

That is the moment when I decided once and for all to change my boat's name to *Jetstream*, and to buy that Loran C I'd been talking about. Of course, our ladies, in fact our entire three families, have never let us forget that day when three navigators couldn't find our way home.

The next time he was in Eleuthera, Bahamas, many of his friends informed Jerry that they had already heard about our misadventure from the crew of the boat that rescued us, proving without a doubt that it really is a small world.

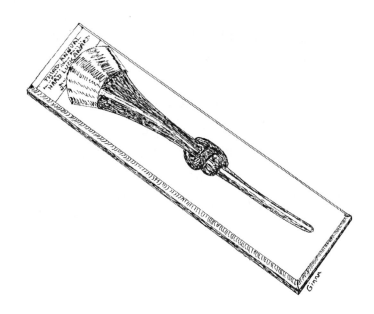

HARD LUCK

Phil McCaleb, the agent who handled our homeowners' insurance, and I became casual social friends shortly after we moved to Virginia's Eastern Shore. We dined at each other's homes occasionally, and attended functions at Broadwater Academy where our daughters went to school. One time he invited me to hunt Canada geese in a big field behind his house. I had recently lost my warm gloves, so the night before our hunt I drove out to the nearest mall, in Onley, VA and bought a nice pair of ski gloves, which I still have. My grandchildren are amazed that I'm still wearing them after 40 years, and believe it or not, every time I wear those gloves I am reminded of that goose hunt with Phil. It was cold and dark and windy as the sun rose, and the ground was frozen, so Phil walked back to his barn and got a maul and an iron spike so we could punch holes in the ground and set up my shell decoys. We shot a few geese, and I remember leaving my decoys stored in his barn, in hopes that he would invite me again.

Sometime later, perhaps a year after I put a new engine on my Mako boat, I invited him to go to Cedar Island with me and do some surf casting. He brought along a gill net which he set in the creek side of the inlet while we fished in the surf. We didn't catch a single fish, either casting or in his net, which he bundled up and returned to the cardboard box he placed on the raised fish box seat just ahead of my almost-new 200 HP Evinrude outboard. On the trip back to the boat ramp, I was going way too fast up Folly Creek, and during a tight turn I hit another boat's wake and that box full of net flew off the stern, taking with it a couple of cast iron window sash weights which Phil used to weight the net down to the creek bottom. Unfortunately, one of those weights smashed against my prop with an awful sounding *thunk* and a piece of cast iron shrapnel flew up and struck the transom, cracking the gel coat. Well, as you might know, those propellers have a big rubber bushing which is designed to slip when the prop strikes a hard object so as to prevent damage to the gears and drive shaft. It didn't slip enough and after inspecting the bent prop, I checked the lower unit and discovered that the magnetic plug was covered with metal shavings and chips from a broken gear tooth. Even though the warranty had expired a few weeks earlier, Phil suggested I send the damaged parts to Evinrude with a complaint about their poor quality gears. Their response was that even though my engine was no longer under warranty, in the interest of customer good will, Evinrude would supply replacement parts if I paid for the labor. So even though I was mad at Phil for bringing those hunks of iron aboard my boat, my anger soon went away, and we remained good friends.

Later that summer I entered our local Marlin Club's tournament, which I did each July. One of my crew was Deacon Saunders, son of my fishing buddy and fellow pilot, Jerry. Deacon lived in California, but he was spending the summer in Virginia with his grandparents while trying to decide where to go to college in another year. He seemed excited about the fishing trip.

After consulting with the president of Mako Marine, I had already installed two twenty-five gallon stainless steel fuel tanks in the bilge, below deck, increasing my fuel capacity to 100 gallons.

Because I had experienced difficulty on more than one occasion finding my way back home from thirty or forty miles offshore, my wife urged me to buy a Loran C navigation radio which I did. We had taken it offshore a few times and inserted waypoints to which it navigated perfectly. It even had ground speed readout, a feature which I found very impressive.

As usual my crew and I eased out of the marina at Wachapreague at 5:30 in the morning in order to be in a good fishing spot by 8:30, the tournament's official "lines in the water" time. On a calm day, those three hours allowed me to be over productive areas for yellowfin tuna and hopefully a billfish. I guess there were thirty boats in the tournament that year and we fanned out over a large area as we departed the inlet. I headed in the general direction of Washington Canyon, passing a couple of intermediate waypoints I had stored in the Loran C. I was proud of that gadget, and my wife has said many times that it was one of the wisest investments I ever made. She was confident that I could find my way home.

In fact, earlier, before I bought the Loran, I took her offshore one clear, calm morning in pursuit of whatever might be biting at a place we called Twenty-Six Mile Hill. I remembered the incident and explained it to Deacon.

"The water was flat," I told him. "There was no wind, and we looked forward to a wonderful day, just the two of us. My first destination was a buoy ten miles offshore, and that is where I headed, intent on impressing her with my dead reckoning navigational skills. I had made enough test runs at various engine RPMs to ascertain my speed, which I reckoned to be 30 knots that morning. The boat was equipped with a speedometer attached to the transom, but I didn't trust its accuracy. Within three minutes of clearing the inlet sea buoy, which was dead astern and still in sight, we ran smack dab into a fog bank. Visibility dropped to less than a half mile. 'Slow down, we can't see anything,' she uttered. 'You'll run into somebody.'"

"She was right," Deacon said.

"I told her we were OK as I carefully observed the compass heading, the tachometer, and my watch. I had penciled the time when we passed the sea buoy onto the center console. 'We'll be fine. There's nobody between us and the next buoy.' Some might consider that comment stupid, but I felt confident, and anyway, if I slowed down, I wouldn't be able to gauge my ETA at the next buoy, and I certainly did not want to run into it. I had no reliable speed data at slower RPMs. I made a mental note to run some more trials at slower engine speeds.

"I maintained a constant compass heading and engine RPM as we continued in the fog bank. She gave me a couple of those looks she has when she raises one eyebrow and scowls, but she stood silently beside me, peering into the fog. I was doing mental calculations as fast as I could. The wheels and gears in my mind were spinning like crazy; I had to get this right. *Hmmm. Let's see now, sixty knots would be one mile per minute, so thirty knots is equal to a half a mile a minute, right, and the next buoy is ten miles ahead, right?* I glanced at my paper chart. Yep, ten miles. So at that speed I should cover the ten miles in twenty minutes. I kept repeating these figures to myself as I watched closely both the compass and my wristwatch. 'Time's up,' I said as I eased the throttle to idle. 'We should be here.' As the boat fell off plane and the bow settled into the water, I switched off the ignition. Silence. 'Listen,' I whispered, 'do you hear anything?' Silence. Then *ooooommmf.* Off to starboard I heard a sound. 'Listen, did you hear that?'

"'Hear what?' she asked, peering into the fog.

"'That sound, that *ooooommmf.* That's the buoy. Look! There it is. We made it.' Much to my satisfaction (and much to her surprise) about one hundred yards to starboard a faint red buoy appeared. I pointed toward it as the fog slowly began to dissipate in the warm sun. 'That's what we call dead reckoning,' I explained. I used the compass, the tachometer, and my watch to get us here. Aren't you impressed?'

"She replied, 'Well, yes, kind of, I guess. But I still think you should get that Loran C you've been talking about.' She was right. I could dead reckon with ease in calm water and as long as I knew my exact starting point. What created my navigation problems was the fact that after fishing offshore for six or more hours, with no visual references at all, I never knew exactly where I was when it came time to head home. A Loran C would easily solve that dilemma."

I told Deacon that story as we headed out to sea with Washington Canyon as a waypoint in the Loran. "Your dad and I used dead reckoning all the time when we navigated across the Pacific, to back up our Loran fixes. Did he ever tell you the story about those P-38 pilots who DR'd more than 950 miles round trip at wave top height on the mission which killed Japanese Admiral Yamamoto? If not, you should read about it. It's an impressive story."

We fished throughout the hot July day, taking turns at the helm so each of us could get in a cat nap. To be honest with you as I write these words many years later, I don't remember if we caught any fish. Definitely not a billfish or I would surely remember that.

What I remember most was our trip back to port. I had tried throughout the day to get both him and Lee (another crewmember) to include the engine water temperature gauge in their instrument scan, but they did not always check it. While trolling for mahi-mahi, we had run into some scattered weeds before noon, some of which hung tenaciously onto the engine's lower unit, blocking the water intake. I pointed to the water temp gauge, reminding him that he should have noticed that the engine was beginning to run hot. We raised the engine, removed the guilty sargassum weeds, and continued to fish.

As we headed for home, it was once again Deacon's turn at the helm. I dozed off and on, trying to get comfortable stretched out on the fish box-seat on the front of the center console. The bimini top was up, providing some shade, but not much relief from the heat. Fortunately, the water was like a mirror, enabling us to maintain a good forward speed. Half asleep, I said to Deacon, "What's the engine water temperature, Deac?"

Before he could answer, I heard that frightening noise which always happens as the lower unit comes completely out of the water and the engine RPMs race toward the maximum, accompanied by a resounding *whaaaack*!

"Take her out of gear!" I shouted. "Put it in neutral."

He did and the boat rapidly fell off plane, came to rest in the calm sea and the engine returned to idle speed. We scanned the water behind us to see what we had hit. Nothing visible. "What'd we hit?" I asked. "Do you see anything? Did you see anything in front of us before we hit it?"

"Nope, not a thing," he answered, "but I was looking at the water temp gauge, remember?"

"Yeah, but you don't stare at it, you just glance at it."

"I was glancing. I wasn't staring."

Realizing that my tone of voice had probably insulted him, I turned my attention to the boat. Everyone looked down along the sides, I stuck my head into the bilge area, and then I crawled forward to inspect the bow at the waterline. We could see no damage, nor could we see any debris. I figured it was not worth going overboard to check the bottom of the boat, so I eased the combination throttle/gear single control lever forward, intent on continuing to Wachapreague. The engine revved up, but the boat went nowhere. I recycled the power lever and tried again. Nothing. We were dead in the water. I raised the lower unit enough to get a clear view of the prop and tried the power lever once again. Not only did the boat not move but neither did the propeller. "Dammit, looks like a broken shaft, maybe the main drive shaft. We ain't going anywhere," I said.

As I scanned the horizon looking for other tournament boats a knot developed in my stomach. There was not a boat in sight. I grabbed the microphone, "Any boat, any boat, this is *Flying Fish.* Do you read me? Over." Silence. Again, "This is *Flying Fish* out of Wachapreague. Does anybody read me?"

"Is that you, Ash?" someone responded. "We hear you. We're at the sea buoy about to enter the inlet. Where're you at?"

I hastily searched the Loran screen, noted the position and the miles remaining to the sea buoy waypoint and replied, "We're eight miles southeast, on our way back from Washington Canyon, and we hit something, maybe a turtle, and broke a drive shaft. We're dead in the water, and don't see another boat within sight."

"There goes one!" Deacon shouted. "I see one, over there on the horizon." He pointed to a small, faint, gray silhouette of boat about the size of mine, which was hightailing it back toward the west, also heading home. It was barely visible, and it did not respond to repeated radio calls.

"Vessel *Flying Fish*, this is Coast Guard Station Parramore. Say again your location. Do you read me? Over?"

"Stand by, Parramore." I checked and double-checked the Loran, finally able to supply him with our latitude/longitude coordinates. "Stay where you are, we'll send a boat, over. Say souls on board."

"Thanks, Parramore, we're not going anywhere. Four souls on board." But I was wrong, we were drifting with the current. Not much, but enough that by referring to the Loran every few minutes we could see our coordinates change; we were moving. *Thank you, Ginna, thank you. Thanks for insisting that I buy the Loran C*, I mumbled under my breath.

Within an hour, we were safely secured to the Coast Guard boat which came to our rescue. "Glad to do it, glad to be of help, but you guys have to put on your life vests," the operator said as he eased his throttle forward, took up the slack line, and headed home. He towed us to the marina, whereupon two of his crew boarded us and made a safety inspection. We had all the necessary gear aboard and passed with flying colors. A couple of my friends helped me load the boat onto the trailer. Thus ended our second and final day of the two-day tournament.

At the awards banquet the entire crowd of tournament fishermen let out a vigorous laugh as we received the "Hard Luck" award.

It was a plaster marlin bill about 14 inches tall, on a walnut base. The marlin bill is tied in a knot. (I still have it, more than thirty years later.)

A few days later, after my mechanic removed the lower unit, he confirmed that the drive shaft had broken at the design shear point. Fortunately, the engine power head was unharmed. I guess the combined forces from that sash weight and that turtle (if it was a turtle) were more than it could handle. I knew Evinrude would not help me this time.

As it is written: "A boat is a hole in the water into which you pour money."

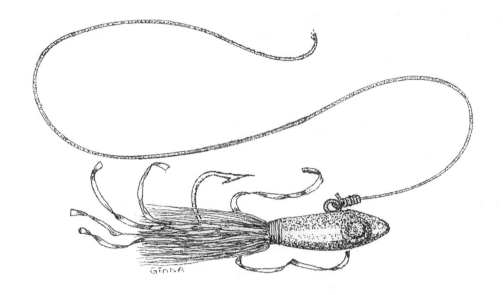

THE GREEN HORNET

"Are you sure we're in the right spot?" I asked my friend and host. "Seems like I've been chunking this red plug for an hour. Why don't we try another place?"

"No! They're here. They're here. They're always here. Every time I've ever wet a line here I've caught fish. We've only been here fifteen minutes and you're acting like a six-year old." He seemed impatient with me, or with the fish, or with both. He was also perplexed as he fussed around with his tackle boxes, obviously searching for something in particular.

"Seems like at least an hour," I said once again. "Did you find that lure yet?" This was my third day in the Bahamas, but our first day of fishing because of the wind. For two days we sat at the dock in Eleuthera listening to the wind whistle and whine through our outrigger lines and through the rigging of the forty-five foot sailboat in the next slip.

"Oh, sure, we could give it a try but it'd be so rough we wouldn't have any fun," he reminded me the first day. "Remember how much you hate it when it's rough. Remember the South China Sea and that typhoon you told me about, don'tcha?"

How could I forget? Two or three days of absolute misery rolling and pitching up and down—two thousand guys puking all over each other—what a mess! Why did the Army have to send an aviation unit to Vietnam on a boat? I promised myself I'd never get on another boat, but promises are made to be broken. Now we each owned a boat.

That's how I happened to be in Eleuthera as a guest aboard my buddy Jerry's boat *Unicorn*, a 41-foot Hatteras, tied up at the dock. He knew I was a fair-weather fisherman; knew I didn't really have sea legs. He knew I had miserable memories of those wretched days in that typhoon, so he wisely chose to remain in port until the weather moderated. It did.

The second day I was able to walk around the cockpit (in the marina) without falling. *Who knows, maybe he'll make a fisherman out of me yet*, I thought. So we spent some time messing about, fixing a few things, changing the engine oil, putting new line on three or four reels, and sharing a beer or two. We told each other a few war stories and a few fish stories—sometimes it's hard to distinguish one from the other. He told me about a nifty lure he bought at a tackle shop in Ft. Lauderdale.

"Wasn't your call sign in 'Nam Hornet?" he asked.

"No, mine was Seahorse 44, but there was a Navy or Air Force unit called Hornet," I replied.

"Well, I found this lure called a Green Hornet and I thought of you. I've been saving it for you because I thought you were a Hornet and I was hoping you'd come down here so I could give it to you as a gift. It's been in one of my tackle boxes for two or three years; I've never used it. I've been looking for it today with no luck, but I'm sure it'll turn up." We continued to relax, quit worrying about the weather and sure enough, as the sun set on the second day his prediction came true—the wind stopped blowing, and I slept like a baby, dreaming of sailfish.

Earlier in the morning we trolled the deep water of Exuma

Sound for four hours without a strike. "Unusual," he said. "Most of the time they bite following a blow like we had. But cheer up, I know a spot on the way home along a drop-off where we can get some action. Reel 'em in."

I cranked in the trolling tackle, secured the loose items, and off we went, headed back toward the reef to his favorite "sure thing" hot spot, the place where he'd often been able to catch a fish or two for the dinner table. It is right at the edge of a vertical drop-off, where the water is only about twelve feet deep on one side of the boat, but drops off to six thousand feet on the other side. "Last year we caught grouper, dolphin, and jacks right here," he said while jockeying the throttles with one hand, skillfully keeping us right on the edge all the while fumbling through a tackle box. "Here it is! I found it! I knew the damned thing was here somewhere. Put this on your line. It's that Green Hornet I told you about."

He tossed me the lure, still in its package, flashed me a familiar grin, and turned his attention back to his controls. He looked happy and content on his flying bridge, my nomad friend, but I suspect he was placing an awful lot of confidence in 1¾ ounces of green lead decorated with white deer hair and a few strands of silver Mylar. I tied the lure directly to the thirty-pound, golden yellow monofilament using a clinch knot, thereby eliminating any possible interference from a steel leader—*better swimming action that way*, I thought to myself, *no bluefish around here anyway*.

The cast was true. From fifty feet away, I plopped that Green Hornet exactly at the edge of the reef, right at the color change. Turning the handle once, I set the bail and - *smack*! - something hit the lure immediately. Hard.

"Striiike!" I shouted, as Jerry slipped the engines out of gear. I felt sure they could hear me back at the marina, about five miles away. The small rod bent nearly double and golden yellow line came screaming off the spinning reel. I knew I was in for a fight.

"Barracuda," said Jerry. "You're on your own, ol' buddy, I've gotta stay up here and handle the boat to keep us off the reef. He's your baby...looks at least twenty-five pounds."

"Don't worry. I've got him. I came here to fish, remember. Say, do you eat these things?"

"Nah. I give 'em away. Some of the locals eat 'em, but I don't. I can't stand the smell of 'em. Robert back at the gas dock eats 'em. Hey! Watch it, he's heading for his hidey hole."

As soon as he said that the line went slack. Gone! The whole thing, from the time I made the first (and only) cast with my new lure until I stood there reeling in the slack line lasted only a half-minute. *Three whole days and now this*, I thought, *thirty seconds of excitement and a lost lure.*

"Sorry, sport. Goes with the territory. Here, try this yellow feather and this steel leader. I forgot to tell you about the barracuda we have around here."

He tossed me another lure and a separate coil of rigged leader wire about four feet long. I was all thumbs. But I managed to rig up again and cast. We had drifted a few yards downwind, but Jerry slipped the engines into reverse, and even as I made my second cast he positioned us right over the same spot. *Plop*! The yellow jig hit the surface and I began cranking. Three turns. Four turns. I jigged the rod up and down a couple of times to impart some action to the lure. Five turns of the handle.

Whack! Splash!

Another strike! I had already set the drag a little bit tighter than before and as I began to reel, Jerry eased the boat forward and seaward a bit to give us a coral-free arena at least a few yards farther from the reef. It wasn't much of a fight. This fish seemed smaller than the first one and once away from the reef I had some maneuvering room. No jumps. No more splashes. No aerobatics. *Definitely not a dolphin*, I thought, *probably a small amberjack.*

"Barracuda," Jerry shouted from the bridge. "I see him. Hang on another minute and I'll come down there and give you a hand. We're far enough from the reef now." I continued to play the nearly spent fish, disappointed that it was only another barracuda, but satisfied that at least I had caught a fish. I lifted the fish box lid just as my friend heaved the 'cuda aboard with his gaff. "Twenty pounds, I bet," he remarked.

Both of us looked down at my catch, lying there on the bottom of the box. At the same time, right on cue as if we had both memorized the same script ... "What the hell?" we both exclaimed, looking first at each other then back at the fish. A twenty-inch strand of golden yellow mono streamed from the fish's mouth, lying right alongside the steel leader wire.

"Are you thinking what I'm thinking?" I asked him.

"Let me get my knife," was his reply as he turned toward his rigging station, three steps away. He returned to the fish box without another word and with the precision of a surgeon he sliced that barracuda's belly open in one smooth stroke. Quickly laying the knife aside, he reached into the opening and gave me another one of those sly grins. "Here's your Green Hornet, ol' buddy. Let's catch another fish."

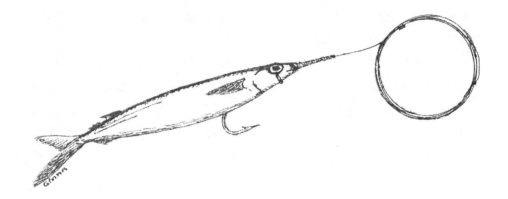

THE IMPERFECT MATE

Many words in our complex and confusing language have several meanings and the term "mate" is one that comes to mind. I'm certain I married one about as perfect as they come. I'd like to think that she did, too, but I know better. At any one time a person can be more than one type of mate, too, I guess. I was in Sydney and Darwin quite a few times and I don't remember anyone ever greeting me with "G'day, Mate," which was made popular the world over by *Crocodile Dundee* a few years ago. I imagine the pairs of critters Noah took with him on the ark became mates sooner or later, and I suppose that if Noah was the captain, then one of his sons (or perhaps his wife) was the First Mate. Every vessel worthy of a captain is surely entitled to have a mate, too.

I have met many mates in my life, on several different kinds of vessels, from the one on the ship which carried me off to a faraway place called Vietnam, to a delightful English-speaking First Mate aboard a German vessel on a cruise down the Rhine, to a pleasant hippie on a salmon boat out of Fisherman's Wharf below the Golden Gate bridge. I don't remember most of their names and they probably don't remember mine, which is all right. Hank Beasley, when he was captain of Lee Tugwell's boat *Top Billin'* out of Pirate's Cove, North Carolina, had a wonderful mate, a college kid from Raleigh, named Finn Gaddy. "Just think of Huckleberry Finn," he would say with a big grin, "And you'll remember my name." Finn always seemed to have a big white blob of sunscreen on the bridge of his nose. What a charming and competent mate he was, and he and Hank could make a day spent fishing with them in the Gulf Stream a real treat, even if you never saw a fish, although I don't remember ever being skunked when they were in charge of the fishing. Finn has become a captain, himself, aboard his boat *Qualifier*, out of Oregon Inlet.

A mate's life can be hard because the hours are long, the work can be difficult, the captain can be very demanding, and sometimes the clients can be impossible to please. My friends and I have been fishing the Gulf Stream waters out of Oregon Inlet and Hatteras and the canyons out of Wachapreague for more than thirty years, some of those trips on our own boats, and we know more than just a little about fishing. We've also done a fair amount of "mating" ourselves, not for pay mind you, but serving in that capacity aboard each other's boats, rigging bally-hoo, scrubbing the deck, gaffing tuna and wahoo, untangling lines, and helping the others aboard have an enjoyable trip. A good mate needs to be a bit of a diplomat much of the time. Some excel at it and some haven't a clue. I think we recently met "Clueless."

Not long ago, as is typical for us, we were at the marina well ahead of departure time because we never seem to be able to sleep very well the night before, and because we were early we got a good parking spot alongside the dock a few short steps from our charter boat. We set our coolers on the tailgate awaiting permission to board and looking forward to a greeting from either the captain or the mate, who were nowhere in sight. Finally, a young man appeared with two bags of ice, climbed down onto the deck, and commenced to put the ice into the fish box. He said not a word even though the six of us were only about ten feet away and watching, with great anticipation, his every move. I've seen such situations before so it did not surprise me. Some mates are shy around strangers. Some don't get a good night's sleep either, for whatever reason. And a few (mercifully only a few) are just plain arrogant and unfriendly.

Finally, my friend, Jerry, introduced himself and each of us as their charter for the day. Jerry tried to make small talk with the man who would spend the next ten hours with us and he asked this mate what kind of success they'd been having the past few days. "Man!" he said, "The last three days we've had our limit of tuna and been back at the dock before noon. Yesterday we were back by 10:30."

Now that kind of response to six fisher people such as our group is a mixed blessing, but he had no way of knowing that. We love tuna. We love to catch them, we love to eat them, and we love to share some with our friends, even with a mate now and then. But we also love a full day on the water, and we have a special fondness for fresh dolphin or mahi-mahi, beer-battered and fried or marinated and hot off the grill.

So in an effort to let the mate know right from the get-go that even though we were excited about the possibility of several nice tuna, we were not particularly interested in being back at the dock by noon. Jerry hinted, therefore, that if we were lucky enough to limit out on tuna (which we have done several times in the past) we'd like to catch a few dolphin also or maybe get lucky and catch a wahoo or a marlin.

"Man, what a greedy bunch of folks you people are. No way! Besides, if we fill the fish box with tuna, we ain't got no place to put any dolphin." I guess I spoke out of turn, but I suggested that we had a little room in our beverage cooler and, if necessary, we could take our lunch out of the lunch cooler. That statement obviously went over like a lead balloon. Maybe he had never seen six clients bring three separate coolers, one for lunch, one for water and soft drinks, and one for beer. Maybe he thought they were empty, waiting to be stuffed with fish, but he never asked. He didn't even offer to help us bring them aboard.

Within minutes, the captain showed up and started to climb up to the flying bridge without so much as a "G'morning, folks. I'm Captain So-and-So. Welcome aboard." Not a word.

As he stood on the gunwale and placed one foot on the first little foot pad step to the bridge, his mate stopped him dead in his tracks. "Hey Harry, these folks want to load the boat with tuna and then fill their coolers with dolphin. Have you ever heard of anything so greedy?" He obviously had a bad hair day or a bad night or he had heard only what he wanted to hear without waiting for a more complete explanation of our desire for a mixed bag. We would have gladly settled for less than a limit of tuna, just for the opportunity to troll alongside a weed line and watch some dolphin light up, or catch and release a marlin or a sailfish. Neither of them ever asked if that is what we wanted.

"Well, folks, which do you want, tuna or dolphin?" asked the captain. An ultimatum—simple as that—one or the other, no mixed bag.

Not wanting to get the day started off any worse than it already was (in less than five minutes) Jerry replied, "Tuna," knowing they were our preference. The rest of us remained quiet, intimidated to be sure, but not wanting to aggravate the situation. Was simply off-loading our gear and demanding a refund an option? We didn't know and we didn't ask. We have enough experience in these waters to know that sometimes the tuna and dolphin can be miles apart and sometimes within sight of each other, and we also know that fuel is expensive. A brief explanation from either of these two men about distance or fuel cost or unfavorable weather or anything reasonable would have satisfied us, but no such explanation was forthcoming.

"Then tuna it is," said the captain, as he disappeared topside.

After we cleared the inlet we settled in, knowing we had an opportunity to get a brief nap, perhaps as much as an hour or more, during the ride to the fishing grounds. The mate joined the captain on the bridge, probably also catching a nap, since he must have been certain he was in for a hard day trying to please this greedy bunch of folks, if pleasing us was his intent. You'd think that someone who chooses a job where a big part of his income is dependent on tips from satisfied clients would try extra hard to get each day off to a perfect start, and try to maintain that momentum all day long. Where was our friend Finn? Why had we not chartered this trip out of Pirate's Cove? Such questions popped into my mind as I dozed on again and off again for the next hour. Off the port beam, I noted one of the Navy towers in the distance as we continued toward the fishing area, and I suspected we were heading about 110 or 115 degrees slightly south of east. I knew where we were because in the past I had caught a few amberjack at the tower and a wahoo very close by.

It was not long before the mate came down and started to rig the cockpit for fishing. We tried to stay out of his way, but at the same time observe his preparations because we're always eager to learn a new trick or two. I politely asked him what our compass heading was and he replied that he didn't know. I thought that was a bit odd, since he'd just spent an hour on the bridge, but I made no further comment. Finally, he broke the ice and asked if we'd ever been deep sea fishing before, a question we were surprised he had not asked earlier, back at the dock. Not wanting to appear both greedy *and* know-it-alls, we replied that yes we had, a few times. As the day progressed we ultimately learned that he was twenty-six and he also had his captain's license but not a boat. Between the six of us clients that day we probably had a cumulative seventy-five years of deep sea fishing, in at least two oceans, and out of more than a dozen ports, much of it before he was born, but we didn't mention that.

Soon we had several strikes, boated a few small yellowfin tuna and lost a couple, a typical morning for us. "Don't pump your rod," the captain shouted down from the bridge, "you give 'em too much slack."

Okey-dokey, I thought, but I also silently wished that he would slow down just a bit so a twenty-five-pound tuna didn't feel like a two-hundred-pounder. *He's the pro here,* I remembered and I let someone else catch the next fish.

One time we had a triple strike and the mate had his hands full, so he condescended to ask a couple of us to bring in the slack lines. I watched him watch us and I guess he realized that we were not a bunch of greenhorns after all. I hoped his assessment of our performance thus far would help break the ice some more. But I was wrong. He maintained a belligerent attitude most of the day, and quite simply, I think he's chosen the wrong profession. I don't think he has a snowball's chance in hell of ever being a good captain, one who has the clients' interest at heart. He may know how to rig baits and gaff a fish (which he did quite well, I must say) and he must do a reasonably good job of keeping his captain satisfied, but he's a long, long way from being the perfect mate.

Out of his earshot we discussed the possibility of a tip. We usually tipped a good mate a hundred bucks or more, and we seriously considered giving this guy nothing, but we got soft-hearted at the last minute and decided on eighty dollars. When we gave it to him back at the dock he said, "I thought y'all wouldn't give me a tip."

We replied, in unison, "We almost didn't."

I hope I never see him again.

MUCHO VIENTO, MUCHO PERDICES

Author's Note: This story first appeared in the March/April, 1992 issue of Shooting Sportsman *magazine. They added a subtitle: 'Three Gringos Go Hunting in Argentina'. Note that it was written twenty-four years ago and many things, such as prices, are probably not applicable in 2016.*

"Mucho viento, senor. Mucho viento." If I am learning any Spanish at all during my visit to Argentina, it is these words that will be forever etched in memory. 'Mucho viento'...much wind.

For three days now it had been blowing hard and cold from the southwest—twenty-five knots or so, with the temperature hovering just above freezing. It is May here, and since the seasonal weather conditions are reversed from what we are accustomed to in the USA it is similar to November. To be more specific, we are here in the last week of May, so in order to get a feel for what it's like, try to think in terms of Thanksgiving weather. In fact, we are right now in the midst of what might be called a Thanksgiving feast. We are the guests of Señor Francisco Castaneiro, landowner, and his foreman Dario Echeverry, at their Saturday noon *assado*, a grilled meat lunch, and it is quite a feast compared to the snacks we've been eating the past few middays.

"Ain't this fun ol' buddy. Lucky our van broke down where it did," says my friend Jim. "And weren't we smart to dump that worthless guide we had a few days ago? Pig hunter, that's all he was. And a thief. He wouldn't believe the fun we're having since we got rid of him." Fun, yes. Good companionship, yes. And fantastic food, yes. But the hunting has been temporarily interrupted this day due to *mucho viento*.

It is now about our sixth day in Argentina. The scene is a small kitchen set apart from the main ranch house. It is a neat, white stucco building, looking on the outside like something you'd find in Arizona or West Texas, or perhaps Mexico, but on the inside reminding me more of colonial kitchens in Virginia. One entire end wall is a huge fireplace, about twelve feet wide and tall enough for me to stand up inside. With the right spit it could easily accommodate a whole steer, but for now there is a small fire roasting an assortment of meats; various cuts of beef and lamb, and *chorizos*, tasty little sausages. Occasionally the tantalizing aroma of succulent roasting meat rises from the fire and wafts across the room, but it is soon dispersed by the drafts coming in through every nook and cranny, courtesy of the wind which refuses to remain outside. Fresh, home-baked bread, a big bowl of boiled potatoes, and your choice of local wine or ice-cold beer round out the feast. What an honor to be an invited guest at these people's humble meal.

They have spent all morning, since sunrise, inoculating cattle, and now it is break time, time for the noonday meal. No siestas, though. These are a proud, hard-working people, descendants of Basque shepherds whose parents and grandparents emigrated from Spain two and three generations ago. They have a love for the land and for their crops and their livestock. And, fortunately for us, they also relish the opportunity to host three Gringo hunters. They are as anxious to learn about us and our ideas as we are to learn about them and their birds.

During lunch the small talk drifts back and forth from politics and economics to cattle prices and dogs and bird hunting; from the value of the dollar to the future of Argentina. It is stimulating with each of us wandering back and forth from Spanish to English to Spanish. None of the dozen or so people in the room is truly bi-lin-gual, but we struggle through with the aid of my little phrase book. As we talk and eat we have a constant companion, that disgusting wind.

"Mucho viento. But it will stop soon, señor, and then you can shoot the perdices aqui." Lots of quail here. Hot dog! That's what I've been waiting to hear. Perdices (per-DEE-ces) or perdiz, those little quail-like birds more properly called *tinamou*, are the reason we have traveled here nearly to the bottom of the earth. We have seen a few so far and shot even fewer. It has taken us a few days to get the lay of the land, convince people that we are not interested in shooting hundreds or thousands of doves and pigeons, and find some suitable places to hunt the perdices. Few locals hunt them. Those who do often revert to road hunting at dusk, pot-shotting a few for dinner now and then.

The hunting guidebook says there are sixteen species of *inam-bues*, or partridges. We are especially trying to locate the perdiz, smallest of the sixteen, but we are also pleased when an occa-sional grouse-sized bird flies up, thus offering a bonus shot and the chance for a real mixed bag. None of these partridges seems to offer the classic bobwhite quail-type shooting I grew up with, or the pheasant hunting to which my companions are accustomed. Each day, even each bird is a surprise. First one will hold so tight that you practically have to kick it out like a rabbit; then the few will flush wildly ahead of you and the dog, sometimes a hundred yards or so away, but most often right at that ragged-edge distance of thirty to forty yards or so. Should I shoot or shouldn't I? Quick shooting with fast, light guns is the name of the game. The three of us are using 20-gauges, which add considerably to the sport. Fortunately the perdices are not found in very heavy cover, but it did take us a day or two of experimenting with different types of cover to zero in on the most likely-looking habitat.

Perdices are edge birds. They avoid the vast grain fields so prevalent in most of Buenos Aires Province, preferring instead a mixture of pasture, some fallow spots, and an occasional small grain field. It is not unusual to find then grazing right along with a few cattle or sheep, never very far from suitable weedy cover, but they seem to avoid the little woodsy areas or montes, small forests, except as escape cover of last resort. They do not necessarily seem to need much water, either, for we often find them far from it. And they are solitary birds, We had expected to find them in large flocks or coveys, but that is not the case. Mostly they are found as singles or in pairs. And unfortunately for my dog, most of their cover is also full of sand burrs.

Francisco has given us free run of his *campos* or *estancias*, cattle ranches, the one here of 10,000 acres and a smaller one a few miles away of only 4,500 acres. We merely have to close the gates behind us and not frighten the cattle, the source of his livelihood. In addition, Dario, the foreman, has provided us with two young guides. Martin and Dorrego. They are excellent retrievers but they can't seem to understand that fetching downed birds is one of the dog's chores. Their presence also causes us to pass up practically every opportunity for a double, for as soon as a bird is hit, they race for it, unaware that we might be considering a shot at a second bird. Running after a cripple is what they have been taught to do. Why waste another shell on a bird that can be run down? Their father has taught them well to be conservative.

Sure enough, after lunch and socializing, and thanks all around for their gracious hospitality, the wind does seem to be a little less menacing. Off we go to a different area of the ranch. The boys instruct us to stop the car here, on top of a low, flat ridge, a three-quarter-mile-long eroded area between a 247-acre pasture and a similar-sized field of newly sprouted wheat planted in last year's wheat stubble. Waving his arm the oldest boy indicates the direction we should hunt. "Perdices aqui." Unfortunately he is pointing downwind. We should be starting at the other end of the field, but we don't know how to say it in Spanish. By now the wind is blowing less than ten knots, calmer than what we've endured for two and a half days, but nonetheless, a force we must reckon with if we try to use the dog.

People who don't hunt with dogs seem to have a problem understanding the necessity for dogs to use the wind. That understanding was one of the reasons we had earlier fired our farmer-guide and left his area. He wanted us to road hunt, or else walk across the fields, beginning wherever he decided to drop us off and ending wherever he decided to park and wait for us. Often this was downwind or crosswind. He was also lazy and wasteful. He did not want to help us clean our birds—women's work! And worst of all he wanted us to shoot all the doves on his ranch. We shot a few dozen along with some pigeons. After the hunt, as I was feeding and watering my dog, Christie, the 'guide' chose ten or twelve big fat pigeons for his grandmother and then began throwing the doves into a hole in the ground. "Nobody keep these leetle theengs, senor. They no good for notheeng."

I guess the problem is as old as modern man; too many doves in a area and eventually they reach the status of pest. At times it looks like the sky is full of doves. I am reminded of the occasional, endless flights of blackbirds I have seen stretching from horizon to horizon. I have read that once the famed passenger pigeon blackened our skies like that, as did the canvasback. And yet, as soon as we start to take a sustainable resource like these birds for granted, look at what happens. Sadly, for all of us, they disappear. The passenger pigeon is history and I haven't seen a canvasback in at least five years. And this particular guide in La Pampa Province, a day's drive from Buenos Aires, has been hosting dozens of well-heeled hunters from France and other places, who spend lots of money to come here and shoot whatever they want, as many as they want, and throw them away if they choose.

From what we could understand from the guide, he normally hosts them in groups of six. They shoot all the doves they like during the day, a few pigs at night, drink lots of wine and beer, eat lots of steak, and go home a week later satisfied that they have had a fantastic time. They probably have. With such a precedent already set, I guess you can't blame the guide for assuming that we wanted to do the same. Unfortunately, the Argentines will probably awaken in a few years to the disappointing fact that they have literally killed the dove that laid the golden egg.

Thus, after two days in La Pampa, we fired the man, paid him half of what he wanted—but easily twice what he was worth—and set out in our rented van to find new hunting territory. We headed south, past Santa Rosa, the capital of La Pampa Province, hoping to find suitable places to hunt perdices. Most of the landowners and caretakers welcomed us graciously, but occasionally we saw 'Posted' signs. We were allowed access to at least half the places we attempted to hunt. Fortunately, for a portion of our expedition we were accompanied by our good friend and hunting companion Julio, an Argentine. He is a 747 pilot for Aerolinas and was able to join us during a short holiday. Thus the language barrier was not quite as much of a problem as it could have been. To our credit, though, we were able to converse almost as well with the locals during Julio's absence.

He was still with us when the van's engine blew a valve. That is how we happened upon the fantastic hospitality of our present hosts. They were customers at the little gas station, miles from nowhere, when we limped in; four airline pilots grounded by a broken valve. While we were trying to negotiate for repairs or a replacement vehicle, I suggested that we ask about the perdiz hunting in the area. One thing led to another, and before we knew it we were hunting on some of the best perdiz habitat available. And except for the wind, we had superb shooting for the next five days, the last half of our ten-day trip. Even the wind cooperated the final two days.

Argentina is difficult to describe. Stretching from about twenty-two degrees south latitude to fifty-five degrees, it is nearly two thousand miles long, with climate ranging from tropical to polar, and from coastal to prairie to desert to mountainous. Such a variety! In area it is about one-third the size of the US, while in population barely more than one-tenth. There are tremendous grain farms and huge cattle and sheep ranches, and vast areas with only dirt roads or no roads. I think it must look a lot like America looked seventy-five or more years ago. It is a country whose inhabitants consist in large part of third and fourth generation descendants of European immigrants, with the largest part comprised of Italians and Spaniards. Most of them are very friendly and hospitable, and every Argentine knows at least one English word—hyper-inflation. They are all concerned about it, but they seem helpless to do anything about it but complain and wonder. It can be such a problem that one is reluctant to change much money at a time for fear of losing value.

As I mentioned, there are sixteen types of partridges in Argentina. You can also find thirty-seven species of ducks and geese. I understand the duck limits are very generous. Read about the duck and goose shooting in George Reiger's fantastic book, *The Wildfowler's Quest*. Outfitters have shown me photographs of a duck hunter standing nearly knee-deep in his morning's kill. I have also seen pictures of two hunters and their eighty-five geese bagged in one hour. There are also, of course, the doves. Doves by the millions. And parrots. The parrots love the sunflower seeds, and although I can't understand why anyone would want to shoot parrots, they're there and available.

In preparation for our trip I corresponded with numerous guides and outfitters all over Argentina. In every instance they hyped the generous bag limits. I have friends who go and take a dozen cases of ammo with them, but I took only two cases and left half of them for my next trip. After all the investigation and inquiry, letters and phone calls, proposals and counter proposals the three of us decided to go it alone without benefit of guide or outfitter. We were fortunate to have our dear friend Julio there, and his wife, Patricia (bless her heart) allowed him to go out and play with us for most of our trip. As a result of a misunderstanding, Julio did get us a guide for the first few days, but he was unqualified. Unless you also have a friend there, I do not recommend that a first-timer hunt Argentina without a guide.

Be prepared to pay $250 per day or more, depending on your level of luxury. As for us, we went Spartan—no frills and do it yourself—because we enjoy the adventure as much as we enjoy the hunt, and we loved every minute of it. The small hotels in the small towns are more than adequate, with private baths, friendly, courteous, helpful staff, and better-than-average restaurants. A few times we provided the cook with a few perdices and we were treated to a sumptuous provincial feast, reminiscent of the home-cooked, wild bird meals of my youth. We shot all the birds we could eat, plus a couple of coolers full to give away to friends and hosts. We never shot our generous limit of fifteen each per day—we didn't need to. And not a single bird was wasted and we're proud of that fact.

"Bird, Gordon!" A flash, a whirr, a blurr. Gone! The wind has calmed down and it is a beautiful clear, crisp morning. Isn't that always the case on the last day of the hunt? But what a pleasant way to finish. The majestic Sierra de la Ventanna mountain range frames the eastern horizon with misty deep purple and golden hues. The cattle graze contentedly a few hundred yards to our flank, along the edge of their two-thousand-acre pasture. And the perdices are here. They get up without warning, for we are hunting this morning without the dog because of the sand burrs. Four abreast, like a skirmish line, we slowly walk across the pasture of grasses, knee-high bushes and occasional clumps of weeds and rushes—good bird cover. It's really too bad about the sand burrs, because otherwise these conditions are perfect for good dog work.

But she can't endure the torture and I've never had any success with those little dog booties.

"Bird! Another flash and another buzz takes off. This time, however, it explodes twenty yards ahead as Julio makes the quickest shot he has made all week. He grew up with this kind of hunting and the three Gringos are novices. Bang! Off to my right another shot as Jim zeroes in on another luckless perdiz. When Jim is hot, he's hot, and today he seems unable to miss. I shouldn't be counting, I know, but I am, and so far he is five for five in about twenty minutes. I had a good day yesterday. Today I think someone has removed the pellets from my ammo. All I see after a shot is a plastic wad and a perdiz sailing off across the hillside...breeding stock.

Bang! Bang! "Hey guys, look at that. Ol' Gordon got another double. Nice shootin' Gordon, but leave some for the rest of us." And so it goes. Another couple of hours of incredibly good hunting, lots of good shooting, a double for each of us, many mysterious misses, and sadly this hunt is over. But the fond memories linger on, and if everything works out right—if our wives and girlfriends give in, if the economy doesn't plummet beyond recovery—we'll go back. After all, each of us still has a case of gun shells down there, ready and waiting.

DAISY

As far as pups go, this was a fairly average litter, except smaller than normal—only four wet, blind, white-ratty-looking little things with pink noses. We had been promised the pick of the litter weeks earlier, so we went right over as soon as Frank called after church that Sunday in March and said, "Sister just had her pups."

Frank raised pointers mostly for fun. He always had too many; it was in his blood, I guess, and it made his retirement more interesting. But when he hunted quail, he normally used his Brittany named Doc Holladay. I never shared it with him, but my suspicion was then, and still is, that Frank's pointers were just a mite too much for him to handle. Doc Holladay never ranged more than forty or fifty yards ahead of us, and he quartered as beautifully as any dog I ever saw. It was almost as if he were an extension of Frank's will, and I don't mind admitting I was envious of their relationship. Frank seldom gave him any commands; it wasn't necessary. "Steady there, Doc. Eeeeasy," was about all I ever heard Frank say to him, and then only when that little bob tail started wagging so furiously that you could almost hear a buzzing sound. You think a hummingbird's wings move fast? You never saw Doc's little half-tail. I liked Doc Holladay except when he had twenty or thirty cock-leburs in his fur.

But nobody in the area had a Brittany bitch so to get puppies Frank bred his pointers again. I knew they were long-legged, bar-rel-chested, hard-running dogs—both parents—but since I was only slightly more than half Frank's seventy-two years, I felt certain I'd have no trouble with one of the pups. In fact, I felt pleased and honored to be offered the pick of the litter. Frank had other hunting buddies, but I might have been his favorite.

I remarked to my daughters, "No, girls, one is all we can have. We have only one kennel, and besides, Frank has grandchildren, remember, and they probably want the others. Which one do you like best?" I wanted them to start thinking ONE so our choice would be easier later.

We briefly handled each pup, one at a time, cuddling up to each little brown face and kissing each little pink nose, which smelled faintly of its mother's milk. We stayed much too long, so long in fact that I'm afraid Evelyn felt compelled to invite us to stay for dinner.

"I've already set the table," she said, "and anyway, it's only left-overs...along with some hot biscuits I just made while y'all were out there 'ooohing' and 'aaahing' those little puppies. Aren't they tee-ny"? So we stayed a while longer, had a quick Sunday evening feast of leftovers, and we went home over-stuffed and full of enthusiasm about the new pup we would bring home in about six weeks.

We returned often the next few weeks. Each time it looked like those little pups doubled in size between our visits. Then one day, we noticed there were only three. "He died Tuesday night," said Frank, "not long after y'all left. Vet couldn't find anything wrong with him. But, poor little thing, he just never did seem able to keep up with his sisters. We buried him over yonder next to the quail pen." The girls and I looked in that direction as Frank pointed, and I could see some fresh dirt under the crabapple tree. I looked at my daughters' sad expressions and I knew they were upset, but I felt they could handle it, having already buried an assortment of goldfish, a parakeet, a stillborn lamb, and a dog or two in our own private pet cemetery beneath the mulberry tree beside the creek.

"Look, girls, look," I said. "See how the others have grown. Look at little Acey, over there sitting in her mama's feed pan. Why they'll be weaned before you know it." I was already leaning toward the little one Frank called Acey, the whitest of the litter. She had a liver head and a little liver spot on her left side. Evelyn appropriately named them Acey, Deucy, and Trey because of the one, two and three spots. I don't remember whether she had named the one who had died. I wasn't especially fond of the name Acey, but as the sixth week rolled around all of us agreed that she was our favorite, although all three were similar in temperament and personality.

"Let's call her Lady," one daughter suggested.

"No, that's a name for a horse," chimed her big sister. We had, indeed, recently sold a horse named Lady.

"Well, we need something that sounds like Acey 'cause that's what she's used to being called," my wife added.

"I've got it...how about Daisy?" I threw in for good measure. It had a nice ring to it and phonetically it sounded enough like what the pup was accustomed to hearing herself called these past five or six weeks that it shouldn't confuse her. "Whaddya think, girls?"

Everyone agreed so Daisy it was, and because we were not strangers (having already handled her so much) she quickly adapted to her new home. One of her favorite pastimes was pacing up and down the creek bank watching the seagulls and terns pitch and dive and splash into the creek.

I had recently read, underlined, and re-read *Gun Dog*, one of Richard Wolters' fabulous dog-training books and I was eager to try his revolutionary techniques. With minimum effort on my part, Daisy practically trained herself. I was so impressed with her progress that I soon began taking it for granted that she would develop into a perfectly finished bird dog. I got lazy. Oh, we had many successful lessons with the bird wing on a string and she eagerly pointed the pigeons I hid in the grass, but she never showed the slightest interest in retrieving anything. I was disappointed at that shortcoming but so pleased with the rest of her performance that I overlooked her failure to fetch.

The hot summer days grew shorter and the shadows grew longer as August slipped away and spilled over into September like the creek lapping steadily at the marsh. Whenever I was at home, the girls and I worked with Daisy once or twice a day, and by the time the first Saturday in September came around, we were pleased with her progress and proud of ourselves as well.

We left her at home, of course, on opening day of dove season. When the four of us returned with a couple of limits of doves, I made the mistake of tossing one a few feet in front of Daisy.

"Fetch, girl, fetch."

How many times during the summer had I given that command only to have it fall on deaf ears? Fifty? A hundred? Two hundred? To my surprise, she pounced upon the still-warm dove, picked it up firmly in her mouth and started toward me.

"Good dog!" I exclaimed.

But my excitement and pleasure were short-lived as Daisy spit out the dove and a mouthful of feathers and looked at me as if I'd poisoned her. She pawed at her face with a front foot to rid her mouth of the remaining feathers. It was a comical scene and I wanted to laugh but I resisted. I had forgotten how easily dove feathers detach.

I tried no more doves. In fact, I made no more attempts at fetch training, concentrating instead on the basics. She responded reasonably well to the whistle, was making excellent progress reacting to hand signals, was rigid on point, and there was not a hint of gun-shyness in her bones. I never worried one bit about the way her tail curved upward on point. Sickle-tail, I've heard it called. No sir, it didn't bother me one bit. I was very happy with my little six-month-old, one-spotted Daisy.

October was a slow month, the highlight being the purchase of that little 20-gauge double I had been promising myself all year; ever since I discovered the Holland and Holland gun room only three short blocks from my hotel in London's Mayfair section. I spent hours and hours in the show room, gazing in awe at the works of art proudly displayed there. In fact, that room has become perhaps one of my favorite "museums" in all the world. No, I did not buy one of those masterpieces, but I did buy a nice little Browning side-by-side for Daisy and me to celebrate the opening of another quail season in November. I put one box of shells through it, breaking nineteen of twenty-five clay targets.

The excitement of opening day was marred by Frank's illness. He was in bed with the flu. The kids were in school and my wife had an all-day meeting, so Daisy and I had the day and our new gun to ourselves. No rush.

I decided to start out slow and easy with the home covey, promising myself not to shoot more than two birds. She found them soaking up some mid-morning sun near some honeysuckle on the south side of the pine thicket. They were edgy, having been caught out in the open, and even though her point was steady, they flushed quickly. I shot quickly as the birds climbed over the honeysuckle and bayberry almost straight up into the pine trees. I shot only once. I tried to mark the downed bird because I knew I would have to retrieve it. As I leaned forward and crouched low to walk beneath some ugly greenbriers, Daisy suddenly trotted up to me, dropped the bird at my feet and then bounded off into the piney woods. I was flabbergasted! What a way to start the day... first bird of the season, first bird with my new gun, and to top it off, little Daisy fetched it as if she'd been doing it for years. I could have quit right then and it would have been a perfect day.

We didn't find the singles. I guess they flew off my property, perhaps even over my neighbor's back acres and into the thick woods across the road. *Let 'em go*, I thought to myself. We hunted two other small farms and found two coveys. I got four birds, all of which Daisy fetched perfectly, and I missed four—not a bad opening day with a new pup. Deer season was also open so I avoided a couple of places where I knew there were birds because I was afraid for my dog. Too many people shoot at a blur in the bushes. *Save those places until after deer season closes,* I thought. The highlight of the day, of course, was Daisy's retrieving. Can dogs smile? I'll swear that every time she brought me a bird that day she looked at me with a knowing smile on her face which seemed to say, "See, I knew all along what to do. No canvas dummies or yucky doves for me, just the real McCoy."

On the way home, I stopped by to see Frank so I could brag a little bit about Daisy. "Come on inside and cheer him up," Evelyn said as she greeted me at the door. "He's been absolutely miserable all day."

I related the day's events to him and he seemed as pleased as I was. His flu was getting better and we promised to hunt together soon.

In December, we hunted Daisy once or twice with her mother, but they never did hunt well together. Daisy couldn't seem to understand about honoring another dog's point so I resigned myself to hunting her alone—but not for long. In mid-December the storms came, some of the worst on record and Eastern Virginia was blanketed with snow. Our farm looked like North Dakota for six long weeks, and my time with Daisy was spent keeping her water bucket free of ice. Then finally, the first few sunny days of February melted away most of January's ice and snow, allowing Daisy and me to hunt together a couple of times. In a few days, another blast of Arctic air swept upon us, without any snow this time, so we continued to hunt.

I particularly remember one of those cold days. Daisy slammed to a halt beside a blackberry thicket between a soybean field and a small marsh. The ebb tide had left behind a thin sheet of ice which concealed the muddy creek bottom. "Whoa!" I said instinctively, as much a command to calm myself as it was a command to Daisy.

It was a classic calendar covey rise, about six birds, one of which afforded me a straight-away shot out over the marsh. The quail folded in flight and then arced out over the creek, sliding to a slow stop like a shuffleboard puck about fifteen yards out onto the ice.

"Dead bird, Daisy. Fetch."

She took the first four or five unsteady steps onto the ice, and then broke through, casting a glance back over her shoulder at me as if she had done something wrong. "Good dog. Fetch. Go on, fetch." I offered the only encouragement I had to offer.

There was no water beneath the thin ice, only air and ripe marsh mud. (I knew she would smell good when she returned.) She continued one slow step at a time, breaking ice with each step, so that by the time she reached the bird her muddy legs had disappeared and she was belly deep in the icy marsh. This was really a job for a Lab or a Chesapeake, not a dainty, little forty-pound pointer, but she never flinched, never faltered, never even slowed down; she just plunged ahead and made the retrieve like it was all in a day's work.

And then the brief season was over. How can ninety days go by so fast and yet the remaining two hundred and seventy until quail season opens again creep by at a snail's pace? It must be the Murphy's Law of quail hunters.

To help pass the time and to keep us both in shape, Daisy and I took long summer walks through the woods and across the fields and along the marsh. Occasionally, she would wade out a few steps into the creek—not quite swimming, but almost—to fetch the bird wing on a string, especially on the hottest days. Why hadn't I thought of that trick the previous summer?

It was while I was walking behind her one July afternoon of her second year that I first noticed her unsteady gait. Her hind end sashayed to one side and then the other, causing her to look like one of those articulated-steering log skidders. You know the kind I mean: they look like the front half is going one direction and the rear half in another as they crawl through the woods. Daisy walked like that. I thought she might have cut a pad on an oyster shell and I wanted to take a look. "Whoa, Daisy. Sit."

When she stopped her hind end simply collapsed. My heart nearly did. I checked her pads carefully but I could find no cut. "Good dog. Good ol', Daisy. Kennel." She raced to her kennel like nothing was wrong. I breathed a sigh of relief, thinking the hot sun was playing tricks on my eyes.

The next day it was worse. I asked my wife Ginna to watch Daisy walk. "Notice anything?"

"Well yes, sort of. Her back end looks funny, like it's going sideways." She confirmed my fears. The vet was down at the south end of the county with a sick horse and couldn't see her until the next morning. By then, she would take six or eight steps, then jink left or right and sit; then get up and do it again. But strangely enough, as I was about to lift her into the truck, she jumped in unassisted and effortlessly. I was puzzled.

The vet was puzzled. "I don't know," he said. I've never seen anything like this. It looks like some sort of intermittent paralysis, but I've never seen it." He pinched her. She jerked her leg away. "Does she jump a lot? Perhaps she fell."

That's it, I thought as a feeling of relief overcame me. "Well, yes, she still chases butterflies and she does jump a lot in her kennel, but it's not concrete, it's sand."

"She probably fell and pulled a muscle. Give it a couple of days and she'll be all right. Keep her confined," he said in his mild-mannered, easy-going, Type B sort of way. "Call me tomorrow," he added.

I called him at home at eight o'clock. "Doc, Daisy can't walk. I mean she can walk with her front legs, but she just drags her rear end around. I'm scared, Doc."

"Bring her over."

I was there in ten minutes. He pushed, pulled, and pinched her in a dozen different places. It made me hurt just to watch, but Daisy had no reaction. She was paralyzed from her shoulders down.

"Why don't you take her up the road to Doc Johnson? He has an X-ray. I'll call and tell him you're coming."

"Thanks, Doc. Tell him I'll be there in forty-five minutes." It's a fifty-mile drive to Salisbury. I don't remember any part of it except the sick, nauseous feeling I had deep down in my stomach. I had been helping one of my daughters with a vocabulary lesson recently and one of the words was "crestfallen." That's how I felt.

I held her steady while Doc Johnson took four X-rays. Then we looked at them together. "Hmmmm. Hips look normal, but there might be a damaged disc right here," he said as he pointed his pencil at the middle of her slender backbone, "but it's hard to say for sure."

"What can I do, Doc?"

"Well, you can take her up to Blacksburg, and for about seven hundred dollars, they'll probably tell you they don't know what's wrong with her. You want it straight?"

"Yes sir."

"Let's try Prednisone. It's a steroid. Give it a week." He looked me straight in the eye. "If she's no better, put her out of her misery and get yourself a new dog." I couldn't return his gaze so I looked away.

"Gee, Doc. It's really that bad? H... h... how much do I owe you?" I just wanted to get out of there and cry someplace where he couldn't see me.

"Well, make it six dollars each for the pictures and five for the medicine, and nothing for the office visit. Twenty-nine dollars. Sorry I don't have better news."

I gave it two weeks; then three. I doubled up on the medicine and still she got only worse. It was horrible to see her hind legs atrophy and to look into her sad little face as she gamely tried to stand. Every day at high tide, I carried her out into the creek...out where it was deep enough that she HAD to swim. I tried to exercise her hind legs. "Physical therapy," said the vet, "might work." It didn't.

I gave her a bath before we took her to the vet, and I stood apart over in the corner of the room and cried like a baby as my wife lovingly held her while he gave her the lethal injection. In about fifteen seconds, she was gone.

She's right over there under the mulberry tree beside Freckles, the parakeet, and the lamb. I think she likes to watch the seagulls and the terns. And sometimes I think she looks over in this direction as I try to teach another pup to fetch.

Author's Note: The events in this story—which is true—took place in the early 1980s before we knew very much about Lyme Disease. Today, in 2016, I read more and more about its effects on people as well as pets. Recently, I read an article which called it "Lyme Arthritis" and told about the possible damage to joints and to the spinal cord and nervous system, causing paralysis among other things. There is no way to tell, of course, but I think Lyme Disease is what paralyzed my little Daisy and took her from me so soon.

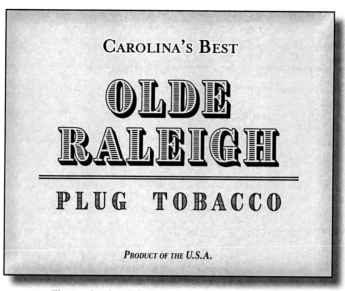

Illustration by Ash Cutchin & Stephanie Fowler

ERNEST AND ERVIN

There aren't many better ways to end a pleasant day of hunting or fishing or just "chilling" with your friends than sitting lazily around a nice fire. We had enjoyed a delicious meal of grilled tuna, grilled veggies, cornbread, and coleslaw. Our day was drawing to a peaceful and rewarding close, the last remains of the charcoal in the grill glowing with a pleasing glow as a few flames flickered and then faded. We had consumed entirely too much food. None of us made a move to wash the dirty dishes as we sat there on the deck of the cottage, overstuffed, each lost in our own private thoughts (perhaps of the day's events) and watching the last dying rays of twilight fade over the Atlantic as the sun dropped behind the rooftops of nearby cottages and the gray waters of Albemarle Sound.

Earlier in the day our friend, Jim Weldon, had flown his Cessna 180 from Pennsylvania down to Nags Head to spend a few days with us. He had landed at the airfield at the Wright Memorial, not realizing they did not sell fuel. He did not think he had enough to continue safely on to Manteo airfield with ample reserve.

The phone rang at about noon. "Ash, this is Ji-im." Somehow he always made his name sound as if it contained two syllables.

"Where are you Jim? We expected you a couple of hours ago. Did you get a late start?"

"Well, yes, but I have another problem. I'm at the airstrip at the memorial, and I need some Avgas to make it over to Manteo. Can you help? Can you drive over to Manteo and get me a few gallons, say two or three gallons of aviation fuel and bring it to me here at the memorial? They won't let me park here overnight."

"Okay, but it'll take awhile. We'll see you when we get there."

"All right, and thanks. I'm sorry to be so much trouble."

So, off we went to a hardware store; we bought three two-gallon cans, drove to Manteo, bought the aviation fuel, drove to the Wright Memorial airstrip, added it to his fuel tank, and then drove back to Manteo to pick him up after he flew his plane there. It took most of the afternoon. In return, he offered to give some of us a plane ride the following morning, flying over the beach down to Buxton to see the famous Hatteras Lighthouse. *Cool,* I thought.

As we sat there on the deck, Jim walked over to the railing, leaned over the edge, and lowered his head.

"Are you all right," I asked.

"Ummm. I wuz um. Um ummmm," mumbled Jim.

"What?"

"He was just spittin' his gross tobacco juice onto the sand dune," said Jerry. "Why don'tcha quit that disgusting habit, Jim?"

"I couldn't agree more," I added.

"I could tell you a story which might help," Jerry remarked. "I didn't tell you this one already, did I...the one about my two uncles, Ernest and Ervin? Sometimes I forget which stories I've told you." He was reminding us of his habit of entertaining us each night with some kind of yarn, a family tradition he picked up from his mother.

"Go ahead," I replied. "Tell your story. We'll stop you if we've heard it before."

Jim mumbled something else unintelligible as he leaned over

the rail once more. He stirred the coals in the charcoal grill and settled back on the lounge chair.

"Well," Jerry began, "This was a long time ago, when I was a kid about nine or ten, I'm not exactly sure. I do remember that I'd had my little shotgun a year or two. I'd shot a few rabbits and a couple of squirrels with it, and a robin, but I hadn't really started bird hunting yet. My dad gave me a real chewin' out, too, about that robin. 'Don't shoot songbirds. The Good Lord put all the birds on this earth for good reasons—some for eatin', like chickens and quail, and some for listenin' to—and robins is for listenin' to.' I got the message. I haven't shot a songbird in forty years. Of course, I think a bobwhite sings a lot prettier than a robin, anyway.

"One Saturday right after breakfast, my two uncles drove into the yard; my mom's two brothers Unca Ernest and Unca Ervin, from over in Cabarrus County near Kannapolis. They didn't come around too often, which seemed to suit my dad all right, but when they did come by, the three of 'em used to hunt birds most of the day. Unca Ervin had a couple of smelly pointers named Beau and Belle; pretty good dogs according to my dad.

"They parked the truck over by the barn. I was real excited because my dad had said I could go with them the next time they came around. My mom rushed out the back door into the yard, gave each brother a big hug, and said, 'You boys hunt all you want to, and take Jerry with you, but his pa can't go. He promised to take me Christmas shopping today.' My dad frowned and looked guilty, as if he were letting my uncles down.

"One of my uncles said that was okay 'cause her husband couldn't hit th' damn birds anyway. He asked her if they were gonna get him some eyeglasses. Both uncles liked to tease my dad and me. My mom told them to never mind what they were shopping for and they could help themselves to lunch. She and Dad went back into the house, and I followed them and grabbed my hunting gear and stuffed three cold biscuits into a jacket pocket.

"Beau and Belle ran around the yard like they'd never seen the place before. Beau hiked his leg on just about everything in sight while Belle eased on over to the chicken pen, coming to a point a few feet away from the fence, like she did every time they visited.

"We hunted the rest of the morning. The dogs did a good job finding birds, and each uncle shot five or six, but I couldn't seem to get the hang of it. About mid-morning, Unca Ervin asked Unca Ernest if he had a chaw of tobacco, and the reply was, 'Naw, I gave it up a few months ago. You should do the same.'

"'Yeah, I reckon so,' was the response. That was the last time anybody mentioned tobacco. Soon we came upon the edge of the neighbor's pasture alongside a weedy fencerow, and Beau locked up on point like he was made out of marble. Belle sneaked up a few steps behind him and honored his point. When the birds flushed, I shot too soon and missed again, but each uncle dropped a quail, one of which fell out into the pasture about forty yards away. Unca Ernest crossed the fence and headed for his bird while Ervin followed the dogs toward a few small pine trees in the opposite direction. So the two of them, my uncles, were maybe eighty yards apart, not really paying any attention to each other, and this is where the fun began.

"Unca Ernest looked carefully toward his brother, then at me, and then he stooped over and picked up his bird and something else, putting each in a separate pocket. He walked over to me with a sly grin on his face, but he said not a word. His brother was still in the woods with the dogs. Unca Ernest put his finger to his lips, whispering 'Shhhhh.' I figure he knew I'd start laughing unless he gave me some advance warning. Then he took his little Buck pocketknife and that nice, ripe horse apple and he started carving. I was sure he'd done this before, judgin' by the precision and speed with which he shaped that horse apple into a small flat shape with crisp edges. A few small pieces crumbled away but mostly it retained its new shape. He smiled as we walked along th' fencerow toward the woods where Unca Ervin and th' dogs were waiting for us.

"'Hey Erv,' he shouted. 'You still want that chaw? I found an old plug here in my huntin' coat. Musta been left over from last year. Prob'ly all dried out by now.'

"'Sure, why not?' Ervin said. One brother walked up to the other and tossed him the prize. I stayed in the background so I wouldn't give away the surprise; I could hardly keep from laughing. Unca Ervin took a big bite off one edge of that small plug of horse tobacco and put the remainder in his shirt pocket. He chomped down a couple of times, kinda scrunched up his mouth in a weird shape and then he spat th' whole mess out with a loud *ptui! ptui!*

"'What kind of tobacco did you say this is, Ernest?'

"'Heck, I don't know... it weren't in no wrapper.'

"'Well, it's awful!' said Unca Ervin. 'It tastes like horse shit!'

"'Maybe that's why I quit,' said his brother. 'You oughtta give it up too.'

"'I reckon I will,' replied Unca Ervin."

Jerry looked away from the fire in the grill and grinned at me. Then he stared ol' Jim straight in the eye as he said, "You boys know what? That was about forty-five years ago, and Unca Ervin is about eighty now, and I reckon he never took another chew."

OL' CASEY

"Come on girl, in you go. Get in the truck. Hup! That's it. Good dog."

I know the professional trainers and the experts say to keep it simple; don't overload a dog's limited understanding of vocabulary with too many commands. I know a simple "hup" or "kennel" would suffice, but somehow I always adopt a conversational tone when talking to old dogs, especially ones I've grown really close to. And we have grown close these past few years, a lot closer than I ever imagined; a lot closer than anyone else in the family ever imagined, too. Hell, this old pickup has almost become her second home, at least her home away from home. My wife is always teasing me about leaving the truck door open just so Casey can sit inside and watch the driveway and house and kennel. But somehow today she doesn't jump up onto the passenger seat with quite the same enthusiasm she used to have.

Tired? Old? Or does she suspect?

How could she have missed my moping around the house these past few days? (Also without much enthusiasm.) They say dogs can't think, can't reason, can't understand or feel. Hogwash! I bet the folks who say that haven't owned any good dogs; leastwise not as good as Ol' Casey here. Look at her. Look at her sitting here beside me and looking at me with those haunting, mournful, sad yellow eyes. Do all chocolate Labs have yellow eyes?

I wonder what she's thinking as we leave the farm and head down the familiar road. She looks outside for a while, observing the same familiar landmarks, making sure I know where I'm going, then settles down comfortably and dozes, her head draped across the seat belt buckle holder. It looks terribly uncomfortable to me and yet it is a pose I'm so familiar with I think nothing more of it.

I don't know what she's thinking, but sad thoughts float through my mind as I try to relive some of the good times we've had together. Why must I be so sad? I mean, after all, they were really good times, even if only borrowed for a few brief moments. And enough dogs have owned me these past forty years that I should know how temporary and fragile such a relationship can be. I guess my happiest memories are of those times when Ol' Casey helped raise a litter or two of pups, pups that weren't even hers. How many times have I seen her race outside to greet a yard full of little pointer pups, giving their mother a break from the drudgery of being a mother by getting right down there on the ground with them... rolling and frolicking and talking puppy talk with them? We even got to the point of calling her Aunt Casey. I swear she used to count them, and if they weren't all there, then she'd search far and wide until she found the one missing, the one over beside the woodshed pointing the butterfly.

Again I wonder what she's thinking about. It certainly can't be ducks. Hell, she's probably the only Lab around who never fetched a duck. It's not her fault, though. We gave up duck hunting a long time ago, before she was even born. But she fetched a goose once. I thought I'd never get it back. It seems that whatever survival instincts passed down to her from her ancestors, those instincts that urged her to keep whatever it is that she retrieves far surpass the "give" command I tried so long to teach her.

Strangely, I did not think I'd ever get her to the point of liking water. I mean, who ever heard of a Labrador retriever not liking water? But she didn't at first. She would wade into the creek or in the pond only up to her belly but no farther. One day, I finally put her in my little aluminum john boat, paddled out into the pond far enough that the water was too deep for her to stand, and tossed her overboard. Once she took those first few dog paddles and realized she would stay afloat, she was okay. She swam to shore and turned right around and swam back to the boat. I was pleased, you know.

She'll fetch, though. By golly, she'll swim the creek all day long and fetch dummies or sticks as long as someone will toss them. I've even thrown an oyster shell now and then, and damned if she won't swim around and around out there searching for it until you'd swear she would drop from exhaustion. I don't think she ever actually fetched an oyster shell, though. She prefers the canvas dummies. Of course, you must have a pair of dummies because she'll only give up the first after you toss another. Loves the water now, she does. No matter if it's a ninety-degree day in August or if she has to break ice coming and going—she's a real water dog. That spot on the vinyl flooring beside the kitchen radiator—the one that's been damp all these years, damp and bleached white where the water got beneath the wax—that spot is going to look mighty empty now.

The miles roll by. A tear rolls down my cheek. I know I'm going to miss Ol' Casey, and I bet she'll miss me too. She'll miss the dummies and the creek and the pointers and all the good times we've had together. And she'll miss this ol' green Chevy truck. But maybe, just maybe she'll get another chance.

She never would have won a field trial, but one thing she was always good at was being able to tell when I turned off a main road onto a gravel one. Even if sound asleep and dreaming of dummies and geese and puppies and other neat things, she could always tell. She sits up now, alert, as the loose gravel beneath the tires wakes her. She's not quite sure what this is all about, I suspect. I've tried to tell her, but she just sits there, staring.

Here's Cathy now. Casey's enthusiasm returns. Recognition.

"Hi, Casey. Good dog. Hi, Dad. Your truck's dirty. Thanks for keeping Casey while I was in college. Come on, Casey, wanna see your new home?"

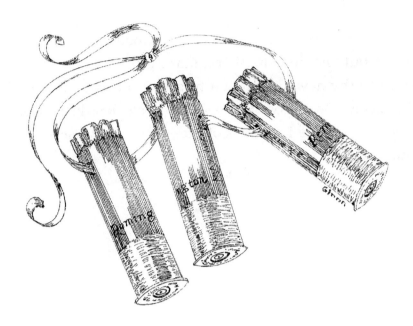

BAD AMMUNITION

Aren't grandchildren just the most funnest, neatest, entertaining things around? They are, but they can also be other things, one of which is unpredictable. Take my second grandson, Trey, for example. The very first time I took him to my farm to go turkey hunting with me, he was probably three and a half years old, and he had heard me and other family members talk about our farm on many occasions. When I stopped the truck a few feet into the farm path, I said, "Well, here we are. This is the farm."

"But where is the barn? Where are the cows?" He had obviously created his own image of the place based on books he had seen, or television shows. There was no barn; there were no cows. It was vacant land, fields and woodland, an emptiness he was not expecting. We saw several turkeys while we were hunched down behind some bayberry branches beside a big loblolly pine tree, but they never came within range. Nonetheless, we enjoyed ourselves.

The next time (if my memory serves me right) he had occasion to return was the following year, Thanksgiving Day, and we were going hunting for deer that time, accompanied by his dad, his uncle, and his cousin who were visiting from out of town. For a few years, we tried to continue a family tradition of spending Thanksgiving holidays together, but that tradition fell by the wayside as folks moved from place to place. Anyway, on that particular morning, perhaps fifteen years ago, the temperature at five o'clock in the morning was 18° Fahrenheit. We bundled and layered as best we could, and off we went. I had previously created a little hidey space for him and his dad, along a well-traveled deer trail within seventy-five or eighty yards of their car, fearing that he would not last until eleven, our predetermined quitting time. I was right. He made it about one hour before his dad decided to return him to the warmth of our living room. The rest of us stayed until eleven, deerless, but eager to return home for some turkey with all the trimmings.

The next time he visited, probably the following summer—I do remember it was warm—I asked Trey if he wanted to go to the farm. He replied, "No sir. It's too cold out there."

I was amused. (He is not amused when I remind him of that day when he incorrectly thought the farm must be cold all the time.)

As he has grown older and he has learned that the farm is not perpetually cold, we have continued to hunt turkeys a day or two each spring gobbler season, sitting on buckets in my little brushy blind. Because he tends to be overly fidgety, I have to hide him well behind branches and brush and other vegetation which sometimes makes it difficult for him to see the turkeys without standing. When he began hunting, he used his Youth Model Remington 870 20-gauge. He has shot two or three gobblers with it and he's been with me when I have done the same. We enjoy the time together. When he was eleven, he joined me, his dad, and my other grandson and his dad on a week-long grouse hunting trip in North Dakota, where we had a wonderful time.

Three or four years ago, I think it was 2012, as a Christmas present, I passed along to him my Belgian Browning 12-gauge Autoloader, given to me by his grandma in 1966. One of my most memorable experiences while flying was a visit to the Fabrique National factory in Liege, Belgium. Another pilot and I rode a train from Brussels to Liege and were given a private tour. It was absolutely delightful and spellbinding to watch those skilled craftsmen and artisans create Browning shotguns and semi-automatic pistols.

Trey took his new Browning the first or second time we went after turkeys the following spring. One morning, it rained like crazy from four o'clock in the morning. when we awoke, until a full hour after sunrise. We sat in the pickup wondering if the rain was going to come through the roof. It finally stopped and while I hid the truck deeper in the woods, he assumed his position on his bucket in a little blind I had built in the pines at the edge of a wheat field. My stealth camera had recorded several gobblers strutting at that location during the previous two weeks.

I placed two hen decoys and a jake about fifteen yards in front of the blind, certain that a gobbler would soon show up and challenge that fake jake to a duel and try to steal his lady friends. As usual, I gave a couple of enticing yelps with my cedar box call. No answer. I called a second time about ten minutes later. No response. We sat quietly, glad that it had stopped raining and just happy to be where we were, together. I don't think twenty minutes passed before I looked up from a sleepy trance to see a lone gobbler approaching the decoys. He had not made a sound as he sneaked around the corner of the piney woods into the wheat field and headed straight for the jake. We watched him. As soon as his rear end was facing us, I told Trey, "He's all yours. Take your time, and don't worry about shooting the decoy."

The blind was bushy enough that my grandson had to stand in order to make a perfect shot. He stood up, took careful aim, and fired. That gobbler looked around to see what was happening, but he did not fall.

"Shoot him again," I said in a loud whisper.

He fired a second time, after which that gobbler began to run away.

"Shoot him again," I said as the turkey lifted off the ground in high speed flight.

He fired his third shot. Missed again.

I won't tell you what each of us said. I know the gobbler had been there because we could see his footprints in the muddy soil. I know those gunshells contained primer and powder, because I heard the noise. I know they contained plastic wads, because they were visible on the ground beside the decoys. But as for pellets, I'm not so sure. They might have been defective shells, somehow making it through the assembly line without receiving any pellets.

We sat in the blind for another hour, nearly ready to leave when we saw five jakes approaching from way across the field. It took them about thirty minutes, but soon they were right in front of us among our decoys.

"Do you wanna shoot a jake?" I asked him.

"Sure. Why not?" he replied. "It's the last day of the season, and they taste good."

"You go ahead and shoot one then," I whispered.

"I'll only shoot one if you do, too."

"But I don't need to shoot a turkey. You shoot one."

"No sir, we've both gotta shoot."

"Okay," I replied, as I shouldered my Ithaca pump shotgun. "I'll count to three, and after 'three' we'll shoot. You take the one on the left."

I aimed at the bird on the far right. I heard myself say softly, "One, two, three," and I squeezed my trigger. My bird fell and the others flew away. "Why didn't you shoot? I asked Trey.

"You never counted," he replied. "You just waited and then you shot. You didn't say a word."

Sadly, I had counted silently, to myself. I felt terrible for him. First he missed a gobbler three times and now I had deprived him of a sure-fire jake. He was not at all pleased with me.

"Let's go to Dairy Queen for lunch, then go home, and come back this afternoon," I said.

Later that afternoon he got a jake. He was happy to be able to take two turkeys home to his mom and dad. He later reported that they were good eating.

I collected the three empty green hulls and saved them. Before Christmas that year, I drilled small holes through each one and tied them together with shiny red ribbon and made a tree ornament out of them. I gave the ornament to Trey as a reminder that some things are imperfect. I hope he saves the ornament as a reminder of the morning we had fun but he missed that gobbler. He insists the camouflage sleeve on the gun barrel interfered with his aim. He's probably correct. He has never used the sleeve again.

LITTLE EMMY

"I never heard of the breed," I said to my daughter when she told me they had ordered a new pup, a Boykin spaniel. There is a small town in southeastern Virginia called Boykins, but I didn't think it was a hotbed of dog breeding. "You mean Boykins?" I queried.

"No, Dad, not Boykins. Boykin, just plain Boykin, singular, without the 's.' They come from South Carolina. Duck dogs. Small duck dogs. Retrievers. Some people call 'em turkey dogs, and the vet says they have good dispositions and are easy to train" ... this coming from a daughter who had owned at least three Chocolate Labs, and who was now getting a new dog for my first grandson. Cathy had arranged to buy a female Boykin puppy from a breeder in Emerald Isle, North Carolina, not far from Moorehead City. They had trouble, a lot of trouble, getting there because it was hard on the heels of Hurricane Floyd when they drove down there to fetch the pup. Roads were flooded; even whole towns were flooded. Try to remember Tarboro and Princeville, and the devastation Floyd wreaked on them in September, 1999. I guess if Emmy had been male, they might have named him Floyd. But they found adequate detours around the flooded areas and were able to retrieve their new pup in a timely manner and bring her to her new home in Virginia.

Once they saw her run, Blair wanted to name her Race Car because she was so fast. Eventually they decided to name her Emmy, after her birthplace. And a cuter puppy I never saw. Even though I am hard-wired to English pointers, I immediately fell in love with little Emmy.

I did some research on the Internet and learned a lot about Boykin Spaniels. If you never saw one, you have missed a real treat. I learned that they are sometimes called "Swamp Poodle" and "LBD" (Little Brown Dog). Even though springers, pointers, and Chesapeakes are part of their lineage, they really look more like a downsized American water spaniel. Legend has it that Mr. Boykin (their namesake) wanted a duck dog that he could carry along in his boat, put overboard to fetch a downed duck, and then lift it out of the water and back into the boat after a successful retrieve. Adult females weigh in at about 25- to 40-pounds. An Internet article says they are high-energy dogs.

"Dad, since Bruce and I both work, will you please help us train her?" my daughter asked in a pleasant and pleading tone.

I said I would. But Emmy was not as much of a people pleaser as we expected. She was hardheaded and stubborn as a mule. High energy is an understatement. Left alone for even a short time, she relished chewing on the corners of my wooden stair treads. Even after weeks of training, "sit" was about the only command she consistently obeyed. Once in a while, she would come to the whistle, but only if nothing else was of particular interest at the time. She loved to chase the bird wing on a string, as well as anything that moved in the yard. Having been born in August, she was still very much a pup when quail season opened, but I let her tag along with Dot and me a few times as we walked along the edges of the soybean stubble and into the cutover pines. Emmy had a good nose for birds, but when Dot would lock up on point, Emmy would imme-diately plunge ahead and flush the quail. I guess I should not have expected anything different from a Spaniel. Flushing is their game. I often wondered if I should take up falconry, but I had no time for another hobby.

Sadly, her owners moved away the following year, taking my lit-tle trainee to Alabama. But a couple of summers later, they let her return to Virginia for a brief refresher course. Since I was dogless that September, they agreed to let me take Emmy with me to North Dakota. We flew to Minneapolis and then took Amtrak to Minot. "We don't allow hunting dogs on Amtrak," the reservation clerk told me on the phone. "Is the dog your companion, your anxiety dog?"

"Well, I do get a little anxious when she's not around," I replied. "Yes, you could say she is my anxiety companion."

"Okay," he replied. "She can go with you. We've had all kinds of anxiety companion pets aboard: cats, parrots, even boa constric-tors."

We departed Minneapolis at midnight and had a very pleasant train ride to Minot. The conductor woke me up at every stop which was long enough for a potty call. Emmy slept at my feet at first, but as the night wore on, she wiggled her way along the bunk until fi-nally we were side by side. We never saw a snake or a parrot.

She loved the prairie and she soon took to sharp-tails like they were God's gift to Boykins. Of course, as long as she could see them, she would chase the birds I missed rather than fetch the ones I knocked down. I had to use a little electronic persuasion, especially one time when she took off after a mule deer we spooked. She wore that little breast-protection vest I had ordered from Ca-bela's, and it performed as advertised. It kept the wheat stubble from rubbing her chest raw, but it was hot. She covered the prairie amazingly well for such a short-legged little critter, and finally she was retrieving like a pro.

Unfortunately, she had only two speeds: race and stop. It did not take long in the early autumn heat for her to be completely exhausted, and I had to let her stay in the kennel the second day. My hosts said she whined and whimpered all day long, but she needed the rest.

By the time we hit the prairie on our third or fourth day, I noticed that Emmy would head straight for a small clump of buckbrush or a Buffalo berry thicket as soon as I released her. I realized that she had quickly learned the most likely habitat which held the grouse.

One time neither the whistle nor the electronic collar performed as I hoped, and that was when she spied a small porcupine running along a fence line. She immediately caught up with it right before it dived into its hidey-hole beneath a small rock pile. Fortunately for Emmy, she only caught some six or seven quills but they were in the tenderest part of her mouth and lips. The ever-resourceful Daryl always carried a little Leatherman multi-purpose tool in a belt holster, and he made quick work of the quills with the needle-nose pliers while I restrained Emmy. It didn't take but about ten minutes, and we resumed hunting. I strongly recommend you carry a similar tool if you hunt in areas containing porcupines.

We had a very successful week in Mountrail County, getting a limit nearly every day we hunted, and I made myself a promise to bring little Emmy back to North Dakota as soon as I could, and bring along her owner, my grandson, as well.

In a couple of years, we made reservations to go back to Minot, this time from Jackson, Mississippi via Amtrak. My grandson, Blair, was nine years old. He had been shooting doves for a couple of years, and had passed the Hunter Safety Test I gave him, even though it was designed for twelve-year-olds. Much to our disappointment, the man at the Amtrak check-in counter informed us we could not take our shotguns aboard the train, even as checked baggage. "Why not? I've done it in the past," I protested.

"Sorry, sir, new rule," he replied as he pushed the little paper toward me, pointing to the section NO FIREARMS. "Blame it on 9/11."

As I closed and locked our gun cases, I said to him, "How about these two violins, then? Can we take them?"

"Sorry, sir, I've already seen that they are guns and not violins. No, I cannot accept them."

So, we left our shotguns with Blair's mom and grandma, and we boarded the train, confident that our friends in North Dakota would see to it that we would have shotguns available. We slept most of the night en route to Chicago, having a sleeper car to our-selves until somewhere in southern Illinois, after midnight, a group of noisy, giggly teenage girls boarded our car. They were obviously very excited about going to Chicago, but they had absolutely no sympathy for us and our desire to sleep. Their chaperone apolo-gized and said that she had been assured they would have the car all to themselves. Surprise! A couple of stops later the kind steward moved us to another car with a private bedroom, where we slept comfortably the rest of the way to Chicago, arriving mid-morning.

Because we had several hours before departing for Minot, we decided to take a little quickie tour of a portion of the city near the train station. Little Emmy accompanied us as we checked our bags into a locker, but she caused quite a stir as she frantically tried to chase the pigeons which seemed to be everywhere in the train station.

It was a beautiful sunny day. We saw the Sears Tower. We ate our lunch in a little park and afterwards, as we rounded one street corner, we noticed a little tour trolley. My wristwatch indicated that we still had about four hours before departure so I asked the man if we could take Emmy with us. "Sure," he replied, "Hop on."

After a brief wait, no more passengers boarded and off we went, Blair, Emmy, me, the tour guide, and the driver. We had a delightful little private tour of Chicago. Blair's favorite site was Soldier Field, the Chicago Bears stadium, which also served as a convenient pot-ty stop for the dog. If you have only a few hours in Chicago, this is certainly the way to see it.

The highlight of our train ride that night to Minot happened while we were in the dining car. Within five minutes of being seated, our steward approached us with a smile. "Your dog is in the crew lounge," he said. "Take your time, and enjoy your dinner, but stop by and get her on your way back." It seems that the door latch to our sleeper compartment was not secure, and shortly after we left, Emmy discovered it and found her way to the crew lounge. A couple of crew members fed her a snack and entertained her while we enjoyed our dinner. What great service.

Our hosts were indeed able to find us suitable shotguns, even a little Remington 870 youth model 20-gauge pump exactly like Blair's which Amtrak would not let us bring. Our first day afield was rewarding enough, with Blair shooting a couple of sharp-tails as well as the very first Hun we flushed. Little Emmy found several coveys of birds, many which she busted out of gun range, but all in all I was pleased. She found and retrieved the birds we downed, and Blair was very proud of her. I was sure that as the week progressed she would slow down, and she did.

On our last day, as we trudged along a half-mile row of choke-cherry trees, one of us on each side, Blair was getting discouraged (and tired) having hunted hard and shot only one grouse that morning, when suddenly Emmy began acting birdy. "Get ready," I said, "There might be some birds up ahead."

As I looked through the brush toward the other side of the tree row I saw Blair bring his gun to his shoulder just as a covey of sharp-tails flushed. I knocked one down on my side of the tree row and then I heard a shot from the other side. Immediately I heard the unmistakable sound of that little pump gun shucking another shell into the chamber, followed by a second shot. Then shuck and a third shot, and feathers flew.

"I got two!" shouted my excited grandson. "I missed the second one, but then another one flew and I got it! I got it! I got two! Where's Emmy?"

"She's retrieving my bird," I answered as I carefully picked my way through the brush to Blair's side of the tree row. "Here Emmy.

Come. Fetch. Good dog."

Then, "Dead bird, Emmy, dead bird."

She dropped my bird at my feet and immediately commenced to search for Blair's two birds. It turned out that both were only winged, and they were running. But Emmy, bless her little Boykin heart, chased down one and then the other, proudly taking both to her owner, my little nine-year old grandson. His first double. I'm sure my smile stretched from ear to ear as I said, "Good job, Blair. You got a double."

"Can we go home now, Ash?" asked Blair. "I have my limit of three. Let's go home."

"As soon as I take a photo, Blair, as soon as we get to the truck and I get my camera. Your mom and dad will want to see a picture of you with your first double. I'm so proud of you. Aren't you proud of your little Emmy?"

TASHA

Her name was Tasha, and she was a beautiful German shorthaired pointer owned by my good friends, Bette and Daryl Belik, of Ross, North Dakota. I had hunted with Tasha once or twice a couple of years ago, but both times with Daryl as her handler. He knew her capabilities and limitations; I was simply an observer and guest. Actually, the Beliks owned both Tasha and (formerly) her father, Sonny, who had recently gone to dog heaven, leaving his daughter behind as the only Belik dog.

I had arrived in Mountrail County two days earlier with my son-in-law, Bruce, this being his first time on the prairie. Bruce flew from Atlanta and I from Norfolk, and we met in Minneapolis and flew together to Minot. Bruce was overwhelmed by the sights as we drove our rented vehicle to Stanley. It seems that every little pothole contained a few ducks, and several flocks of geese flew overhead from time to time. "Wow!" he kept saying every few miles, "I wish my dad could see this." Bruce had grown up in southwest Georgia, and I don't think he had ever before traveled to this part of the country. I loved the prairie, having hunted several times in both

Dakotas, but this was the first time I had come without a dog, having just buried my beloved pointer, Dot, the week before. Daryl was busy harvesting his wheat, so he could not join us this week, and I was curious to see how successful Bruce and I could be hunting sharp-tails without a bird dog. I had done it a few times in South Dakota with great success, but it was not as much fun.

Things got off to a bad start. We arose that day to a beautiful sunrise, but it was accompanied by a strong low pressure system with a cold north wind howling down from Saskatchewan. We trudged along that morning, hunting mostly into that wind which slapped into our faces like tiny whips, and by noon it was accompanied by little rain drops. We soon discovered that the grouse were extra skittish, most of them flushing well out of gun range. It was very discouraging, and by midday we were tuckered out and frustrated. Our rosy cheeks and earlobes were cold, and even inside our gloves our fingertips were starting to hurt. After lunch we tried again, and were successful only as sunlight began to fade and the wind moderated. I like that word "moderated" having known what it meant for a long time, but only heard it describe the wind by my friend and neighbor, George Reiger, who not only authored several books, but who also wrote for *Field and Stream* magazine for many years. George was their Conservation Editor, and he likes fancy words.

Several times during that uncomfortable day, I thought of the book, *Remember the Wind*, which I had read a few years earlier. It is a beautifully written story about life on the prairie authored by William Chapman. He wrote about the time he spent as Headmaster of St. Elizabeth's School on the Standing Rock Reservation in South Dakota. I had hunted sharp-tails on the Standing Rock Reservation around Timberlake three or four seasons, and I have fond memories of the birds and the friendly people, but I hated the fact that my dogs kept getting their feet full of prickly pear cactus thorns. I tried those little leather dog booties a couple of times, but Christie didn't like them and kept removing them with her teeth.

The South Dakota cactus is one of several reasons I began hunting in North Dakota.

"You guys didn't do so well today, eh?" Daryl remarked during dinner. "You should let Tasha tag along with you tomorrow. She should behave herself fairly well, and you know how she loves to hunt sharp-tails."

I knew, but I was reluctant to accept his offer, and I told him so. I had seen Tasha range 300 or 400 yards ahead of us in the past, and I liked a closer-working dog.

"Ah, go ahead," he insisted. "You'll do fine. I'd go with you, but if this wind keeps up tonight, it should dry things enough that I can combine wheat all day long tomorrow. Try those tree rows over at Carl's place and maybe along my north prairie. I see grouse up there all the time."

Bruce and I went to sleep that night reinvigorated. I can't say that visions of sugar plums danced in our heads, but I know I dreamed of a better day.

It was cloudy and windy as we ate a quick breakfast. The wind had backed off and was now out of the west, and it was not quite as cold. Daryl had already started his combine and was headed out the driveway as Bruce and I followed Tasha down the path through the barnyard toward the north prairie pasture. Actually, the dog made a brief detour and ran down along the north side of a row of trees, circled a small field of wheat stubble and returned to us, satisfied that she had not missed any birds. I had shot several Hungarian partridges along that same tree row in years past, and I wondered where they were today—perhaps just ahead.

With her head held high and her nose pointed into the west wind, Tasha skirted a second tree row before responding to my whistle and returning to our side. "Good dog. Good girl," I told her as I gently stroked her smooth, liver-colored head. It was beginning to look like we would have a great companion today, and I was certain that these little jaunts had helped her run off some of her boundless energy.

As we walked abeam a small cluster of assorted abandoned farm implements, relics from Daryl's dad's farming days, we passed through an open gate and transitioned from row crop fields to short grass prairie pasture. The gate was open because Daryl no longer raised any cattle, having given up that endeavor two years earlier. About six widgeon flushed from a small pothole in a wet slough as Tasha nosed and sniffed about along the edge. I studied the pasture, which was a quarter section or 160 acres of gently rolling hills with little draws, trying to decide how best to work it. I wanted to take advantage of the wind, but we were in the wrong location, upwind of the entire quarter section. I silently scolded myself for not doing a better job of planning ahead and approaching this area from downwind. Bruce ambled his way a few yards north toward a clump of buffalo berry shrubs and small trees. "I'll check out those bushes," he said.

Tasha, meanwhile, decided that she knew more than we did about this particular piece of real estate, and she headed south, crosswind, like a greyhound along the edge of some buckbrush toward a small rock pile off to my right. I whistled a couple of blasts, but she paid no attention to me, and continued crosswind. All of a sudden, as if she had run into an invisible brick wall, she stopped dead in her tracks, firmly planted her feet, and literally angled her body into a ninety-degree arc of muscle and nose. *Point!*

"Birds!" I shouted toward Bruce. "Birds! Tasha's on point! Get over here!"

I was afraid that the birds would not hold very long because of the wind, and I wanted Bruce to get in position for a shot. I stayed where I was until he was about thirty yards from the dog, and then we both eased closer to Tasha, who was still solid as a statue. Suddenly, about eight grouse rose vertically from the brush, and most of them quickly banked to their left and flew downwind, directly away from us. However, one of them flew straight toward me, passing within five or six yards, and continued into the wind behind me. I was able to turn around and drop it at about forty yards. Bruce was fortunate to get off a quick shot and his sharp-tail fell into the buckbrush downwind of us. Then the covey was gone, straight over the rock pile, across a half section of wheat stubble, and onto the prairie south of us.

Within a few seconds, Tasha was at my side with one of the birds. *What a great dog!* I thought. "Good dog," I said as I took the bird from her mouth. "Dead bird, Tasha. Fetch the bird." She quickly retrieved the other grouse. We had been hunting less than thirty minutes, and I was excited about our prospects for a very successful day.

We returned to the house, loaded Tasha into the back seat of our rental-car, and drove one mile south along a dirt path toward an area Daryl says his dad always called "Chicken Hill." It contained a small clump of brush about a quarter acre in size, and, depending on the time of day, it usually held birds, either in the brush or in the surrounding short grass. It was bordered by a field of alfalfa on the south, wheat stubble on the west, and prairie on the north and east sides. I imagined that it had been home to many generations of sharp-tails for several hundred, maybe even a thousand years. Perhaps the birds we had flushed earlier had flown this far.

Because we were now east of where we wanted to hunt, this time the wind was more in our favor. As soon as she exited the car, Tasha looked around, and as if she knew exactly where she was and what to do, she slowly headed straight for that little patch of brush. I say slowly, because her gait was a bit unsteady and she seemed to favor her left foreleg. Because she was fairly close to me, I called "Tasha, come," and she immediately came to me. I knelt beside her and examined both front paws, expecting to see a cut or something (perhaps a small stone) lodged between two toes. Nothing. I gently squeezed each foot and she had no reaction, so I stood up and motioned her forward. As Bruce and I followed her, she stopped a few feet short of the brush and made a classic point. I eased over to the left and Bruce to the right so at least one of us could get a shot as the birds flushed. I had hunted this little clump of brush in the past, and I knew from experience that it was possible for the birds to flush straightaway so that no one got a shot.

Birds began to flush from the thicket in all directions. I felt like I was in the middle of an artist's watercolor print of a dozen hunting scenes in outdoor magazines. I fired twice, dropped one grouse and missed the second. Before I could cram more shells into my Ithaca pump gun, a "sleeper" or late bird arose almost at my feet and I dropped it also, filling my limit. "Nice shot, Ash," Bruce shouted. "I got a couple also. Looks like we can quit for the day." We had been hunting for about one hour and we had our legal limit of three grouse each.

"Well, yes, we can quit hunting sharp-tails, but there might be some Huns around," I replied. "Let's take Tasha and the birds back to the house and then walk those chokecherry rows over on Carl's place."

We left the dog at the house with Bette, field dressed the birds, and then spent the next two hours leisurely walking along Carl's tree rows and onto an adjacent section whose owner we did not know. We did not see any "posted" signs, so we felt comfortable that we were not trespassing. Finding no Huns, we called it a day and decided to see if Daryl needed any assistance moving grain trucks. After all, we were his guests, and we would gladly help in any way we could.

Tasha slept most of the afternoon while we cleaned the birds and helped Bette with dinner. After a wonderful meal of freshly grilled sharp-tail breasts and some of Bette's homegrown vegetables we drifted off to bed, tired but happy with our day's hunting success. Daryl had finished harvesting about half his wheat.

I arose early next morning to find Bette sitting on the living room floor, sobbing, with Tasha cradled across her lap, whining and whimpering. "She didn't sleep at all during the night," said Bette. "She cried and moaned all night long, and she has licked her left leg nearly raw. I'll call the vet up in Powers Lake and take her up there."

"I'll take her," I said. "I feel responsible for whatever is wrong with her. After all, I was the one who took her hunting."

"No, it's not your fault. It's nobody's fault, but she's in terrible pain." Bette could hardly withhold her tears. Tasha was Bette's dog, and I felt like a total jerk for whatever was wrong with her.

Powers Lake is about twenty miles and twenty minutes north of the ranch, and Bette, Tasha, and I were there within the hour, as soon as the vet opened the door. Sensing an emergency of sorts, he took her right away. After a brief exam he decided to x-ray her left foreleg. A few minutes later, he informed us that she had chipped a small, sharp fragment off her leg bone and it was causing inflammation in the muscle tissue and therefore the pain. He said he could not repair the chip, it would require a specialist, either in Bismarck or Fargo. He did put a splint on the leg joint and gave her some pain medication. He showed us the x-ray. I could see the small chip, maybe three millimeters long. It looked like a toenail clipping. The vet said the pain would subside in a day or two, and she should be almost as good as new within a couple or three weeks if we let her rest as much as she needed. I paid the vet and we departed for home, unhappy that such a jewel of a hunting dog was injured.

Much to my extreme disappointment, Tasha never did recover good as new. She walked with a limp the remaining six or seven years of her life and she had to be confined to the yard, because if she ever got any distance from the house, she would go grouse hunting all by herself. Even with her disability, she loved to hunt grouse. She always seemed glad to see me whenever I returned, and I still remember that awesome point the day she injured her leg. I can still see her nearly bent like a pretzel, with both her hind end and her nose pointing into the wind.

What a dog, that Tasha!

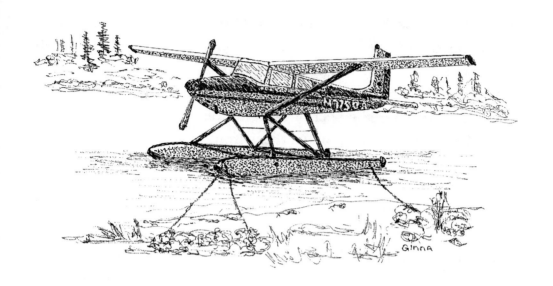

ALASKA

Several of my close friends at Pan Am either owned their own planes or shared ownership with others. Jim Weldon, who hunted grouse with me in South Dakota and who went with me to Argentina to hunt perdiz, had a Cessna 180. Harry Shepard had a fancy Italian acrobatic plane and put on air shows for a fee. Another such friend was Jack Meyers, from St. Louis. His co-owner, Kim Kimball, had died in a plane crash in a box canyon in California, leaving Jack as sole owner of a 180 on floats. One of my favorite people, Jack was the quintessential playboy bachelor without being obnoxious about it. Jack was a down-to-earth kind of guy, and everyone who knew him loved him.

His commute apartment in New York was a couple of blocks from mine, and when we were there together between trips, we shared some meals and some yarns. He had flown DC-3s for Ozark Airlines before being hired by Pan Am, and he spun many interesting tales about flying the Gooney Bird. Jack was also an outdoorsman; he loved to hunt and fish, two hobbies we shared. He enjoyed telling me about hunting turkeys in Missouri, and I liked to brag about my skill with bobwhite quail and bird dogs. Jack also dearly loved Alaska, and he showed me many pictures of his Cessna 180 floatplane and of the scenery around his campsite on Nonvianuk Lake, northeast of King Salmon. I sat and watched him tie many dry flies as we shared a beer or two and told yarns, and I promised him I'd save him some quail feathers from Virginia, not knowing if he ever used them or if he even wanted any.

One day in early 1982, he asked me to help him unload a tent from his car trunk and carry it into his apartment. It was heavy canvas and definitely a two-man job. "I had this custom-made in New Delhi," he told me. "I didn't know it would be so heavy. It's for my camp in Alaska. Ash, I've asked you several times to come fish with me up there, and if you keep saying 'no,' I'll have to ask someone else. I have lots of friends who want to come."

"But I've got to consider my wife, Jack. I go off and leave her too much as it is; she'd never stand for my spending ten days up there with you."

"Hell, bring her along. She likes to fish, doesn't she? I bet she'd have a wonderful time."

"Well, yes, she likes to fish all right, and I guess her parents could stay with the girls while we're gone. I'll ask her. Thanks. I'll let you know. Oh, would there be any other girls in camp?"

"No, you're the only guy I know who takes his wife along on these kinda jaunts. Some take their girlfriends, but she'd be the only one this time. Jim is bringing his two sons, and Erroll is bringing his teenage boy, and Ralph comes by himself. Ginna would be the only girl. Tell her we'd love it if she'd join us."

And that is how it went that day. My wife was excited, but very curious and a little skeptical when I explained the plans I had discussed with Jack, but I convinced her she'd have a good time and she definitely would not have to spend a week cooking and washing dishes for a group of pilots and one teenager. I promised.

Because we were eligible to fly non-rev (but space available) on most other airlines, it was always "iffy" if we would arrive at our chosen destinations on time, but we planned the trip and went anyway. Jack promised to meet us at King Salmon airport in Alaska on our chosen arrival date in July, and if we were not there, he'd meet every flight from Anchorage until we showed up. What a great guy! As it turned out we had to make an unscheduled stop in Seattle instead of getting on an Alaska Air direct flight out of San Francisco, but otherwise things were flawless, and Jack was there to meet our flight from Anchorage, as he had promised, sporting a four-day beard along with his normal bushy mustache. He was standing beside the terminal building as we disembarked. If we'd been late, we had no way to get in touch with him; this was way before cell phones.

"I came to meet you yesterday, but then I realized I'd messed up and got the wrong date," he exclaimed as he gave Ginna a bear hug. "Welcome to King Salmon."

He and Ginna hit it off immediately, as if they were old friends; Jack was like that.

"Do you like Klondike Bars?" he asked, wiping some chocolate from his mouth onto his sleeve. "Here, have one. Eat it fast before it melts." He gave each of us a chocolate-covered ice cream snack, loaded our gear into a jeep, and said, "Hop in. I have to make a quick stop at the grocery store."

We did, and within a block or two after we departed the rustic terminal, he stopped in front of the store, went inside for a few minutes, and soon returned. I saw him place two six-packs of Klondike bars and several steaks into a styrofoam cooler. "Here, hold this," he ordered, "and don't drop it; it's our dinner."

After a very short drive to the river, we unloaded our gear and stowed it in his plane which was parked alongside a small wooden pier. He parked the jeep, which belonged to a friend. I had been worried about our spinning rod cases fitting inside his plane and was pleased to discover that there was plenty of room for them inside a compartment on one of the floats, right next to a wooden paddle and some spare rope. "Ash, you take the copilot seat; Ginna, you ride behind him. Have you ever seen a bear?" he asked her.

"Only in a zoo," she replied.

"Nice plane," I told him. "Not too different from what I flew in 'Nam, except mine had wheels. How far do we have to go?" I was concerned about Ginna and small planes because she had gotten sick at least once when she flew in small Cessnas with me. Not wanting to put any subliminal thoughts in Ginna's head, I didn't ask Jack if he had any sick sacks aboard.

"Just a short hop along the river."

He made a quick radio call to ground control, started his engine, taxied out into the middle of the narrow river, parallel to the main runway, and asked the tower for permission for a water takeoff, to which the controller replied, "Cleared." Then he pushed the prop lever and throttle lever forward and off we went on another adventure. He quickly turned north, raised the water rudders, leveled off at about 800 feet, reduced the throttle setting, and continued to look around outside. I could see ahead and out each side window and could tell that we were flying over isolated marsh-like terrain dotted with small ponds and creeks and very few trees. He turned northeast, pointed to the front, and said, "That's Lake Iliamna way up there. We're not going that far. Beautiful, ain't it?" I could tell he was loving this. "That's Alagnak River right below us. Not much farther."

Within a few minutes, he chopped the throttle to idle, banked sharply to the left, and said, "Look! Look down there! See the salmon? Just below the wing tip in that bend in the river." He pointed with his right arm toward the left side window, pointing almost directly beneath the plane. "See all that red? That's a school of salmon." Then he rolled to the right, nearly standing the 180 on a wing and pointed his arm across my face to the right window. Sure enough, we could see what looked like a red blanket just below the surface, hundreds of salmon. It was hard to make out individual fish, of course, and that float outside my window looked as big as an aircraft carrier, but as he leveled off at about one hundred feet above the river they came into view more clearly.

Then he shouted, "There's a bear!" Neither of us saw it, but he insisted he saw one. He flew a tight 360° circle, but I guess his bear ran into some heavy brush, because we still did not see it. He climbed back up to about five hundred feet altitude.

Within another few minutes, he began a slow, descending, circling turn, saying, "That's our camp down there, right where the lake empties into the river. See the tents? See the guys waving at us? They're expecting some ice cream. They just love those Klondike bars."

He flew beyond the camp, made a 180° turn, lowered some flaps, made a slow final approach, and touched down onto Nonvianuk Lake which was as smooth as a mirror. After the plane settled down firmly on the floats, he lowered the water rudders and added enough power to taxi to his parking spot beside the camp. Ginna and I were both excited; we had arrived.

"Ash, you know Jim and Erroll, don't you? Heck, y'all just introduce yourselves all around."

After sharing the ice cream with his friends and helping us unload our gear, he said, "That's the tent you helped me unload in New York," pointing to a sturdy, straight-wall tent about eight feet by ten feet. Then he pointed to a small nylon tent about thirty yards from two other ones which were clustered together beside his large tent and a screened shelter along the rocky beach, saying, "You two take the honeymoon tent," he chuckled, "so you can have some privacy."

Everyone laughed.

"Follow me and I'll show you our toilet facilities." He led us away from the tents, along a faint path, back away from the river maybe fifty yards. There we discovered a small privy, a wooden shed whose sides and top were covered with roofing felt. "Don't come over here alone," he cautioned us. "Always bring a friend." It was a two-holer, but I figured he did not mean Ginna had to share it with anyone.

We returned to the main campsite where Jim and Erroll had

already begun to prepare the steaks and home-fried potatoes. Jack served us some chips and salsa, gave me a cold beer from a mesh sack in the river, and offered Ginna some chilled white wine. She looked around, saw a fish make a splashing jump about twenty yards from the shoreline, and said, "Are you guys catching anything?"

"A nice trout now and then, but no salmon," remarked my friend Jim. "I think we're a little too early."

"Well, I'll get up and catch our breakfast," my wife said. "What time do we get up?" I looked at my watch, and to my surprise, I noted that it was already nine o'clock, but it was barely dark. It looked more like four in the afternoon. Time had slipped away from me.

"Yeah, you catch our breakfast," Jack said to Ginna, sounding unimpressed, "but we have bacon and eggs just in case. And it won't get very dark, maybe from around eleven until two or so. Sometimes it's hard to sleep, 'cause it's never very dark."

I think he figured she'd sleep in and not keep her promise. But he was wrong. After about six hours' sleep, maybe seven, she was up and at 'em before anyone else in camp. Surprising all the guys, using a little plastic lure I had bought in Tokyo, she caught a nice trout, and snagged a salmon, enough to feed about half of us. She and I were using light-weight spinning tackle. Everyone else was using fly rods. I cleaned the fish and Jack cooked them, saying he was impressed with her success. He also made some pancakes and fried some bacon.

He warned us that if we caught anymore fish, we were NOT to walk along the riverbank with them hanging on our belts, but to bring them immediately into camp and clean them. "A bear can smell a dead fish a mile away, and one can sneak up behind you and you'll never know he's there until you smell him, and then it's too late. Most of 'em stink." We took his advice seriously. "In fact," he continued, "we release most of the fish we catch. In a day or two, if the weather is nice, we'll fly over to Brooks Falls and fish there, but you have to use barbless hooks and release everything you catch." We didn't bring any barbless hooks.

The weather remained nice, cloudy and cool, and with enough wind that the mosquitoes were not so bad. Ginna caught one, saved it in a Ziploc, and brought it back to Virginia to show our neighbors how small they were compared to Accomack County's. (On more than one occasion I've told people our Eastern Shore mosquitoes are so big it takes only six to make a dozen.) We fished each day, took a short nap each afternoon, and just relaxed, glad to be where we were and glad to be in the company of such a great group of folks.

Having thought all along that we would be really, really way out in the boonies, far from civilization, not seeing anyone but our campmates, we were surprised to see a nearly constant flow of people. A park ranger and his young wife, whose cabin was nearby, joined us for several meals, and float plane after float plane landed on the lake beside our camp—several each day. Some planes would unload two or three passengers with heavy-duty inflatable boats and depart immediately. Their passengers drifted away down the river toward the west. Some planes would simply stop along the edge of the lake, disembark two or three people who would make several casts, re-board within thirty minutes or so and fly off to another location. Once in a while a small group would eat lunch right across the narrow river from our camp and wave goodbye to us as they departed.

Ginna and I hiked along the river two or three times, casting and casting and casting with our little spinning rods, using lure after different lure, the same way we did along the Outer Banks, but usually catching nothing more than a small trout or two. Some of our companions joined us, using their fly rods, having no more success than we did. We had come to catch fish, but soon realized—like our friends—that simply being here was what the trip was really all about. The sky was usually clear, the breeze was just right, and the view of the snow-covered mountains to the east was awesome. It was perfect.

But before we knew it, Jack said, "Time to go, folks. Anybody who wants to go to Brooks Falls, get ready. Tomorrow we have to go to Anchorage, but today I'm running a shuttle service."

And so, loading us into his plane, four of us in seats and one person crouching in the baggage compartment, off we went to see the sights. He even let me make a takeoff and a landing, something I'd never before done in a seaplane. It was fun. When it came time to set down on the lake near Brooks Falls, he told me, "Just before you think you're ready to touch down, look outside at the float on your side. Ease the throttle back and fly the float onto the lake, keeping the wings level." I did as he instructed, and we glided onto the lake like I'd been doing it for years. Cool! I think Jack was impressed, but he said, "Beginners luck."

After he brought his second load of passengers from our camp, we assembled with about two dozen other tourists for a little briefing from the park ranger before taking the short hike to the falls. "Welcome to Katmai. This is the bears' park," she said. "We are their guests. They usually won't bother you as long as you make some noise while walking along the river. They are accustomed to people, but they don't like surprises. Remember you must use barbless hooks and release every fish you catch. Enjoy your day."

Ginna and I had not even brought along our spinning rods, but Jim and Jack and Erroll's son made an occasional cast with their fly rods as we hiked along the river. We talked and laughed and whistled, and we made certain we did not surprise any bears along the way.

I did not know what to expect. I had been to Niagara Falls. I had been to Yosemite. I had flown over Angel Falls in South America and over Victoria Falls in Zimbabwe, Africa. I did not think I would be impressed. I was mistaken. Brooks Falls is probably one of the most photographed places on this planet, and it doesn't take but a few minutes to see why. The waterfall itself drops only about six or eight feet and the river appears to be less than one hundred yards wide, but the view is fabulous. Ginna and I (both wearing waders) walked slowly out into the river maybe fifty feet downstream below the falls, keeping a sharp eye on the brown bear along the far edge. There were salmon everywhere all around us, bumping our legs as they swam upstream toward the falls, ready to leap up, and continue their journey to their place of birth. I tried to reach down and touch one with my hand, but was unsuccessful. We saw the bear grab one in its mouth after ducking its head below the water for a few seconds.

"This is so cool!" Ginna remarked. "I'm so glad we came. Aren't you?" I was. I didn't care whether we caught another fish.

We spent about an hour there, inching our way closer to the falls before returning to the bank, and walking farther upstream abeam the falling water. This was many years before they constructed the wooden viewing platform which is there now. It was exciting. It was raw Mother Nature. All too soon Jack shouted, "That's it, folks, time to go."

We returned to our camp and spent one more night before Jack flew us back to King Salmon. Before leaving the camp site, we broke camp and packed the tents and other gear inside a wooden storage shed to protect against possible bear damage. Jack left his equipment because he would return in August and again in September, bringing other friends, but we had to go home.

"Is he clean shaven? Is he dressed neatly?" Those were the words I heard the Wein Air captain ask his operations clerk over their company radio when told that a Pan Am pilot was requesting the jump seat to Anchorage. There was only one seat available in the passenger compartment of the 737, space for my wife. If the jump seat were not available, I would spend the night in King Salmon and join her the next day.

Wein had a short turnaround time, and the captain stayed on board the plane. "Yes sir, Captain, no beard. He's even wearing a sport coat and a tie," I heard the clerk reply. They were talking about me. Fortunately, I was dressed the way I always did whenever I flew non-rev/space available on an airline, my own or another. As I write this in 2016, I can't help but reflect on the fact that on my last six or seven flights in the U.S. I have noticed that I have been the only passenger wearing a tie. I saw one passenger in Houston wearing one, but he was in line for another flight. Times have changed.

Ginna departed the terminal through the regular passenger door, and the clerk escorted me from his office door directly to the plane so the captain could get a good look at me before he approved my jump seat status. I passed and flew to Anchorage in the cockpit. Ginna rode in the economy section.

We stayed in Anchorage two days waiting for nice weather so Jack could take us on a scenic tour around Denali in his plane. Didn't happen. It drizzled rain constantly, with visibility less than one mile. We satisfied ourselves with doing a little shopping and taking a short self-guided walking tour of Anchorage. Our hotel was adjacent to Lake Hood, the Anchorage float plane base (which is the busiest seaplane port in the world) on the north edge of the airport. Ginna was most impressed with the little boat slips along the lake shore. She thought they were boat docks and was shocked to learn, upon closer inspection, that each one was a slip for a float plane, not a boat.

We fell in love with Alaska, and we have returned several times since, but we have decided it is a summer place. I transited Fairbanks once when the temperature was minus 35° F, and I thought my feet would freeze to the ground while I did my exterior pre-flight inspection. No sir, Alaska is fine in the summer, same as Kitty Hawk.

Kitty Hawk is where we were in June the following year—my friend, Jerry, and I with our families. We returned to the cottage from an all-day offshore fishing trip at about four o'clock. While the kids were helping me unload the four yellowfin tuna which needed cleaning, Jerry said, "I have to call crew scheduling to find out if I was awarded that trip I requested." I hoped he was not simply avoiding helping us clean the fish.

In five minutes he returned to my boat, which was parked in the driveway, and he was as white as a sheet. It looked like all the blood had drained from his face. "Did ya get the trip?" I inquired.

"Yeah, but you won't believe what Harry in crew scheduling just told me. You won't believe it." Harry was one of our favorite crew schedulers, having driven down from his home in New York, and joined us once on an offshore trip. He caught a forty-five pound wahoo. Harry knew we were at Nags Head, and he knew we were friends with Jack Meyers. "Harry said Jack Meyers is missing, Ash, and they're pretty sure he crashed his 180 in Alaska."

"Oh no!" I heard myself say. "Are you sure?"

"Harry said Jack didn't call in for his London trip three days ago and they had to call out a reserve pilot. From New York, Jim Duncan tried to check with Ralph up in Anchorage, only to learn that Ralph was with Jack."

(Jim Duncan later became Vice President of Operations and Ralph was the Snap-On tool distributor in Anchorage and Jack's best friend.)

"Ralph's wife says she's pretty sure they crashed near the lake in bad weather, and probably overloaded, she said, but no one can find the plane. The Coast Guard and several friends have been searching for two days. Not a sign."

I was crestfallen and heartbroken. Jack was my friend, my good friend who introduced me to Klondike bars and who planned to take me caribou hunting in the fall, and had promised that we could hunt ptarmigan together in the future. He knew I loved to shoot birds.

Later in the summer of 1983 we held a memorial service for Jack and Ralph de la Ronde at the chapel at JFK. I think several years passed before the wreckage was ever located, and I find conflicting references to the accident on the internet. One report says two were killed, and one report says four. Both reports indicate what all of us suspected: overloaded with an aft center of gravity.

Four years later, on September 15, 1987, Erroll Johnstaad was flying a Mercer Owl Formula One Racer nicknamed "Harvey's Wall-banger" while practicing for an air race in Reno, Nevada. One witness told investigators that Erroll made an abrupt left turn, snap rolled, and crashed into the ground from an altitude of forty feet. Erroll was also practicing to become a part of Harry Shepard's acrobatic team. He was an excellent pilot, a line pilot as well as a 747 flight instructor at our training academy in Miami. I heard other friends say that his engine quit during the Reno flight, and Erroll did what all pilots were told over and over never to do. Instead of landing straight ahead, he tried to make a 180° turn and land on the closest runway in the opposite direction. He didn't make it. We'll never know exactly what happened those last few seconds. Official reports state that the NTSB was never able to determine the probable cause.

They say flying consists of hours and hours of sheer boredom punctuated by moments of stark terror. All too often that is exactly what it is.

JACK MYERS

ERROLL JOHNSTAAD

DOT

It seems like just last week, that chilly 1988 night around midnight when she came running inside, shouting, "Mom! Dad! Come look, Christie has puppies!" Cathy was right; first six, then seven, and by dawn we were all very tired, but excited over our first litter of Elhew pups, at least part Elhew. They don't come any better, as far as I'm concerned.

We played with them two or three times every day so they would be properly "peopled" by the time we offered them for sale. As the pups grew, their mama watched while her babies frolicked with Casey and me outside the kennel, and her facial expression seemed to convey a look of relief from her maternal chores, even for short periods of time. Casey was our chocolate Lab (who we called Aunt Casey, because she acted like an old maid aunt around these pups). She loved to play with them, and she treated them as if they were her own offspring.

We named each pup according to some distinguishing markings, the way they do with whales. The shy one with only one liver spot on her side was named Dot. We called the little orange-headed one Julie, after that refreshing beverage "Orange Julius." We knew the names were probably only temporary, certain that their new owners would rename them.

We also gave each one a collar, and I used an old trick I read about to acquaint each one with a leash. For a few minutes every day, I connected two of them together with a short leash, about thirty inches long, and let them tug away at each other. That way the pups themselves taught each other the futility of resisting, and I was not the culprit. It wasn't very long before they were well-peopled and reasonably well-mannered. I eased them along with the whistle also, blowing two short chirps each time I placed a bowl of puppy chow within their sight. Soon they would come running every time I whistled. Of course we weren't raising show dogs but bird dogs. Even so, we wanted our buyers to see that our pups were special and that they knew how to behave around people as well as around birds.

They surely did know how to behave around birds. By the time they were four or five weeks old, each pup would point the bird wing on a string attached to the cane pole. In fact, a few times when I let them all play together, all seven would be pointing it at the same time. I always wondered, *where's the camera? I never seem to have it handy at the right time.*

They were born on my birthday, October 21, so they were six weeks old in early December. It came to pass that by the time they were weaned at day 42, I was already taking them on short walks across the weed patch and into the piney woods where my wild training covey of bobwhite quail lived. I usually took my little 20-gauge double because bird season was open.

Sure enough—and a lot of people are skeptical about this, but it's true—three of these little pups paused briefly, rigid on point, and Julie, the little orange one, rolled her eyes in my direction, as if awaiting instructions. I brought the gun up, not really believing what I saw, when about six quail flushed and flew toward the bayberry thicket over by the marsh. I winged one, which quickly ran into an old, hollow locust log, followed immediately by the little orange-headed Julie. She nearly disappeared, poking first her nose, then her body into the hollow as far as she could reach, with only her little dog tail visible. In a few seconds she backed out, holding in her mouth a quail almost as big as she was. She proudly pranced around, displaying her expertise to her litter mates, several of whom tugged this way and that, trying to take away her prize. Fortunately, I was able to retrieve the little bird before it was completely mangled.

We cut the lesson short rather than pursue the singles and returned to the kennel. I reminded my wife once again that they sure did show lots of promise, and we should consider keeping at least one of them as a companion (and later replacement) for Christie. "I don't want one unless she's well-mannered," she remarked, "especially if we're going to keep her in the house."

"They're all well-mannered," I replied. "You should have seen them fighting over that quail, trying to take it away from Julie. All except little Dot, who just watched from a distance."

Both of us had noticed Dot's shyness and her tendency to play away from the group, occasionally preferring to pursue a butterfly over near the apple tree, rather than join her siblings playing with my bird wing on a string. Dot was becoming the quintessential introvert, and if that was a negative quality, it certainly did not bother my wife, who took more and more of a liking to Dot as time went by. Because she was shy, she never ran up to the prospective buyers who came and went those weeks and days shortly before Christmas. She just kind of hung around the edge of the yard, watching the kids (little and big, young and old) as they zeroed in on her braver, more aggressive, and apparently more lovable litter mates. Most bird hunters want a bold dog, and as a pup Dot was anything but bold. So most of the pups were sold, many to be Christmas gifts, and by the end of the month, we were left with Dot, the shy one, and her sister, Holly, so named because her two little brown spots reminded me of two holly berries. Later we gave Holly to a friend, Frank, who lived and hunted over near Wachapreague, on the sea side. I was happy to give her to him because four or five years earlier, Frank had given Bogey, another pointer, to me. Bogey was simply too much dog for Frank, too hard to control.

Thus, Dot adopted my wife Ginna as her new person. She was easy to house break, always eager to please, and showed little shyness when pointing and retrieving quail. Because I have usually been a one-dog person myself, I never successfully taught a dog to honor or back stand another dog on point, and it was no different with Dot. That shortcoming never seemed to be a problem, however, because the few times I hunted her with her mama, they always seemed to find the birds at exactly the same time, or else they were far enough apart that it didn't really matter to me, or to them. We hunted them together in South Dakota in 1990, and several times in Virginia, but mostly we hunted them one at a time. Christie lived to be eleven, and finally Dot was the only one left.

Not long ago I read Bill Turner's delightful book *East of the Chesapeake*, and in one of his stories he wrote these words, "He was the best dog in the world, and I am sure every reader has had one as good or better." I trust that this is a Turner original saying, and I gladly give him the credit, but I'm envious because I wish I had said it first. It applies to Dot. She took to the training regimen as naturally as any dog that has ever owned me, and there have been several. She coursed into the wind, checked over her shoulder for my location every so often, came to the whistle (most of the time) and retrieved birds two, three, no, ten times better than any other dog I ever hunted with. I never hunted birds from horseback and I never intend to, but Dot didn't know that. Her inherited trait to run farther ahead of me than I like was easily brought under control during several sessions with the electronic collar, exactly like I had done with her mama. Such is the fate of a walking hunter who ends up with offspring of field trial champions and one who hunts mostly on small farms.

Dot became a house pet, a sentry, a member of the family, and a beloved companion in a very short time. The grandchildren called her Dotdog, and she patiently tolerated them. She also became a minor celebrity of sorts, too, having her photo appear in an issue of North Dakota Outdoors magazine in 1992. Throughout it all she became a superb bird dog, and I'll probably never have another like her, although, in actuality, she was Ginna's dog not mine.

She loved to hunt and retrieve sharp-tail grouse. One or two months before her first trip to North Dakota, there appeared on the cover of one of my outdoor magazines an impressive photograph of a dog pointing a bobwhite quail; they were nearly nose to nose and eyeball to eyeball. "Fake!" my wife remarked. "Fake. That's either a stuffed quail or a stuffed dog." She absolutely refused to believe it was real. Later, on one of our first hunting days in North Dakota, Dot pointed a covey of Hungarian Partridge (Huns) and Ginna and I both missed our shots during the flush. I took note of the flock as they sailed across a field, most flying onto the next ranch. However, a single landed not too far away in a clump of brush. Dot and I headed for that spot, as Ginna trudged along behind us, her boots heavy with mud. Dot immediately locked up on point and as I inched forward closer and closer she remained steady and motionless. I came up behind her, close enough that I could have touched her, my gun at the ready. Nothing flew. Then, much to my surprise, I saw that little Hun—probably scared nearly to death—no more than twelve inches in front of Dot's nose, staring up at her. They were nose to nose and eyeball to eyeball, almost an exact duplicate of that magazine cover. Ginna came close enough to observe the scene, convinced that it was not fake, but she missed the shot when I reached toward the little bird and made it fly. I would have given you a hundred dollars for my camera.

Later in the week we were hunting with Daryl and his German shorthair, Sonny, a bold dog if ever there was one. Dot raced to retrieve a downed grouse, took a healthy mouthful, and turned to bring it to me. Immediately Sonny hit her broadside like a blitzing outside linebacker blind-siding a quarterback, and Dot rolled over in the dust, truly sacked. Sonny proudly took his purloined prize to Daryl, never realizing the trauma he inflicted on Dot, who would not retrieve another bird all week. In fact, it was several weeks and several birds later, back home in Virginia, before she would pick up another dead bird, preferring, instead, to stand guard over it while I walked to her and picked up the bird. Finally, her old habits returned and once she sensed that Sonny was not around to sack her, she resumed retrieving. She even hunted side by side with Sonny a few years later, older and wiser, usually allowing him to retrieve all the birds he wanted to.

My friend, Ron Livingston, (grandfather of the Hollywood actor with the same name) from Iowa, encouraged me to let her run a little farther and wider, which she did in classic style, but she remained steady on point when she found the birds. She demonstrated once again her failure to honor another dog's point when she darted past Sonny and Tasha (who were pointing a skunk) and received a large shot of skunk juice full in her face. "Rub some tomato juice on it," suggested Ron as we headed for the truck, certain that Dot was finished as an effective bird dog for a few days. Not so. A few yards away, Dot locked up point (which the other dogs did honor) and we flushed several grouse, bagging three, one for each dog to retrieve, which they did. Good old Dotdog.

But over the years, the quail became more scarce in Virginia as did the opportunities to hunt them in places where you can walk and see. Loss of habitat and predators other than humans have taken their toll, I'm afraid, but that's the subject of another story perhaps. Dot stayed with us through it all, eleven years in fact, same as her mother, ever the perfect lady, never begging table scraps—always eager to go for a ride in the pickup and getting especially excited at the sight of a shotgun.

One day in early September 2000, Ginna and I decided to shoot some clay targets over at the farm. We chose to take Dot with us, even though the vet had already shown us the "hot spot" on the x-ray, and Dot had lost her appetite for just about everything but warm chicken soup. Dot limped to the truck and waited for me to help her climb up behind the wheel. She slowly jumped over the front seat to take her place on the rear seat of the extended-cab Chevy. When we reached the farm, she stayed in the cab until the first shot was fired, whereupon she bolted out like an excited pup, racing to and fro among the soybean stubble and broken clay fragments in search of the dead bird which she would never find.

Even though the season was closed, if I'd seen a quail that day I would have shot it for Dot. As it was, we powdered a few more clay targets, missed a few, and then brought her home, both sad and happy at the same time.

I cried the entire time I was digging the hole in the ground. As I had done with her mama, Christie, and with Freckles and Daisy and Bogey and several others, I held her close while the vet tied the rubber tubing and found the vein in her foreleg. I counted nine heart beats and then she left us, without a whimper, ladylike and shy as ever... the best dog in the world.

GOOD GARDEN SEED

Author's Note: This story, a tribute to my father, was published in the October/November, 1990 issue of Shooting Sportsman *magazine, along with another story, "Spreadin' A Little Corn." That was the only time I ever had two stories appear in the same issue of a magazine.*

The dog stood motionless, at the edge of some greenbriars, motionless except for moving her eyes. She always did that. I think she was looking to see if we were ready. She knew what would happen in a few seconds. She just wanted to make sure we were ready. She was as tense as the spring on a steel trap.

"Move up a little closer, Greg," I said. "Granddaddy and I are ready, are you?"

"I think so," my thirteen-year-old nephew replied. He was new at this game of quail hunting, but he was having fantastic beginner's luck. I had been patting myself on the back all day as I had watched him. I was pleased to be a part of his training. He had missed the first few shots, but as the day drew to a close he seemed to gain the self confidence so necessary to becoming an accomplished wingshot.

I eased forward toward the dog. It was difficult trying to handle the dog, help Greg correct his mistakes, and get in a few shots myself, The covey flushed straight away. I heard shots on both sides of me as Greg and my father fired. I saw birds fall. The dog bolted ahead to retrieve, proof again that I had never yet been able to train one to be steady to wing and shot. A sleeper sailed out in front of her and I raised my gun to fire, but I hesitated, uncertain about how many birds from this covey had just fallen.

"Fetch, Daisy. Fetch. Dead bird. Fetch." I didn't have to give her any commands, because she was already returning with one of the birds, but I was hoping it would sound like I knew what I was doing. "Give. Good dog. Fetch." She darted off like a greyhound in pursuit of another quail. "Good shooting guys," I added. "I saw birds falling everywhere. How'd we do?"

"I think I got two!" my nephew shouted. "I found one but I don't see the other one."

"Two!" I said in mock jest. "I didn't even get a shot off and you say you got two? Who are you trying to kid?" The dog returned with my father's second bird. I felt certain Greg was right, that he had, indeed, knocked down two birds, but I couldn't resist the temptation to tease him. "Come on Daisy. Dead bird. Dead bird. Fetch the bird. Good dog." Suddenly she slammed on brakes beside a pine top. We were hunting a large cutover. "Whoa!" I said, but it was unnecessary because she looked like a statue.

"Prob'ly a cripple," said my father. "You take him, Greg. It's your bird anyway." Dad was reminding me not to shoot the bird. Greg eased in close to the dog, his gun at high port, ready to fire. But the dog sprang forward, dived headfirst into the brush pile, and came out with a mouth full of bobwhite, the other half of Greg's first double. "Boy! She's a retrievin' fool, ain't she? Good Garden Seed!" my father said. There was that expression again. I hadn't heard it for quite a while, having been away so much, what with college and the military and the new job and all.

"Good Garden Seed!" How many times had I heard it in my youth? It was about the most profane expression he ever used. Once in a while he threw in a 'damn' or a 'hell' but not often. I heard him say "Goddammit," a couple of times—once when he dropped a new Zippo lighter overboard in the deepest fishing hole in the millpond, and another time when a wrench slipped and he banged up his knuckle pretty hard working on somebody's refrigerator—he took me with him once in a while when I was a kid. Mostly, however, he usually just said, "good garden seed," and he reserved those three words to express amazement or excitement or delight when he felt those emotions. I guess he felt them less and less as the years wore on, a widower the last twenty-one, so consequently, I heard that expression less often.

They put their birds into their game vests and we started walking back to the truck. I had always intended to ask him about that expression but I never got around to it. Suddenly, as if he had been reading my mind, Greg asked him, "Granddaddy, why do you say that? I never hear anybody else say it. What does it mean?"

"Well, Greg, I'll tell you now that you asked. When I was about twelve, just after I started smokin' cigarettes, it was, and I started smokin' 'em when I was eleven, so this had to be somewhere 'round nineteen-eighteen. Well, I was a lot like you kids are today—thought I knew more than my mama—thought she was old fashioned. I learned to cuss before I learned to smoke. She hated both. One day Mama and me was walkin' out to th' barnyard to feed th' chickens when a big ol' hawk swooped down and grabbed a young fryin'-sized chicken and flew off with it. He didn't kill it right away, 'cause it was hollerin' and squawkin' and makin' all kinds of racket and I said, 'Good God Almighty, Mama, look at that hawk yonder stealin' that chicken!'

"Well Mama, she said, 'What'd you say, boy? Did you take the Lord's name in vain again? Now you git yourself up to th' kitchen right this minute, you hear me? Soon as I feed these chickens I'm gonna wash your mouth out with soap.' So I went slinkin' away kinda like a puppy with his tail tucked between his legs, you know, and I sat there in th' kitchen waitin' for her. She had already washed my mouth out with soap one time before, that disgustin' ol' Octagon soap, tasted awful. Worst part about it was—well, there was really two worst parts about it—one thing was I didn't really think I had taken th' Lord's name in vain. After all, I'd heard th' preacher say 'Good God Almighty' lotsa times, and th' other thing was, Mama didn't seem at all upset 'bout that hawk gettin' that chicken. She was only upset with me. Now if papa hadda been there he would have taken his shotgun and gone after that hawk and shot him. But papa had died th' year before, and I wasn't quite big enough to handle this big ol' Lefever 12-gauge double. It was this same gun. Only one I ever owned. Mama gave it to me the next year. Anyway, when she returned she said, 'Now you listen young man an' you listen good. You're just getting' too big for your britch-es. I reckon you're getting' too big to spank and too big for me to wash your mouth out with soap, but don't you ever let me hear you take the Lord's name in vain again. You want to swear, you say something like 'good garden seed!' So that's how come I use that particular expression."

We arrived at the truck as he finished his story. He laughed as he sat on the tailgate and he leaned his head back and he smiled with his eyes the way he always did and then he started coughing. I know that hunt took place at least ten years ago, because my nephew has finished college now.

So I heard him say it again, that same expression, a few days ago. "Good Garden Seed," he said, "Look at that point. Solid as a rock. You got yourself another real bird dog there, son." This time the two of us were sitting on the seat of my pickup truck bird hunting behind a new pointer bitch I was trying to train. We weren't really hunting, just following the dog. It takes patience and hard work to train a dog, and he had tried so hard for so long to teach me how to do it that whenever I had a real promising prospect I liked to show him the results. I used to take him out of the nursing home a few afternoons a week, but there never seemed to be enough time left over to do things together like we did when I was the child and he was the hunter. Somehow, without my realizing when or how, the tables had turned. I was the hunter and he was the child.

As we sat there in my truck and I looked over at him, many pleasant memories floated across my mind. Time seemed to stand still. I remembered how this frail old man had once tipped the scales at two-thirty-five. And yet he could sneak through the woods as silently as a deer. He tried to teach me how, but I never learned. We used to try to sneak up to the edge of the pond to surprise some unsuspecting wood ducks, but I'd usually cough or sneeze or step on a dead stick. We could hear the ducks splashing as they took off and then hear their mournful whistles as they sailed away through the cypress trees, well out of range. But he rarely lost his patience with me as he tried to teach me many things about being an out-doorsman. "Sneakin' up on wood ducks is hard to do," he said. "Next time we'll try the boat. It's quieter."

I remembered other times, the times he used to carry me pig-gy-back across the wide wet spots, places where the water was too wide for me to jump across and too deep for me to wade. Some-times, when I was only four or five he'd carry me and his gun at the same time, and later, as I got a little bigger, he'd make two separate trips, me first and then the gun, as we headed for his favorite hick-ory tree up on that low ridge near the far side of the millpond to shoot a few squirrels. We shared many sunrises together along the banks of that pond. At other times we went up to the other end of the farm to the broomstraw patch beside the graveyard to look for that covey of quail that almost always seemed to be there.

"Take care of the birds," he used to say. "Take care of the birds and they'll stick around year after year." Every spring he had the tenant farmer plow and disc a couple of spots and leave them and we'd go up there and sow some game bird mix that my uncle got from the Game Commission. My uncle was a game warden and he and his boss liked to come by once or twice each year and shoot a few birds, but they didn't shoot many once I reached my teens because they knew Dad liked to save most of them for me. I didn't shoot many in those days either, because it was a long time before I learned how to pick out a single bird and not try to shoot the whole covey with one shot.

I smiled inside as I remembered how he used to encourage me to forget about the explosion of eight or ten feathered bombshells all around me, and to concentrate instead on one bird out on the edge of the covey. "Shootin' singles is easier," he said, "'cause you can concentrate all your thinkin' on one bird. But try to think of a covey as nothin' more than a bunch of singles, and pretty soon you'll get the hang of it. Once or twice I succeeded and it pleased him. "Don't ever shoot out the whole covey, either," he always said. "Now you take this graveyard covey—been here 'bout as long as I can remember. We always quit huntin' 'em after they get down to six or seven birds so they can have some protection at night when they sleep in a little circle with their tails together and their heads stickin' out in every direction, and also so there'll be some breedin' stock left over to produce a new covey next year." Respect the law and respect your game were two of the things he tried to teach me. Don't shoot more than the limit and don't decimate a covey.

One Saturday we came close. It was an accident. It was late in the season and there had been lots of snow and we hadn't hunted birds at all for about a month. We were in the broomstraw by the graveyard and Rusty, that red setter we had for a few years, locked up on point. He was hard to see 'cause he was kinda light red, almost golden, and in the afternoon sun with only a few small patches of snow still on the ground in the shady spots, when he stopped moving he nearly disappeared into the scenery; he looked just like any other clump of broomstraw. But there he was, pointing birds. "Easy boy, easy there Rusty," Dad said as he motioned for me to walk up a little closer to the dog so I'd have a good shot. I felt goose pimples starting to form all over my body, because I knew what was about to happen. I was using my cousin's borrowed 20-gauge double because the firing pin was broken on my little four-ten. Dad was using his Lefever.

A small covey flushed and flew out over the bare field where the peanuts had been harvested and Daddy shot and I shot, and then I shot a second time because I had seen two birds kinda peel off to the left. I got them both. My first double! Rusty never was very good at retrieving and he was running around all over the place because it was full of bird scent. I could see both my birds on the ground not fifteen feet apart so I ran over to them hoping that Daddy had not also shot at the same birds, thereby robbing me of my double. I ran back to the broomstraw patch about as excited as I had ever been (except for that time in the seventh grade when Cindy stopped by my desk on the way to the pencil sharpener and kissed me right on the mouth right there in the classroom). "Did you see that?" he asked. "I got two birds with one shot. Good Garden Seed! First time I ever done that." He held his two birds in one hand and I showed him my two birds and we stood there at the edge of the broomstraw looking at the four birds.

"It took me two shots," I said. "I don't guess I'll ever get to be as good a shot as you are."

"No sirree," he said, "you're wrong. Mine was luck. Yours was good shootin'." He seemed genuinely prouder of my accomplishment than of his and I'm sure he was. "Let's go home. Here, Rusty. Here. Come on boy." He called the dog. "Can't shoot any more birds outta this covey or there won't be any left to pair up in th' spring. That was good shootin' son. Bet your mama will be proud too." We walked home across the bare peanut field side by side in the warm afternoon sun and I felt like a grown man even though I was only fourteen.

As we sat there in my truck and I glanced at Daddy again, I couldn't help but be pleased that he was, indeed, enjoying our outing. We didn't shoot any birds because it was August and the season was closed and I was only training a dog anyway and taking Daddy out of the nursing home for a couple of hours to give him some fresh air and let him relive the excitement of the point and the flush. I knew I would never be able to repay him. How does one repay such a debt? Some say you repay your debt by passing along your knowledge and skills to someone else. I can't think of a better way. We made a good start with Greg. I'll continue to try to do that. It would make Dad happy, I know.

I walked over to the dog and the birds flushed out of a small patch of foxtails and panicum missed by the herbicide and they sailed across the soybean field to the cutover timber two hundred yards away. It was a big covey, two adults and at least a dozen young birds. I guess he'd seen bigger coveys in seventy-nine years. He sat there on the pickup seat, smiling as I whistled the dog in and put her back into the dog box in the truck and closed the tailgate. "I reckon you'll have some good shootin' this fall," he said. "That's three coveys just on this one farm. Wish I could still shoot, but these ol' eyes and these ol' legs ain't what they used to be. How 'bout takin' my gun out a couple of times and shootin' a couple of birds with it." I promised him I would. "Guess we'd better get on back to th' nursin' home, Son. I gotta take my medicine and it'll be dinner time soon and anyhow I'm kinda tired. That sure is some fine dog you got there."

"Elhew," I said, "one of the best there is, but she loves to run like a racehorse." I never did tell him about the special collar. He was such a gentle person that I didn't think he would understand. Three days later I stopped by to see him again, this time without the dog because I was on my way to work and I was in a hurry and didn't have much time. Where does it go? I took him a vanilla milkshake.

He told me he'd had the weirdest dream the night before about being a kid and waking up in the middle of the night one night and hearing the chickens squawking and the dogs barking. He grabbed the shotgun his papa had left him and he went outside in the moonlight and fired into the air and a tramp came running out of the chicken house yelling, "Don't shoot! Don't shoot! I ain't stealing nuttin'. I'm jes lookin' for a place to sleep." The tramp ran off toward the railroad track. He laughed and said he didn't know why he dreamed such a silly dream because nothing like that had ever happened as far as he could remember, but it seemed so real. He said he'd been having lots of dreams lately and they were mostly weird, but so vivid, and that maybe he'd been watching too much television. "Not much else to do," he sighed.

He also told me he'd had an especially bad dream a few nights ago about my getting hijacked to some place in the Middle East and it had frightened him. I told him not to worry because I was going mainly to South America these days and anyway if somebody hijacked me I'd just say to him, "Where do you wanna go sir?" and that's where I'd take him because I wasn't interested in becoming a hero. To change the subject I told him his granddaughters had been reloading shells because dove season would open soon. I added that both were planning to hunt with me on opening day.

"Good Garden Seed!" he said. "You're still tryin' to make tomboys outta those girls, aren't you?" As he said that he slapped his right thigh the way he always did and he grinned a big grin and then he leaned back against the pillows and the emphysema made him cough and he looked away toward the window and a tear rolled down his cheek. And a cold chill started at the base of my neck and quickly worked its way down my spine as I shivered and started to cry and then we hugged each other and I told him I loved him. I promised him we'd take the dog out again a couple of times next week and we'd have him over for dinner one night and have a mess of doves with wild rice and some squash and some fresh tomatoes. And a beer.

"Hot dawg!" he said. Then I left to go to spend the night in New York and then go to Europe for a week. "Have a safe flight," he said. "Hope you luck." He always said that when I left.

They called me early the next morning in New York before I had a chance to fly to Paris. He died in his sleep sometime between four and six in the morning. It was painless they said.

He said he had vivid dreams. I like to think he died dreaming. Not about me and airplanes getting hijacked or blown apart, but about young bird dogs on point and doves on the dinner table and his grandchildren finding big coveys of quail. And that the Good God Almighty forgave him for taking his name in vain a few times back in 1918 and a few times since.

"Good Garden Seed!"

ABOUT THE AUTHOR

Ash Cutchin was born in October, 1941 in a farm house in Isle of Wight County, about two miles from Franklin, Virginia near a Naval Auxiliary Airfield which was later named in memory of his friend and school mate, Army helicopter pilot, John Beverly Rose. As a youngster he spent many nights kneeling at his bedroom window watching Navy carrier-based planes make touch and go landings at the airport.

He graduated Windsor High School in 1959 and then attended VA Tech for two years, studying Architecture. Realizing that he simply did not have the math and engineering skills required to be the next Frank Lloyd Wright, he transferred to the College of William and Mary, graduating in 1963 with a Bachelor of Arts Degree in English, with plans to become a college professor. He also received a commission as a Second Lt. in the US Army Reserve. While in college, he trained at Ft. Eustis, VA, and Ft. Bragg, NC. During his three-year Army stint he was based at Ft. Sill, OK; Ft. Rucker, AL; Ft. Meade, MD; Camp A.P Hill, VA; Ft. Hood, TX; Dong Ba Tin, South Vietnam; and finally Ban Me Thout, South Vietnam as a reconnaissance pilot, flying the O-1 Birddog.

Following his military service Ash spent 25 years as an airline pilot with Pan American, flying both the Boeing 707 and the Boeing 747, first based in San Francisco and then New York. Much of that time he and his family lived on Virginia's Eastern Shore, and they spent many hours fishing the Chesapeake Bay and the Atlantic Ocean, as well as training bird dogs. He operated Pan Am Flt. 103 five times during the month of December 1988, and was at home on Dec. 21st when a Libyan terrorist bomb in a suitcase exploded over Lockerbie, Scotland killing 270 people, 17 of whom were his friends and fellow employees.

Ash has visited 78 countries. He has two daughters, and six grandchildren. He and his wife Ginna live near Courtland, VA. He was a Certified General real estate appraiser from 1992, until his retirement in 2015, after having been gainfully employed since age 14.

CPSIA information can be obtained
at www.ICGtesting.com
Printed in the USA
FFOW01n1541131216
30153FF